T0369402

INTERNATIONAL DEVELOPMENT

INTERNATIONAL DEVELOPMENT

A CASEBOOK FOR EFFECTIVE MANAGEMENT

FREDERICK KEENAN AND **CHRISTINE GILMORE**

iUniverse, Inc.
New York   Bloomington

International Development
A Casebook for Effective Management

iUniverse books may be ordered through booksellers or by contacting:

iUniverse
1663 Liberty Drive
Bloomington, IN 47403
www.iuniverse.com
1-800-Authors (1-800-288-4677)

Because of the dynamic nature of the Internet, any Web addresses or links contained in this book may have changed since publication and may no longer be valid. The views expressed in this work are solely those of the authors and do not necessarily reflect the views of the publisher, and the publisher hereby disclaims any responsibility for them.

ISBN: 978-1-4502-5526-4 (sc)
ISBN: 978-1-4502-5527-1 (ebook)

Library of Congress Control Number: 2010916423

Printed in the United States of America

iUniverse rev. date: 01/06/2011

NOTE TO INSTRUCTORS

There is an *Instructor's Manual* to accompany this textbook, which is available to lecturers who have prescribed this textbook in their courses. The *Instructor's Manual* contains detailed and comprehensive teaching notes for all of the cases in the book.

Case teaching notes typically contain most or all of the following:

- learning objectives of the case
- suggestions for identifying, and dealing with, the issues
- suggested strategies for teaching the case
- sources of additional relevant information, including download-able slide shows
- student assignments
- detailed answers to the assignments
- an analysis of the decision process
- follow-up cases with their teaching notes.

Course instructors are invited to contact Dr. Frederick Keenan at ipps@rogers.com to obtain a copy of the *Instructor's Manual*.

Contents

CHAPTER ONE

EFFECTIVE DECISION MAKING IN INTERNATIONAL DEVELOPMENT: THE CASE METHOD

One of the greatest pleasures obtained from working in international development is watching highly effective managers, Westerners as well as our partners in other countries, as they repeatedly make good things happen. These individuals are quite a disparate lot. They could be academics or students, they might belong to international or indigenous NGOs, they might work for associations of educational institutions, they may be community leaders or trainers in developing countries, they can be found working for government or bilateral or multilateral agencies at home and abroad, they might be businesspersons or consultants, they could be enthusiastic volunteers meeting around a kitchen table.

Although many of the individuals who do international work are very good at the business of managing development activities, there are too many—unfortunately—who are less effective, resulting in a poor use of scarce resources, and in disillusionment and chagrin on the part of their partners.

What nurtures the ability of solid international development decision making? In striving to answer this, the authors spent considerable time over the past three decades observing effective managers of international cooperation projects, and trying to determine what it was that they had in common. For example, was it the kind of academic training they had; was it their religious, ethical, family or community backgrounds; was it the types of projects and the countries they had their early formative experiences in?

The conclusion we came to was that, although all of the above influences can contribute to preparing someone for productive international work, the most dominant widely shared characteristic of effective managers is the thought processes they use, either deliberately or intuitively, for the following:

1. to accumulate and organize the available information
2. to establish various potential alternative courses of action
3. to set criteria for evaluating the various alternatives
4. to make the decision
5. to formulate plans for implementing the decision reached
6. to establish a system for monitoring and evaluating the results of the work, and
7. to convincingly explain and defend the decision and the implementation plans to their peers.

In many cases, moreover, they do all of this in the context of incomplete, irrelevant or contradictory information being available!

Because we are often asked to teach, to counsel, and to evaluate international management, we have struggled with how to cultivate this kind of thought process. Even though there are lots of tools and information, and countless opinions, nevertheless there are no "answers in the back of the book" in international work. We eventually came to appreciate that one of the most powerful tools for developing the ability to make good decisions in the face of incomplete information was the *case method* as used, for example, by the Harvard Business School in the US and the Richard Ivey School of Business in Canada[1], and (in different forms) in certain medical and engineering schools.

A *case* is a description of an actual situation (a problem, a decision, an opportunity, a challenge, a dilemma) that a real individual in a real organization has recently been confronted with. Readers are invited to put themselves in the shoes of the decision maker to evaluate the information that was available to the decision maker at that moment in time, and with a time frame in which to make a decision. The available information may be relevant or irrelevant, and is often incomplete. Students go though the seven-step process described three paragraphs above. They then present, and defend, their decisions to groups of their peers. This process is fundamental to the case method and will be used repeatedly in the book, starting in Chapter Seven where the first full case will be encountered.

When we say that students are invited to put themselves "in the shoes of the decision maker", this means that the same incomplete information is placed in front of the students as the decision maker had available at the time of the case, and that the students are challenged to make and justify the most effective decision to be made in the circumstances of the case, just as the original decision maker had been. (This is not the same as trying to be in the *mind*, rather than the shoes, of the decision maker because that is just not possible.)

The teaching philosophy behind the case method is that the best way of learning how to make good decisions is to be confronted every day with a wide range of complex decisions that need to be made and defended. Students in the highly rated Ivey School, for example, regularly face up to three cases per day during their education. One learns to be an effective decision maker by repeatedly going through the processes required for making tough decisions, and successfully arguing those decisions in front of peers. The evident abundant success of Harvard and Ivey in preparing professionals as decision makers in a wide variety of organizations is a testament to the utility of the case method.

> *This then is what the book is all about. In partnership with your course instructors, we will provide you with a solid introduction to all the elements of international development, and then sharpen your abilities as effective decision makers by taking you through a wide range of decisions that real development managers were actually faced with.*

In the use of the case method in a teaching and learning environment, students use **casebooks**, which are textbooks in which a large number of cases are interspersed with the instructional material. We have written this book as a casebook. The cases contained in this casebook are all real[2], and the individuals described have given written permission to use their situations in classrooms. The cases are of different types of decisions in a wide range of countries, and are of differing levels of complexity and difficulty. Cases are included to give students, under the guidance of their instructors, the opportunity to work a situation all the way through to a decision.

In addition to cases, we make extensive use of **case analyses**. Case analyses are used to describe development situations (again, real and recent ones), the decisions that were actually made, and the actions taken. Case analyses are presented to illustrate the thought processes that various managers went though in reaching decisions and how they implemented the decisions. Students are welcome to "second guess" the decisions that were made, and possibly to improve upon them.

The decisions in the cases were made using both individual and collective approaches. In some cases, it was an individual who struggled with choices. In

3

other cases, there was a striving for consensus by a group of Westerners and their partners in other countries.

Here are the opening paragraphs of four of the cases contained in this book. We invite you to put yourself in the shoes of the four managers who are the focal points of these cases. Now, what are you going to do? What possible activities can you imagine doing? Out of all these possible activities, which ones will be the most effective? How will you determine if and when they are effective? What information will you seek to help you make your decisions? What development concepts and principles apply here? Are there other professional disciplines that you will you need to draw from? How much money will you need? Where will the money come from, and how will you convince the funding agency to support you? What time scale is appropriate? Will your decisions bring about an efficient use of human and financial resources? How will you select your partners in the other countries? How do you plan to respect the knowledge, experience and aspirations of your partners? Whom, specifically, are you trying to help? Will you achieve sustainability, and gender equality and empowerment? How will you defend your decisions to groups of your peers? Will you really make a difference to someone's life, or are you just engaging in tourism?

- Case: Ghana & Don Sawyer
  The new Ghanaian leader stomped out of the meeting at one point with no indication of when, or even if, he would return. Sawyer's colleague turned to him and said, "Don, I don't think we can work with these guys. I think we should just leave." Sawyer had to decide, and quickly, what to do.

- Case: Peru & Andrew Nelson
  On May 6, 2002 Andrew Nelson, an Associate Professor of Anthropology, had just returned from a trip to Peru where he wanted to establish a museum of cultural history and an accompanying international bioarchaeological research center. Nelson had successfully gathered all the necessary information and arranged all the required legal agreements while in Peru, and he turned now to fundraising. Nelson understood that, when he approached the private sector for funding, a proper business plan for this venture would be required. Never having previously been involved with such documents, Nelson set out to inform himself about business

plans and to prepare one for the Peruvian museum within the next few months.

- ### Case: CESO & Gordon Cummings

  During the first week of September 2003, Gordon Cummings, President & CEO of the Canadian Executive Service Organization (CESO) was busy in CESO's Operations Centre in Toronto preparing for a meeting of the Executive Committee of his Board of Directors, which was going to be held on September 27, 2003. He knew that the CESO organization was at a crossroads: CESO could either choose to continue operating as it had for more than three decades, which would probably please most of its staff and its roster of over 3000 volunteers, or it could undergo fundamental strategic changes in order to follow the new directions urged upon it by the Canadian International Development Agency (CIDA), the major funder of its international activities.

- ### Case: Ethiopia & Christine Gilmore

  On September 7, 1993, Christine Gilmore, the Administrator of an NGO called *Future Forests, Partners in African Community Development,* had just returned from the annual monitoring trip to their project in northern Ethiopia. She was starting to write a proposal to be submitted to the Board of Directors of *Future Forests* for the next phase of the project, and she was faced with making fundamental changes to the project in response to the wishes of the Ethiopian villagers.

Again, these are all real, and fairly recent, situations. Sawyer, Nelson, Cummings and Gilmore have all given written permission to use their experiences in this book and in courses that use this book.

Each of the cases in the book continues beyond the opening paragraph to provide the reader with the information that was available to the decision maker at the moment of the case. The information may be relevant or irrelevant, and is usually incomplete. The reader is then challenged as to what to do, and how to do it.

In addition to cases and case analyses, we include a large number of brief illustrative *examples* of actual activities that were useful in development projects in working towards intended results. There are also three *conversations* between Keenan and individuals who possess valuable insights that can be helpfully used in international development cooperation.

Cases don't start appearing in this book until Chapter Seven (some examples extracted from the cases appear as early as Chapter Three). Before then, we will introduce you to the concepts, principles and information that you will want to have at hand when tackling the cases.

This brings us to the structure of the book. In Chapter Two, we discuss the nature of international development cooperation—what it is, who does it, what are the needs and priorities of our partners in other countries, the fashions in international assistance over the years. Chapter Three (the longest chapter) explains what works in successful international development projects, and what doesn't work. What Canadians do in international development— the kinds of contributions Canadians are making-are in Chapter Four. Chapter Five explores where the money comes from to pay for these projects and programs, and what are the priorities and requirements of the funding agencies. Using this basic information, in Chapter Six we then go through the process of creating good projects, paying particular attention to the discipline provided by Results-based Management.

In Chapter Seven we start inserting cases, and we continue to provide new cases and case analyses throughout the remainder of the book. At the same time we introduce much more information of potential value to the reader, such as how to get projects properly started, establishing and managing NGOs, private sector development, business plans, international consulting and contracting, corruption and challenges to integrity, monitoring and evaluation, successful exchange programs, security and health hazards, how individuals get started in international development work, preparing yourself and your family for an overseas assignment, problems of re-entry to Canada, the role of research in development, some protocol advice on courtesies and taboos, and much more.

We have been asked who would benefit from using this book and by participating in courses based on this book. In general, we have written this book for the women and men at home and in our partner countries who are called upon to make international development decisions, as to what to do, and how to do it. These people include, for example, university and college undergraduate and graduate students in arts, social sciences, engineering, agriculture, and information sciences who are taking courses in international development, students of international business, senior university and college officials responsible for the internationalization of their institutions, university and college administrators responsible for international activities such as student exchanges, study abroad, preparation of project proposals and management of projects, employees of government departments and agencies involved in international cooperation, employees and volunteers of NGOs, private sector involved in international business and consulting, the general public and media interested in effective international development, as well as our partners and counterparts in other countries.

The book is intended to prepare the reader, first, to be an effective *practitioner* of international development cooperation, and also to be an effective *manager*. One successful academic model for achieving this is to use this book as the textbook for third year and fourth year courses in international development that contain a summer internship in a developing country between third and fourth years. The third year course prepares students to be practitioners; the fourth year course (enriched by the students' summer experiences) enhances their skills as managers.

Finally, as a note from the authors to the reader who is considering devoting all, or a portion, of her or his life to international development: there are an enormous number of truly important things for you to do, and you will find it fundamentally satisfying when you help to improve the quality of life in a community. It is our goal with this book to develop and sharpen your knowledge and your decision making skills so that you will do *effectively* whatever it is you choose to do with your life in international development.

CHAPTER TWO

THE NATURE OF INTERNATIONAL DEVELOPMENT: OBJECTIVES, NEEDS, PRIORITIES, AND FASHIONS

In its simplest terms, international development is sustainable improvement in the quality of life, especially for those in the world most in need. Working in international development is an attempt to make the world a better place.

That was the easy part. Now the questions get tough. What does one mean by "the quality of life"? What needs to be done to bring about an improvement in the quality of life? How will you know when (or even *if*) you have made such an improvement? How does one make the improvement sustainable? *Why* do it, i.e. why does it matter? Who can do it? Who *should* do it? How can we best work together with our partners in other countries—what are *their* aspirations, experiences and capabilities? How does one go about doing it? What does it cost? How should the work be organized? What countries should be targeted·for improvements? Which sectors of society should be helped? How do the concepts of fairness and gender equity come into play?

Moreover, how does one, in the context of chronically inadequate resources for foreign aid and development, make choices as to whom to help and what to do? What should we do first? How does a country that provides international assistance make resource allocations among emergency aid, post-disaster reconstruction, development cooperation, and debt relief? What training should one receive to do work of this kind? What personal characteristics are needed for doing development work?

HUMAN DEVELOPMENT INDEX

First, with respect to the quality of life, one place to start assessing this rather vague concept is the Human Development Index (HDI), listings of which for individual countries are found in the annual Human Development Reports of the United Nations Development Programme:

> *The Human Development Report (HDR) was first launched in 1990 with the single goal of putting people back at the center of the development process in terms of economic debate, policy and advocacy.*[3]

The HDRs were created under the leadership of Pakistani economist and finance minister Mahbub ul Haq, whom we quote here:

> *The basic purpose of development is to enlarge people's choices. In principle, these choices can be infinite and can change over time. People often value achievements that do not show up at all, or not immediately, in income or growth figures: greater access to knowledge, better nutrition and health services, more secure livelihoods, security against crime and physical violence, satisfying leisure hours, political and cultural freedoms and sense of participation in community activities. The objective of development is to create an enabling environment for people to enjoy long, healthy and creative lives.*[4]

The Human Development Index is based on four indicators:

- life expectancy at birth
- adult literacy rate
- enrollment in primary, secondary and tertiary schools, and
- GDP per capita.

In the 2004 HDR, HDI values were given for 177 counties. The *top* ten (in descending order) were Norway, Sweden, Australia, Canada, Netherlands, Belgium, Iceland, USA, Japan and Ireland. The *bottom* ten were Chad, Democratic Republic of the Congo, Central African Republic, Ethiopia, Mozambique, Guinea-Bissau, Burundi, Mali, Burkina Faso, Niger and Sierra Leone. The bottom ten are all in Africa. In fact, all but four of the bottom 37 countries are in Africa.[5]

For the top ten countries, the median HDI value was 0.94; for the bottom ten, it was 0.35. To understand what this means in human terms, one can compare a country in the midst of the top ten, for example Canada, with one in the bottom ten, say Burundi: at birth a Canadian can expect to live to the age of 79, but a newborn Burundian can only expect to reach, with some luck, the age of 41. Most adult Canadians are literate, but only half of Burundi's adults can read and write. GDP per capita in Canada is US$29,480; in Burundi, it is US$630.

An excellent presentation of this information is a wall-size map of the world produced by *Canadian Geographic* magazine and the Canadian International Development Agency (CIDA)[6]. Entitled *A Developing World*, it displays the HDI data for all countries. For each country, data are given for:

- surface area
- population
- life expectancy at birth, women/men
- net primary school enrolment rate, women/men
- Gross Domestic Product (GDP) per capita in US$ Purchasing Power Parity (PPP)[7]

On the map, each country is color-coded to indicate whether its HDI is high (yellow), medium (orange), or low (red). Yellow is the color of, for example, North America, Western and Central Europe, the Southern Cone of South America (Argentina, Chile, Uruguay), Japan, Australia, New Zealand, and Brunei. Red is seen almost exclusively in Africa.

MILLENNIUM DEVELOPMENT GOALS

In response to the terrible inequities revealed by the wide range in the values of the Human Development Index, in 2000 all 191 member countries of the United Nations met and pledged themselves to meet the following eight Millennium Development Goals (and the corresponding targets for each MDG) by the year 2015:

Eradicate extreme poverty and hunger.
- Reduce by half the proportion of people living on less than a dollar a day.
- Reduce by half the proportion of people who suffer from hunger.

Achieve universal primary education.

• Ensure that all boys and girls complete a full course of primary schooling.

Promote gender equality and empower women.

• Eliminate gender disparity in primary and secondary education preferably by 2005, and at all levels by 2015.

Reduce child mortality.

• Reduce by two thirds the mortality rate among children under five.

Improve maternal health.

• Reduce by three quarters the maternal mortality ratio.

Combat HIV/AIDS, malaria and other diseases.

• Halt and begin to reverse the spread of HIV/AIDS.

• Halt and begin to reverse the incidence of malaria and other major diseases.

Ensure environmental sustainability.

• Integrate the principles of sustainable development into country policies and programs; reverse loss of environmental resources.

• Reduce by half the proportion of people without sustainable access to safe drinking water.

• Achieve significant improvement in lives of at least 100 million slum dwellers, by 2020.

Develop a global partnership for development.

• Develop further an open trading and financial system that is rule-based, predictable and non-discriminatory.

• Include a commitment to good governance, development and poverty reduction—nationally and internationally.

• Address the least developed countries' special needs. This includes tariff- and quota-free access for their exports; enhanced debt relief for heavily indebted poor countries; cancellation of official bilateral debt; and more generous official development assistance for countries committed to poverty reduction.

- Address the special needs of landlocked and small island developing states.

- Deal comprehensively with developing countries' debt problems through national and international measures to make debt sustainable in the long term.

- In cooperation with the developing countries, develop decent and productive work for youth.

- In cooperation with pharmaceutical companies, provide access to affordable essential drugs in developing countries.

- In cooperation with the private sector, make available the benefits of new technologies—especially information and communication technologies.[8]

The United Nations Development Programme (UNDP), as the UN's global development network, links and coordinates global and national efforts to reach the Millennium Goals. Then-UN Secretary-General Kofi Annan asked UNDP Administrator Mark Malloch Brown, in his capacity as chair of the UN Development Group, to be the coordinator of the Millennium Development Goals in the UN system—to make them an integral part of the UN's work worldwide. UNDP does so by integrating the MDGs into all aspects of the UN system's work at the country level. For more than 70 of the poorest countries, the main strategic tool is a nationally-owned poverty reduction strategy paper, which relates to national budgets, development activities and other assistance frameworks. National poverty reduction strategies are discussed a few paragraphs below.

The Millennium Project was commissioned by the United Nations Secretary-General in 2002 to develop a concrete action plan for the world to achieve the Millennium Development Goals. In 2005, the independent advisory body headed by Professor Jeffrey Sachs presented its final recommendations to the Secretary-General in a synthesis volume *Investing in Development: A Practical Plan to Achieve the Millennium Development Goals.*[9]

The World Bank evaluated in 2004 the progress being made towards meeting the MDGs and concluded, disappointingly:

> *...if current trends in growth and poverty reduction continue, the goal for eradicating extreme income poverty is within reach. But it may well be the only goal to be attained, for many of the other non-income goals—*

such as universal primary education, promoting gender equality and reducing child mortality—current rates of progress are too slow.[10]

NATIONAL POVERTY REDUCTION STRATEGY PAPERS[11]

With respect to the first Millennium Development Goal above, "Eradicate extreme poverty and hunger", developing countries have been urged by the World Bank (WB) and the International Monetary Fund (IMF) to create and implement national poverty reduction strategies. Poverty Reduction Strategy Papers (PRSPs) describe a country's macroeconomic, structural and social policies and programs to promote growth and reduce poverty, as well as associated external financing needs. PRSPs are prepared by governments through a participatory process involving civil society and development partners, including the WB and the IMF.

As of February 28, 2005 some 44 developing countries had prepared their national PRSPs and 10 more were in the process of doing so. The PRSP for each country is located on the IMF's web site.[12]

According to the World Bank,

> *For the most part…PRSPs to date have focused on economic and structural policies to achieve higher growth rates and on social sector investments. Documents have also highlighted the importance of transparency, accountability, good governance, and empowerment of the poor in this process…Ideally, a country-owned poverty reduction strategy will enjoy the support of all of a country's development partners, and will provide a common framework for their assistance programs in the country…Many governments have begun to use the PRSP process as a means to improve aid coordination.*

Because it is important that donor countries not trip over or duplicate each other while working in a particular developing country, agency coordination is one of the basic principles to be followed in the project creation process. The national PRSPs are one of the more useful documents to be carefully considered in ensuring complementarity of assistance efforts.

With respect to the large multilaterals we have been mentioning such as the UN, UNDP, WB, and IMF, explanations of who and what they are, and of their funding programs in support of international development that the reader can tap into, are presented in Chapter Five. Canada's own international assistance agencies are first introduced in Chapters Three and Four, and their funding programs are described in Chapter Five.

FUNDS DEVOTED TO FOREIGN AID

By now, the reader has an idea of the enormously wide range of what needs to be done in order to bring about (in the words we used at the beginning of this chapter) "sustainable improvement in the quality of life, especially for those in the world most in need". This is going to be costly. How much is the world—and how much is Canada-prepared to spend on international development?

In the fiscal year 2005-2006, Canada spent $3.7 billion on international aid.[13] A UN commission led by former Canadian Prime Minister Lester Pearson proposed, in 1970, a target of 0.7% of GDP as the amount of money to be devoted to foreign aid by rich nations. According to the Globe and Mail[14], in 2005 (four decades later) Canada was contributing only 0.28%. At that time, "Just five rich countries devote 0.7 per cent of GDP or more to foreign aid: Denmark, Norway, Sweden, the Netherlands and Luxembourg".

FASHIONS IN INTERNATIONAL DEVELOPMENT

Let's spend a few minutes to take a glimpse at how those in the development business actually go about their work. For this, we are going to turn to the writings of Jack Westoby. Westoby was an almost legendary economist and statistician who retired in 1974 from the Forestry Department of the Food and Agriculture Organization of the United Nations (FAO) after 22 years of distinguished, and occasionally controversial, service. During this time, he was one of the leading thinkers struggling with the questions of how forests can be used to serve mankind and, more generally, how the process of development takes place. At one point he wryly observed that, in order to make a contribution to international development, "it was necessary to lose one's illusions while keeping one's faith".[15]

In 1978, Westoby looked back on the thirty or so years since the end of the Second World War (when modern global development efforts had their start) and reviewed, humorously but somewhat ruefully, the many changes in the fashions in development thinking over that time:

> *In the late 1940s, it was assumed that countries that were less developed were that way because they were "late starters". They were further behind on the road to development than other countries and, therefore, in order to catch up, they needed know-how. So, says Westoby, "Experts started to flood into the underdeveloped countries, and the era of development by exhortation was under way". This was the 'tell me' phase.*

Shortly thereafter, "the fatuity of disembodied advice, advice not backed up by concrete help, became obvious. The international assistance effort was stepped up, and development aid moved from exhortation to demonstration: from the 'tell me' phase to the 'show me' phase. The walking know-how of experts was supplemented by increasing amounts of hardware."

Later, emphasis shifted to the need for education and training, and a "flow of young and serious Third World students trekked north and west to assimilate irrelevant knowledge and master inappropriate technologies".

Next was the realization that investment was the key to development. We had entered "the era of pre-investment surveys, feasibility studies, leading to 'bankable' projects and actual investment. To sustain the flow of development assistance funds, articles appeared in the business weeklies showing how aid not only soothed the donor's conscience but lined his pockets too. It was possible to do well by doing good."

"Down the years, the international apparatus for dealing with development problems grew by leaps and bounds, as attention concentrated on this or that piece of the development jigsaw…Non-industrialized nations are poor. Industrialized nations are prosperous. Therefore prosperity lies in industrialization. Thus, after a struggle, the United Nations Industrial Development Organization (UNIDO) was born, in the teeth of the opposition of the already industrialized nations."

"Worsening terms of trade more than wiped out the flow of aid. Came the new cry, 'Trade, not aid'…eventually the United Nations Conference on Trade and Development (UNCTAD) was born, in recognition of the intimate connection between trade and development."

"The poor nations' efforts to develop were being frustrated by their propensity to breed too fast, so the UN Population Fund was set up. "And so on and so forth."[16]

Each of these development assistance methods ran into difficulties insofar as they were *single-mode* approaches to development. We have reached the stage where we recognize the need to use *all* of the above components listed by Westoby (and more) in a comprehensive approach that is tailor-made to the needs and possibilities of each individual case. We need direct technical assistance and advice, we need demonstration projects, we need capital, we need assistance with industrialization, and we need training and education, in working with developing countries. And, above all, we need to work *with* the countries.

The target is national and community self-reliance. When the countries no longer need us, we will have accomplished our objectives, and the international assistance organizations can go happily out of business.[17]

CHAPTER THREE

SUCCESSFUL DEVELOPMENT PROJECTS: WHAT WORKS AND WHAT DOESN'T

The authors hope that you enjoyed reading the ironic reflections of Jack Westoby at the end of the previous chapter. With the benefit of hindsight, Westoby identified a number of approaches that were *not* very successful in international development, some of which were:

- talking rather than listening

- taking a single-mode approach to development rather than a comprehensive approach

- transferring irrelevant information and inappropriate technologies, and

- expecting that Western entrepreneurs and investors would use their money to provide developing countries with what they most needed.

The follow-up question, therefore, is what *does* work well in reaching the goal identified in Chapter Two of "bringing about sustainable improvement in the quality of life, especially for those in the world most in need"? This chapter contains a compilation of the most significant elements and characteristics of development projects that have proven to be helpful in achieving this goal. They have been assembled into two categories:

(a)   choosing the **desired results** to be targeted, and
(b)   choosing the **approaches and methodologies** to be employed in working towards the desired results.

In creating successful development projects, the objective is: after understanding the needs, aspirations, experience and capabilities of your partners and the possibilities available in the development situation, to utilize the approaches and methodologies discussed below to achieve as many as are applicable of the desired results.

The desired results and the approaches and methodologies covered in this chapter are summarized in the list below. The reader is encouraged to examine the various cases and case analyses presented later in this book to determine which of these results and approaches are included in each case.

Several examples are given in this chapter of actual specific activities that were usefully carried out in achieving the desired results. Many of these examples are extracted from the cases and case analyses that are presented later in the book. Some examples are used more than once where there are different aspects of the example to be highlighted.

Desired Results

- Reduction of extreme poverty and hunger
- Education and training
- Gender equality and empowerment
- Improved health and nutrition
- Combating HIV/AIDS, malaria and other diseases
- Protection of children and women
- Reduced environmental impact
- Sustainability of intended results
- Increased awareness through public advocacy and development education
- Financial assistance
- Local ownership, equality and accountability
- Improved infrastructure
- Provision of appropriate equipment
- Improved language skills
- Good governance and human rights

Approaches and Methodologies

- Listening to your partners
- Building capacity, including research capacity
- Training the trainers
- Getting started properly
- Benchmarking and baselines
- Thinking outside the box

- Choosing the right partners
- Donor coordination and Sector Wide Approaches
- Extending intended results through effective communication
- Management structures, processes and communication
- Results-based Management
- Achieving consensus through collective decision making
- Flexibility and adaptability
- Creating long-term partnerships
- Managing expectations
- Monitoring, evaluation, and mid-term corrections
- Maintaining good links with the Canadian mission in the country

DESIRED RESULTS

REDUCTION OF EXTREME POVERTY AND HUNGER

Poverty is thought of, primarily, as the lack of money or other resources to enable an individual (or a family, or a community, or a country) to obtain the food necessary to avoid persistent hunger and chronic malnutrition. More broadly, poverty can also be thought of as the lack of resources to obtain shelter or clothing or health care or education or security. Most broadly, however, poverty has been described as (in addition to the above) the absence of opportunities or options in one's life, e.g. the lack of an opportunity for a child to obtain an education, the lack of choice for a woman to be married or to be educated (or both), the absence of the option for a man either to survive by a life of violence or to build a life of dignity, security and service to others.

Child poverty and hunger: Two Afghan children in an internally displaced person camp about 15 km west of the western Afghan city of Heart. Most of the children in the camp are barefoot and poorly dressed. (Photograph: UNICEF Afghanistan/2001/ Ahmed Masoud)

Eradication of extreme poverty and hunger is the first of the eight Millennium Development Goals[18] (the MDGs were discussed in Chapter Two). In that context, one indicator of extreme poverty is living on less than US$1 per day. In 2006, the UN reported:

> *In 1990, more than 1.2 billion people – 28 per cent of the developing world's population – lived in extreme poverty. By 2002, the proportion decreased to 19 per cent. During that period, rates of extreme poverty fell rapidly in much of Asia, where the number of people living on less than $1 a day dropped by nearly a quarter of a billion people. Progress was not so rapid in Latin America and the Caribbean, which now has a larger share of people living in poverty than South-Eastern Asia and Oceania. Poverty rates in Western Asia and Northern Africa remained almost unchanged between 1990 and 2002 and increased in the transition economies of South-Eastern Europe and the Commonwealth of Independent States (CIS). These two regions had previously nearly eradicated the worst forms of poverty, and recent survey data suggest that their poverty rates are again dropping. In sub-Saharan Africa, although the poverty rate declined marginally, the number of people living in extreme poverty increased by 140 million...*
>
> *Chronic hunger—measured by the proportion of people lacking the food needed to meet their daily needs—has declined in the developing world. But progress overall is not fast enough to reduce the number of people going hungry, which increased between 1995-1997 and 2001-2003. An estimated 824 million people in the developing world were affected by chronic hunger in 2003.*
>
> *The worst-affected regions—sub-Saharan Africa and southern Asia—have made progress in recent years. But their advances have not kept pace with those of the early 1990s, and the number of people going hungry is increasing. Of particular concern is Eastern Asia: in the early 1990s, the number of hungry people declined; but again it is on the rise.* [19]

Recently, the World Bank raised the poverty line from US$1 per day, which is the criterion used above, to US$1.25 per day as a result of extensive research on the actual cost of living around the world. The change in this criterion has increased the estimate of those living in poverty from 900 million to 1.4 billion.[20] The expression "The Bottom Billion" is sometimes used for these unfortunate souls.[21]

One method widely used in development projects to reduce poverty is the **stimulation of economic activity**, such as the nurturing of entrepreneurial activity to create small and medium size enterprises. Economic activity can be stimulated by:

- the provision of skills training for the technology of the enterprise
- the provision of skills training for the management of the enterprise
- the multiplicative approach of "training-the-trainers"
- the provision of microcredit or revolving loans
- encouraging gender equality and empowerment
- improving health and thus the ability to learn and to work
- creating essential physical infrastructure such as roads and communication systems
- improving access to the services of government agencies
- creating a governance system that supports-rather than impedes– small scale economic development.

» Example: Egypt & rural women

One nice example of the stimulation of economic activity is a project carried out by Mansoura University in the Nile Delta of Egypt, with the cooperation of the University of Guelph, to create formal and informal extension programs for rural agricultural communities. The informal ones are directed towards villagers, and utilize personal contacts, appropriate training, and extension materials. One is called the Rural Small Enterprises Program. This is a program designed to help poor girls and women in the villages (aged about 18 to 35), by technical assistance through training and the use of pamphlets prepared in the project, to create microenterprises.

Related to this, the program helps NGOs in the villages, "Social Care Societies", to manage the projects. They are forming groups of about ten women, each with a facilitator, to deal with the marketing of the products (e.g. agricultural or animal production, or handicrafts) of the microenterprises. They organize marketing courses of a few days duration, following which the women spend about two weeks going to the places where they intend to market their products, e.g. factories. They then return to the course to discuss their findings, especially any apparent obstacles. After all this, they make final decisions about the products they want to produce, and therefore what training they would like to have for this purpose.

The project also conducts training-of-trainers courses so that they can replicate the training for other groups of women and possibly for other nearby villages. The microenterprises have a value of 1000 Egyptian pounds or less (for example, growing mushrooms, raising poultry or rabbits), and therefore local resources of the villages, or even of the women themselves, can be mobilized. [22]

» Example: Peru & *pro-poor* tourism

In Chapter Ten, there is a case entitled *Peru & Andrew Nelson*. Closely related to this case is a proposal to create a Northern Tourism Circuit in Peru that will take pressure off the major sites in the south, notably Cuzco and Machu Picchu, which now receive virtually all tourists to Peru. As a result, these southern sites are undergoing significant degradation.

The Northern Tourism Circuit is also a *pro-poor* international development concept that was elaborated in 2002 on the basis of research done under the auspices of the British Embassy. Tourism is seen as a vehicle that can bring about positive change in this region. The idea is that local people along the route of the Circuit could obtain income from food sales, hostels, guiding, guarding, and handicrafts (e.g. carving and weaving). The inputs needed for this project are infrastructure enhancements such as improving the roads and re-opening an airport, training courses for guides, providing security for the archaeological sites, some language training, marketing assistance, and loans to providers of food and accommodation.

A weaver using a backstrap loom in the Utcubamba Valley on the proposed Northern Tourism Circuit of Peru

» Example: CESO & economic development

The Canadian Executive Service Organization (CESO)[23] is a not-for-profit organization of Volunteer Advisors founded in 1967 to provide social and economic development assistance in developing nations, in emerging market economies of Eastern Europe and the former Soviet Union, and in Canada, especially in aboriginal communities. There are over 3000 Volunteer Advisors on its roster, with experience in more than 150 professional, management and technical areas. These VAs serve as trainers, advisors and mentors in about 1500 assignments annually, of which 700 are international and 800 are in Canada.

Historically, CESO has worked in virtually any area in which there was a skill on its roster that was needed by a client. These included a broad number of sectors including economic development, education, health, governance and social development, among others. Compared to the other eight Volunteer Cooperation Agencies (e.g. WUSC, CUSO and CECI), CESO's activities a few years ago were much more diverse and much less focused in regard to programmatic impact or to geographic coverage. However, CIDA, the major funder of CESO's international activities, was looking for considerably tighter focus in regard both to areas of development assistance and to geographic range. If CESO has a single predominant sectoral strength of interest to CIDA, it is private sector development or economic development. In fact, most of the work done in recent years, both for aboriginal peoples and internationally, has been in the economic development area. About 70% of the entire roster of volunteers comes from the business and economic development sectors.

CESO therefore reduced its range of activities to its core strength of economic development assistance. This includes help with:

- drawing up business plans
- marketing
- inventory
- production management
- quality control
- bookkeeping
- building physical infrastructure in support of economic development, such as water resources.

Moreover, CESO has wisely taken a *broad* approach to fostering economic development, e.g. human resources development, including training and precursor activities such as increasing literacy, and governance in support of economic development.

Chapter Ten, *Small Enterprises*, discusses these concepts in greater detail.

The discussion on poverty and hunger in this book is centered on the situation in less developed countries (LDCs), but poverty, malnutrition and hunger are also present in some highly developed countries, such as Canada. Development should be thought of as a global set of issues, rather than just in the global South. In Chapter Two, we talked about the Human Development Index and the enormous disparities in HDI values among countries, e.g. for the top ten countries, the median HDI value is 0.94; for the bottom ten, it is 0.35. However, the median value of a particular country, whether high or low, does not reflect the range of living conditions within that country. The ratio of the comfort level of the economically top 10% within a country to that of the lowest 10% can be enormous, for both developed and developing countries. For this reason, organizations such as CESO provide their services both internationally and in Canada.

An indicator of the disparity of family incomes within a country is the Gini Index (or the Gini Coefficient)[24]. At one extreme, a Gini Index value of zero means that every family in the country receives exactly the same income (there is zero disparity—every family receives the same income); at the other extreme, a Gini Index value of 100% means that just one family in the country receives all the income (there is 100% disparity). Sweden and Norway, not surprisingly, have the lowest Gini Index values (23% and 25%, respectively); Canada is 32%, South Africa 65%, Namibia 71%.[25]

In contrast to direct small scale economic activity, the concept that an increase in the total wealth of a country (e.g. its GDP) will lead through a "trickle-down effect" to improvements in the life of the poorest members of society is generally seen as being much less effective than direct income generation. The economics cliché that "a rising tide floats all boats" is not very helpful when, like many African villagers, you live far from the sea and you don't have a boat.[26]

Another strategy in reducing chronic hunger and malnutrition is helping to increase *food security* in the community, in the region, or in the country. One method, dating from the story of Joseph in Egypt in biblical times, is the establishment of storage facilities such as grain warehouses to smooth out the variations between "the lean years and the fat years". Other methods are maintenance of biodiversity, increasing agricultural productivity, education and training, agricultural trials and research, and capacity building.

» Example: Inca food security

"At the time of the Spanish conquest, the Incas cultivated almost as many species of plants as the farmers of all Asia or Europe. It has been estimated that Andean Indians domesticated as many as 70 separate crop species[27]. On mountainsides up to four kilometers high along the spine of a whole continent and in climates varying from tropical to polar, they grew a wealth of roots, grains, legumes, vegetables, fruits, and nuts.

"Without money, iron, wheels, or work animals for plowing, the Indians terraced and irrigated and produced abundant food for fifteen million or more people—roughly as many as inhabit the highlands today. Throughout the vast Inca Empire, sprawling from southern Colombia to central Chile—an area as great as that governed by Rome at its zenith—storehouses overflowed with grains and dried tubers. Because of the Inca's productive agriculture and remarkable public organization, it was usual to have 3–7 years' supply of food in storage."[28]

Inca terraces for intensive food production

» Example: The Green Revolution[29]

The Green Revolution is a term used to describe the transformation of agriculture in many developing nations that led to significant increases in agricultural production between the 1940s and 1960s. This transformation occurred as the result of programs of agricultural research, extension, and infrastructural development, instigated and largely funded by the Rockefeller Foundation, along with the Ford Foundation and other major agencies.

The Green Revolution has had major social and ecological impacts, which have drawn intense praise and equally intense criticism.

The projects within the Green Revolution spread technologies that had already existed, but had not been widely used outside of industrialized nations. These technologies included pesticides, irrigation projects, and synthetic nitrogen fertilizer.

The novel technological development of the Green Revolution was the production of what some referred to as "miracle seeds." Scientists created strains of maize, wheat, and rice that are generally referred to as HYVs or "high yielding varieties." Cereal production more than doubled in developing nations between the years 1961–1985. Yields of rice, maize, and wheat increased steadily during that period. The major purported achievement of the Green Revolution has been that the production increases have helped to avoid widespread famine.

The transition from traditional agriculture in which inputs were generated on-farm to Green Revolution agriculture, which required the purchase of inputs, led to the widespread establishment of rural credit institutions. Smaller farmers often went into debt, which in many cases resulted in a loss of rights to their farmland. The increased level of mechanization on larger farms made possible by the Green Revolution removed an important source of employment from the rural economy. Because wealthier farmers had better access to credit and land, the Green Revolution increased class disparities. Because some regions were able to adopt Green Revolution agriculture more readily than others (for political or geographical reasons), interregional economic disparities increased as well.

The new economic difficulties of smallholder farmers and landless farm workers led to increased rural-urban migration. The increase in food production led to a decrease in food prices for urban dwellers, and the increase in urban population increased the potential for industrialization. However, industry was unable to absorb all of the displaced agricultural labor and some cities grew at unsustainable rates.

Green Revolution agriculture increased the use of pesticides, which were necessary to limit the high levels of pest damage that inevitably occur in monocultures...problems with pesticides include the poisoning of farm workers, the contamination of water, and the evolution of resistance in pest organism populations.

Irrigation projects have created significant problems of salinization, waterlogging, and lowering of water tables in certain areas.

The spread of Green Revolution agriculture affected both agricultural biodiversity and wild biodiversity. There is little argument that the Green Revolution acted to reduce agricultural biodiversity, as it relied upon just a few varieties of each crop. This has led to concerns about the susceptibility of a food supply to pathogens that cannot be controlled by agrochemicals, as well as the permanent loss of many valuable genetic traits bred into cereal varieties over thousands of years.

EDUCATION AND TRAINING

This intended result embraces primary education for children, secondary education, post-secondary education, postgraduate education, adult education, continuing education, and skills training.

Achieving universal primary education for children is the second UN Millennium Development Goal, with the target being to "ensure that, by 2015, children everywhere, boys and girls alike, will be able to complete a full course of primary schooling". In 2006, the UN reported[30]:

> Educating all children presents a significant challenge due to the large number of children who live in remote, rural areas of developing countries. High rates of poverty in rural areas limit educational opportunities because of demands for children's labor, low levels of parental education and lack of access to good quality schooling. Based on household surveys in 80 developing countries, 30 per cent of rural children of primary-school age do not attend school, compared to 18 per cent in urban areas. And because rural areas have larger populations of children, they account for 82 per cent of children who are not in school in developing countries...
>
> Globally, more than one in five girls of primary-school age are not in school, compared to about one in six boys. Oceania, Western Asia and Southern Asia are the regions where the gender gap is most evident. Of particular concern is the wide gender gap in sub-Saharan Africa and Southern Asia, where almost 80 per cent of the world's out-of-school children live.

All three examples in the previous section *Reduction of extreme poverty and hunger* utilized training programs of different types in efforts to stimulate local economic activity in order to reduce poverty. The following are three more examples of how education and training have usefully been incorporated into development projects.

» Example: Afghanistan & schooling for girls

An example of the extreme difficulty for girls and women to receive primary level education was the situation in Afghanistan a few years ago. When the Taliban held power in Afghanistan, it was forbidden for girls and women to go to school.

In 2001, after the fall of the Taliban, an inter-faith grassroots fundraising campaign in London, Ontario raised almost $200,000 for the children and women of Afghanistan during the rebuilding phase. This campaign originated from a group of concerned citizens and included students in the public and separate school system, the university and the community college, Christian leaders of the various churches, and Muslim organizations in the city.

The campaign organizers chose to direct the funds to an international organization with a consistent track record of successfully delivering funds to designated groups with minimal administrative costs involved, with an unquestioned international reputation for supporting the welfare of children, and with a long term experience in providing developmental assistance across the world. They chose UNICEF because it meets these criteria, and because of its work in Afghanistan in childhood education, with emphasis on girls having access to schools.

Nigel Fisher, the President of UNICEF Canada, had been in Rwanda with UNICEF in 1994 after the genocide. It was UNICEF's across-the-board policy to get children back into schools quickly as an important response to an emergency, and so, by September 1994 (just three months after the genocide ended) UNICEF had managed to assist in getting roughly 200,000 Rwandan children back into schools. In 2001, days after 9/11, Fisher was assigned by UNICEF to lead its programs for Afghans in Afghanistan and neighboring countries. Prior to the fall of the Taliban, UNICEF and other organizations had been supporting schooling for girls through a secret school system, "home schools", in which teachers, often women, were teaching small groups of children (mostly girls) in homes. Education of girls was forbidden, and so probably less than 1% of girls were being schooled at that time. When the Taliban fell, UNICEF worked with the new government to develop a major back-to-school program for children. Fisher and his UNICEF colleagues had gone around to Afghan refugee camps in September and October of 2001 and asked "As you return to Afghanistan, what would give you hope for the future?" The predominant answer was "Education for our kids." UNICEF then began to engage Afghans, both educators in Afghanistan and from the diaspora, in discussing the launch of a rapid nationwide back-to-school program.

Once UNICEF could resume full-scale operations in Afghanistan after the December 2001 Bonn peace agreement, preparations accelerated. Working together with a very new Afghan education minister and his team, UNICEF rapidly built up a strong education and logistics team, partnering with other agencies, including USAID and international curriculum experts, to develop curricula and textbooks. UNICEF also signed on a Japanese NGO to augment its own logistics capacity, mapped existing schools, called on teachers and former teachers to report for duty through the media and then fanned out over the country to organize logistics, identify sites for schools, arrange for quick repairs, establish new schools, recruit and train new teachers, provide school materials and textbooks. In March 2002, President Karzai, together with Carol Bellamy (then Executive Director of UNICEF) and Nigel Fisher (at that time an Assistant Secretary-General and Deputy Special Representative of the U.N. Secretary-General in Afghanistan), launched the back-to school program. Between 3 and 3½ million children went back to school in March 2002, one-third of those being girls. This has continued to progress to the point where today there are over 9000 functioning schools, six million children in school, of whom two million are girls (compared with less than 10,000 girls in secret home schools in 2001), continued teacher training, continued upgrading of facilities, and continued building of new schools.[31]

Afghanistan: Girls raise their hands in a tent classroom at Phool-e-Rangeena Government School in the north-western city of Herat. Like many schools throughout the country, the facility has been overwhelmed with children returning to classrooms after years of conflict. (Credit: UNICEF/ HQ07-1086/Shehzad Noorani.)

» Example: FSU & educational reform

In the early 1990s, the countries of the Former Soviet Union (FSU) were undergoing dramatic changes towards democracy and market economies. Educators in Canada and their counterparts in Belarus and Russia, with funding from the Gorbachev Foundation, developed new curricula, textbooks and classroom support materials in civic education to replace the Communist era materials. At the same time, students from the business school at the University of Western Ontario delivered intensive introductory business courses for managers, entrepreneurs and university students in several cities throughout Russia and Eastern Europe.

» Example: Vietnam & social work[32]

The rural poor have not fully benefited from the recent impressive economic progress made by Vietnam following its transition from a centrally planned economy to an open market economy. On the contrary, this group appears to have suffered from the effects of globalization, as well as from other problems. Symptoms include increases in the presence of street children, family violence, abuse of children through labor practices and sexual exploitation, prostitution, trafficking of women and children, abuse of the elderly, emotional stress, unrelieved poverty, HIV/AIDS, drug and alcohol abuse. The need for trained social workers to help deal with this is growing very rapidly, with regard both to the numbers of social workers and to their training and qualifications. There are currently many people in Vietnam who provide social services, but most are untrained and work "according to their hearts and their intuition".

The University of Labor and Social Affairs (ULSA) in Hanoi, with the cooperation of Memorial University of Newfoundland, has provided training workshops in various aspects of social work. When the mid-term evaluators of this project were in Vietnam, they travelled to the town of Ha Nam south of Hanoi and met in the Vocational Orientation Training Centre with seven government-employed social service providers (four males, three females) who had received training from the project. Six had attended short-term training workshops, and one woman had taken an 8-month course. They work, respectively, in seven different communes (mainly rural), and provide services such as the following:

- providing health care insurance for poor people
- disseminating information on health care matters, including family planning, reproductive health, and HIV/AIDS

- vocational orientation training, e.g. sewing and woodworking
- support services to families with disabled children, including Down Syndrome sufferers and those deformed from birth or developmentally delayed as the result of a parent having been exposed to Agent Orange during the American War[33]
- helping to look after invalids and veterans
- implementing the local and national poverty reduction strategies, such as helping to set up businesses, counseling re taxes, and encouraging young people to study
- re-settling and re-integrating street children
- cultural activities for the communities
- investigating reports of family violence and, through mediation groups, helping to take action
- helping to obtain microcredit loans to set up small enterprises to supplement family income from rice growing, e.g. weaving, handicrafts, woodcarving.

When asked what affect the new training had on their provision of social

A trainee at the Ha Nam Vocational Orientation Training Centre in Vietnam

services in their local communities, interesting replies were received: one said that previously he had thought of family violence simply as a husband beating his wife. Afterwards, he realized it was more complicated—there is abuse of children, abuse of elderly parents, etc., and he had developed a fuller understanding of the causes of family violence. This gave him the ability to be more effective in mediation groups and in taking action against violence. Another said that, prior to the workshop, he looked down on people with AIDS and their families: "I thought they were dirty things." The workshop helped him to remove his prejudices: "Now, I'm not afraid of them." Another: "As a result of the workshop, I understand better the needs of vulnerable people. I help to re-settle street children, and give them information about HIV/AIDS and counsel them about child labor and abuse." Another: "To help street children stay away from drugs and violence, I help them organize clubs and sports." One more: "We used the teaching manuals from ULSA to educate our family members and neighbors."

In Chapter Seventeen, we will introduce the Centre for Intercultural Learning[34] (CIL) of the Canadian Foreign Service Institute of the Department of Foreign Affairs and International Trade (DFAIT). CIL provides training programs to develop intercultural effectiveness in Canadians who are about to go abroad to work or to volunteer in CIDA-funded projects. CIL has studied the effectiveness of training in international projects and has published *Re-examining the role of training in contributing to international project success: A literature review and an outline of a new model training program*[35], which is recommended reading for Westerners who will be trying to create or deliver training activities in other countries.

GENDER EQUALITY AND EMPOWERMENT

Women hold up half the sky. (Mao Zedong)

Gender equality and the empowerment of women is another of the Millennium Development Goals[36]:

Women represent an increasing share of the world's labor force – over a third in all regions except Southern and Western Asia and Northern Africa. However women remain at a disadvantage in securing paid jobs. Wage differentials, occupational segregation, higher unemployment rates and their disproportionate representation in the informal and subsistence sectors limit women's economic advancement. Sociocultural attitudes, employment policies and a lack of options for balancing work and family responsibilities or for controlling the timing and spacing of births contribute further to inequality in the labor market.

Women's political participation has increased significantly since 1990. One in five parliamentarians elected in 2005 are women, bringing the percentage of parliamentary seats held by women in 2006 worldwide to almost 17. In 20 countries, more than 30 per cent of parliamentarians are women.

Much has been written and published about gender equality, for example, by the Canadian International Development Agency (CIDA)[37] and by the Association of Universities and Colleges of Canada (AUCC)[38]. Fundamentally, however, the reasons for wanting to have gender equality as a cross-cutting feature in development projects boil down to just two: *fairness* and *effectiveness*. Fairness is an obvious objective to anyone educated in the liberal humanistic tradition. As for effectiveness, there is abundant evidence that development—international and national development—just works better when barriers to women are removed.

Indicators of gender equality include:

- The relative numbers of women participants
- The number of women having decision-making roles at various levels
- Lack of impediments—formal and informal—to either women or men participating in, or receiving benefits from, the program
- The economic rewards from a paid activity are the same for men and women
- Absence of prejudice or stigma against either men or women participating in certain activities.

Although gender equality overwhelmingly refers to removing impediments to *women*, it also applies to men, e.g. there should not be obstacles facing men enrolling in nursing schools or joining the nursing profession after graduation.

» Example: Empowerment of rural Ethiopian women

A group of Canadian volunteers spent over a year in Ethiopia providing emergency relief to agricultural villagers during the terrible drought and famine of the mid-1980s. When the crisis eased and the Canadians came home, they realized that they could not simply close the door on the friendships they had built up in Ethiopia. Consequently, they decided to form an NGO called *Future Forests of London: Partners in African Rural Development*, and made the transition from emergency relief to development cooperation.

Subsequently, while working in the villages, *Future Forests* urged the Ethiopian villagers to hold local elections in order to create a grassroots Partnership Committee that would have representatives of all four villages (three Muslim, one Orthodox Christian) who could speak to the development aspirations of all four villages.

The Partnership Committee was to have several subcommittees, such as the Water Committee, the School Committee, the Health Committee, the Adult Literacy Committee, the Oxen Loan Committee. Astoundingly, when the nominations for the elections were being made, village men insisted that women should be on the committees "because they know more about what is going on in every household in the villages than the men do—the women know the water situation, the food situation, the schooling situation, the health situation". Economic or political status in the community was not a factor in the choices—rather, they nominated some very poor women who had known bad times and who had brought their families through the bad times. The elections were held, and several women were elected. The elected women participated, strongly and wisely, on the Partnership Committee (four of the ten members were women) and on the subcommittees. The committees worked very effectively, in large measure because of the knowledge the women brought to them.

Some subcommittees were composed entirely of women. One such committee (consisting mainly of orphaned girls and widows), had the idea to create a fruit and vegetable garden. This was unusual because creating and tending food crops were traditionally male roles but, because of the warfare, many men had died or were off with the army, and thus some women were heads of households. *Future Forests* helped get the garden started. The garden was successful: the women solicited and secured contracts to supply juice stores, their produce was sold in the market, and the women accumulated a cash profit. Rather than keeping the cash in their homes, they had the unprecedented idea of opening a bank account in a major nearby town. After twice being laughed at and rebuffed, they eventually managed to open a bank account, the first one that had ever been established by rural women in this part of Ethiopia.

Empowered by this success, the women began to think about establishing a local grinding mill so that they would not have to make long trips either to the north or to the south of the villages in order to have their grain milled. *Future Forests* learned about a special fund (the *Canada Fund*) administered by the Canadian

Embassy in Addis Ababa intended to assist rural women with entrepreneurial projects. *FF* and the women of the committee obtained the appropriate application forms, and worked night after night to answer the questions and fill in the forms. They also created a business plan, which was required to accompany the application! The forms were submitted, the funds were approved, and the women arranged for the construction of the mill. Then the women successfully operated the mill, including soliciting tenders for the equipment, buying the equipment, maintaining the equipment, advertising, arranging electrical service, hiring a young man to lift the heavier grain bags into the hopper, bookkeeping and accounting, the weighing, and all the decision-making.

The women's grinding mill in Bette, Ethiopia (Photograph courtesy of Future Forests)

» Example: Mongolian women & geology[39]

The Mongolian University of Science and Technology (MUST) is encouraging women to become professional geologists. This is going well, as evidenced by several indicators:

- At the Master's and Doctoral levels in geology, the number of women students exceeds the number of men. At the undergraduate level, the number of females is only slightly less than the number of males.

- There are no gender impediments in admission requirements or degree program activities.

- The Head of the Geology Department is a woman, and she is actively encouraging women to join the profession of geology.

- A half-day gender conference ("Mongolian Women in Geoscience & Community") was held in Mongolia in October 2005. Women from government, the mining industry, the NGO community, and the University participated in the conference.

- At the conference, the Mongolian women founded the Mongolian Association of Women Geoscientists. Membership includes women employed in and/or studying geosciences, in all types of occupations. The primary objective of the association is the continued professional development of its members. The Association works to increase the awareness of gender related issues among relevant individuals and institutions, including mining companies, and to develop strategies for the further integration of women into all spheres of geoscience related research and careers.

- With the assistance of Saint Mary's University in Halifax, the Mongolian partners collected data on socioeconomic and gender issues. The first results on the employment and role of women in the field of geoscience in Mongolia were reported at three conference presentations.

- Modules on gender will be incorporated into a specialized course (Economic Geology), and into an introductory course (Introduction to Environmental Geoscience) for all first year geoscience students and a new elective course on ethics in geology.

- Mongolian women geologists are participating in international geology conferences. A poster on "Mongolian Women in Geosciences: The appearance and reality of changing gender roles" was presented by two Mongolian team members at the Atlantic Geoscience Society Conference in February 2006.

However, there is one aspect that bears further examination: the presence of both men and women in geology field camps. There is reluctance on the part of some managers to have women in field camps ostensibly because of the expectation that women will be at a disadvantage in the physical demands of the work, e.g. in a typical four-month stay in the field in a mapping survey.

Attempts are being made to determine what precisely are the logistical and attitudinal obstacles to the presence of women in the field camps and then what should be the strategies to address these.

Fossilized dinosaur eggs from the Gobi desert displayed in the Geology Museum of the Mongolia University of Science and Technology

IMPROVED HEALTH AND NUTRITION

» Example: Rebuilding the health sector of Rwanda[40]

Longstanding tensions between the Hutu majority and the Tutsi minority erupted in a bloodbath on April 7, 1994. For the next 100 days, killing squads of extreme Hutus massacred some 800,000 Tutsis and moderate Hutus, using mainly machetes, axes and clubs. Canadian General Roméo Dallaire was the commander of the United Nations (UN) peacekeeping forces in Rwanda at that time but was prevented by the UN bureaucracy from intervening in the killing. The genocide ended when the Rwandan Patriotic Front army, led by Paul Kagame, who subsequently became President of Rwanda, defeated the Hutu fighters or forced them into exile. Kagame then had the challenge of rebuilding an officially unified, but still simmering, country.

One of the instruments of the genocide was rape, and this led—intentionally—to a significant increase in the rate of HIV infections. Almost one-third of Rwandan women between the ages of 18 and 35 were HIV-positive. Countless women and children were traumatized by the killings and the rapes.

In mid-1999 the Office of International Research at the University of Western Ontario received a letter from the rector of the National University of Rwanda (NUR). The rector said that the number of doctors in the country had literally been decimated in the 1994 genocide and asked UWO to assist NUR to rebuild the medical sector in the country. The letter was forwarded to medical professor Dr. David Cechetto, who reacted immediately and positively to NUR's request, and travelled to Rwanda to learn as much as possible about the situation in the country.

When Cechetto was in Rwanda, he visited NUR in Butare to talk about the training of doctors, but he quickly became aware of the wide range of other health sector participants that Rwanda needed, e.g. nurses, traditional birthing assistants, psychologists, nutritionists, community health workers. In this latter context, he met the Director and her colleagues of the Kigali Health Institute (KHI), which is the main government supported training center for nurses. Cechetto decided to partner with both NUR and KHI, with KHI taking the lead Rwandan role. In order to make the best possible contribution in the area of *primary* health care in Rwanda, he needed the skills of doctors, of nurses, and of all health sector practitioners who work at the community level.

Cechetto and his colleagues and partners developed a project, of which the intended outcomes were:

- Increase the capacity of the Kigali Health Institute to develop and deliver relevant and current educational programming, particularly in areas related to HIV/AIDS and mental health, including trauma.

- Improve the ability of nursing students and graduates to provide comprehensive and community-based nursing care and counseling to individuals with HIV/AIDS and to women and children experiencing the effects of trauma due to the genocide or sexual violence.

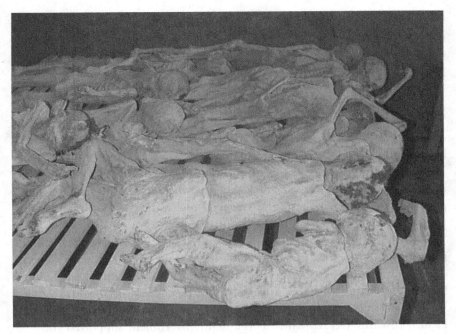

Some of the 800,000 victims of the 1994 Rwanda genocide
(Photograph courtesy of Dr. David Cechetto)

» Example: Clubfoot care in Uganda[41]

Clubfoot is a birth defect that is characterized by the bones of a foot being pulled sideways by an imbalance in the muscles and ligaments. A significant proportion of children born every year, especially in the developing world, suffer from clubfoot.

Dr. Shafique Pirani, a Professor in the Department of Orthopaedics at the University of British Columbia, was born in Uganda, and was part of the group expelled by dictator Idi Amin in 1972. He was trained as a doctor in the UK and as an orthopaedic surgeon in Canada, and later decided to specialize in clubfoot. Initially he managed clubfeet surgically and then became aware of the Ponseti Method, which is a nonsurgical treatment involving accurate manipulation of the foot and the successive applications of five plaster casts, followed by four years in a brace. This treatment has been shown to work with remarkable success if initiated on children up to the age of 12 months. For older children, surgery is possible, but is not an ideal solution.

Pirani wanted to rid affected children in Uganda of the burden of the clubfoot deformity. However, instead of the more usual approach of involving just one or two partner training institutions and a small number of community-based organizations, Pirani involved *all* of Uganda in the project—all the hospitals, all the community health workers, and all newborn children suffering from clubfoot.

His project has two intended outcomes:

- Integrate the Ponseti Method within the Ugandan healthcare system such that by the end of the project, a Ugandan child born with a clubfoot would be "detected", taken by the parent to the hospital for treatment, and that treatment would be available and effective.

- Build capacity for Uganda's healthcare training institutions to train Uganda's future healthcare workers in the detection of clubfeet and its management by the method of Ponseti.

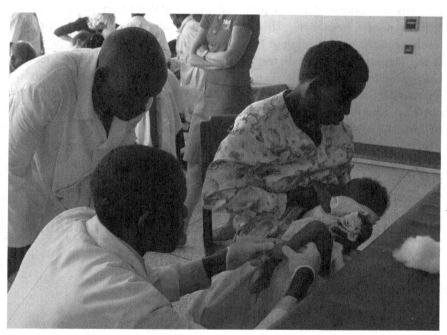

A baby with a clubfoot (in Mom's arms) having its clubfoot gently manipulated and casted by the Ponseti Method. The teacher is demonstrating to the trainee Orthopaedic Officer how the foot is manipulated, whilst the trainee observes. (Photograph courtesy of Dr. Shafique Pirani)

» Example: Belarus & post-Chernobyl health problems

Unit 4 of the Chernobyl nuclear power generating complex in northern Ukraine exploded at 1:23 a.m. on April 26, 1986. The roof was blown off, releasing a cloud of radioactivity over Eastern Europe that was detected as far west as France. Because of the prevailing winds, two-thirds of the air-borne radioactivity was carried into nearby Belarus. The death toll in Ukraine, Belarus and Russia as of today has been estimated at over 100,000[42]. There was a significant increase in birth defects after the accident, as well as thyroid gland cancers and other unusual tumours in children.

Many Canadians, and the Canadian government, provided assistance to Ukraine and Belarus, including the sending of medical volunteers and medical supplies. A number of families in various Canadian cities volunteered to have children from Belarus stay in their homes for several weeks in order to get away for a while from the residual radiation and the effects of poverty. Dentists in London, Ontario provided free dental services to the visiting "Children of Chernobyl". This activity evolved into a five-year project resulting in the modernizing of 12 dental stations with up-to-date equipment at the Department of Paediatric Dentistry of the Belarusian State Medical University. Six dental teachers studied at the University of Western Ontario for six-week periods during the time of the project. Substantial assistance to purchase equipment came from the Ministry of Health of Belarus and from Belarusians in Canada, the US, the UK, and Australia.

The paediatric dental program subsequently expanded into other health areas: cardiology and the treatment of heart patients, training of nurses, ophthalmology, and occupational therapy.

COMBATING HIV/AIDS, MALARIA AND OTHER DISEASES

In 2006, the UN reported:[43]

[HIV/AIDS]

Several countries report success in reducing HIV infection rates, through interventions that promote behavior change. However, rates of infection overall are still growing. And the number of people living with HIV has continued to rise, from 36.2 million in 2003 to 38.6 million in 2005 (nearly half of whom are women). There were 4.1 million new infections in 2005. The number of AIDS-related deaths also increased that year, to 2.8 million, despite greater access to antiretroviral treatment and improved care in some regions.

The epidemic remains centered in sub-Saharan Africa. With just over 10 per cent of the world's people, the region is home to 64 per cent of HIV-positive people and to 90 per cent of children (under 15) living with the virus. Twelve million sub-Saharan African children are orphans. Around 59 per cent of HIV-positive adults in sub-Saharan Africa—a total of 13.2 million people—are women.

Rates of new HIV infections in the region peaked in the late 1990s, and prevalence rates in Kenya, Zimbabwe and in urban areas of Burkina Faso show recent declines. HIV prevalence among people aged 15 to 49 in sub-Saharan Africa appears to be leveling off, though at extremely high levels. This apparent stabilization reflects the fact that as new people acquire the virus, nearly the same number die from AIDS...

[Malaria]

A growing awareness of malaria's heavy toll has been matched with greater commitment to curtail it. Increased financial flows from the Global Fund to Fight AIDS, Tuberculosis and Malaria, the World Bank's Global Strategy and Booster Programme, the United States President's Malaria Initiative and the Bill and Melinda Gates Foundation, among others, are expected to spur key malaria control interventions, particularly insecticide-treated net use and access to effective anti-malarial drugs. In just four years (1999-2003), distribution of insecticide-treated mosquito nets increased 10-fold in sub-Saharan Africa. Despite this progress, urban dwellers are six times more likely to use the nets than their rural counterparts, according to data available from a number of countries in the region. Similarly, the richest fifth of the population are 11 times more likely to use them than the poorest fifth...

[Tuberculosis]

New tuberculosis cases are on the rise, even excluding those associated with HIV...The number of new tuberculosis cases is growing by about 1 per cent per year, with the fastest increases in sub-Saharan Africa. In the Commonwealth of Independent States, incidence increased during the 1990s, but peaked around 2001, and has since fallen. Tuberculosis kills 1.7 million people a year. Of nearly 9 million new cases in 2004, 741,000 were among people living with HIV.

» Example: Africa & generic drugs[44]

From the July 25, 2005 newsletter of the Stephen Lewis Foundation:

> *In May 2004, Parliament unanimously passed the Jean Chrétien Pledge to Africa Act. This legislation effectively allows Canada to implement an August 2003 decision of the World Trade Organization (WTO). This decision allows WTO member countries to override patents so that they can produce lower-cost generic drugs for export to countries that lack the capacity to make the drugs themselves.*
>
> *The process of drafting the regulations and passing the Act took more than twelve months, but it should come into force this year. It's been an excruciatingly slow process. In the interim, NGOs and some generic manufacturers have held discussions about which drugs to produce and high on the list is the fixed-dose combination anti-retrovirals recommended by the World Health Organization.*
>
> *If politicians, manufacturers and activists continue to move forward in the spirit of the original legislation, this could well be a breakthrough. Nothing should stand in the way of rolling out treatment to hundreds of thousands in the immediate future. And it's equally clear that huge numbers of African lives could be prolonged and saved by generic drugs because they're at a fraction of the cost of brand-name drugs.*[45]

However, one year after the above newsletter appeared, the *Globe and Mail* carried an opinion piece entitled *Canada's generic drug law is all talk, no action* by Rachel Kiddell-Monroe, the Canadian head of the Médecins sans frontières [MSF] Campaign for Access to Essential Medicines[46]. She pointed out that MSF was one of the first organizations to place an order for antiretroviral drugs as soon as the law was passed. "But, two years on, not a single pill has left Canada." She attributes the blame largely to the decision of the WTO as "unworkable, hugely complex, and involves jumping through a series of bureaucratic hoops." Making the situation worse, "the Canadian government chose to add to the bureaucratic complexities mapped out by the WTO."

The good news is, at the time of writing, the pills are finally moving from Canada to Africa.

» Example: Africa & ABC

A major strategy in the struggle against HIV/AIDS is packaged as "ABC": Abstinence/ Be faithful/ use a Condom. This three-pronged strategy seems to be working, but there is considerable debate as to how much relative emphasis should be placed on each of the three components. Some individuals and organizations, because of their social and/or religious views, want to stress (and to fund) abstinence programs far more than condom use. For example, the US President's Emergency Plan For AIDS Relief (PEPFAR), a US$15 billion five-year program announced in January 2003, stresses changes in sexual behavior, including a delay in "sexual debut", while other authorities maintain that condom programs are more effective, and more cost-effective.[47]

» Example: Smallpox & polio

Smallpox was eradicated in the world in 1979 (by completely eliminating the virus that causes smallpox), and there have been recent predictions that polio could likewise be eliminated, if only the political will to do so could be found.

A 15-year effort called the Global Polio Eradication Initiative, involving more than 200 countries, 20 million volunteers and [US] $ 3 billion, succeeded in driving the number of polio cases worldwide from 350,000 in 1988 to fewer than 700 cases in 2003. This popped back to nearly 1,185 in 2004, largely because of the continuing spread in Nigeria. From Nigeria, polio has now spread to more than a dozen neighboring countries. [48]

PROTECTION OF CHILDREN AND WOMEN

In 2006, the UN reported[49]:

> *Though survival prospects have improved in every region, 10.5 million children died before their fifth birthday in 2004—mostly from preventable causes. The vast majority of these children (94 per cent) lived in 60 countries. Sub-Saharan Africa, with only 20 per cent of the world's young children, accounted for half of the total deaths, a situation that has shown only modest improvement. In contrast, child survival has improved markedly in Latin America and the Caribbean, South-Eastern and Eastern Asia and Northern Africa, where child mortality rates have declined by more than 3 per cent annually.*
>
> *Disparities in child deaths are pronounced both within and among countries. Survival rates for children of mothers with at least a secondary education are twice as high as those for children with less educated mothers. Similarly, children living in the wealthiest 20 per cent of households are twice as likely to survive as those in the poorest 20 per cent of households...*

The vaccination of three quarters of the world's children [against measles] has proven to be one of the most cost-effective public health interventions on record. Nevertheless, the disease killed 454,000 children in 2004, leaving others blind or deaf. Two thirds of the world's unprotected children live in six countries: China, the Democratic Republic of the Congo, India, Indonesia, Nigeria and Pakistan. Latin America and the Caribbean made the greatest strides in immunizing children, with sub-Saharan Africa showing significant progress as well. Sub-Saharan Africa also achieved the largest reduction in deaths from measles: a decrease of nearly 60 per cent between 1999 and 2004. This overall progress masks wide inequalities within countries: In Chad and Nigeria, for example, children of educated mothers are two to almost four times, respectively, more likely to be vaccinated than children of mothers with no education. The gaps are even wider when children from richer and poorer households are compared...

Though the issue has been high on the international agenda for two decades, ratios of maternal mortality seem to have changed little in regions where most deaths occur (sub-Saharan Africa and Southern Asia). Unreliable data and wide margins of uncertainty make it difficult to tell for sure. Adequate reproductive health services and family planning are essential in improving maternal health and reducing maternal mortality. But some 200 million women who wish to space or limit their childbearing lack access to contraception. Skilled attendants at delivery, backed up by referrals to timely emergency obstetric care, can reduce deaths further, as a growing number of countries have demonstrated...

Within countries, the presence of a skilled attendant at delivery is the most inequitably distributed among child and maternal health indicators. Impoverished and rural women are far less likely than their urban or wealthier counterparts to receive skilled care during childbirth. Inequality between urban and rural care at delivery is particularly significant in sub-Saharan Africa: For 33 countries with data, urban women are over three times more likely to deliver with health personnel than women in rural areas. And women in the wealthiest fifth of the population are six times more likely to deliver with a health professional than those in the poorest fifth.

In addition to protecting children from preventable diseases, another large area of concern is protecting children from being abducted and used in warfare.

According to Amnesty International:

An estimated 300,000 children under the age of eighteen are currently participating in armed conflicts in more than thirty different countries on nearly every continent. While most child soldiers are in their teens, some are as young as seven years old…As of 2004, Africa [had] the largest number of child soldiers with up to 200,000 believed to be involved in hostilities. Child soldiers [were] being used in armed conflict in Burundi, Cote d'Ivoire, Democratic Republic of Congo, Rwanda, Sierra Leone, Somalia, Sudan, and Uganda. The Ugandan Lord's Resistance Army [was] particularly notorious for its use of child soldiers [as fighters, spotters, observers, message-carriers, human shields, sex slaves, cooks and porters] [50].

Moreover, even if the fighting ends and the children are returned to civil society, there is a huge problem in re-integrating them into social activities utterly different from the lives they have known:

» Example: Sierra Leone & child soldiers

Ishmael Beach was twelve years old in the 1990s when he was kidnapped and forced into joining the Revolutionary United Front, a rebel group fighting against the government of Sierra Leone. He has recently written an articulate and poignant account, *A Long Way Gone: Memoirs of a Boy Soldier*, of how he survived during his years of fighting, the drug addictions forced on him to deaden the realization of the horrors he was participating in, and his eventual difficult rehabilitation into civilian life. Reviewer Lynne Jones writes:

"…Ishmael's story has a happy ending. He makes new friends in New York who rescue him when his uncle dies and war begins again in Sierra Leone. In 2002, the recruitment of child soldiers becomes a war crime, and the first indictment against Thomas Lubing, a Congolese warlord, is issued in 2006. But active recruitment continues and there are still at least 250,000 child soldiers worldwide, 1500 of them in Northern Uganda where I write this, 70,000 in neighboring Somalia.

"Ishmael's story shows both the horror and the possibility of redemption." [51]

» Example: Costa Rica & prevention of violence against women [52]

This project began with the active encouragement of two First Ladies of Costa Rica. The University of Western Ontario and their Costa Rican partners, the University of Costa Rica and the National Institute for Women/ Plan of

Action to Eradicate Intra-Family Violence, are studying the economic impact of violence against women in that country. Awareness of the economic costs of violence against women will influence policy development in favor of victims in Costa Rica.

> "...special laws for the prevention of domestic violence against women have been put in place, but access to justice and services for victims and survivors are still limited", says Dr. Laura Guzman, Director of the Centre for Research on Women's Issues at the University of Costa Rica. "One serious handicap is the lack of appropriate data and information systems to adequately measure the extent of violence against women. This is an excellent opportunity to develop a methodology and train a team connected to several government agencies..."

REDUCED ENVIRONMENTAL IMPACT

This desired result refers to the reduction, or (even better) the reversal, of damage being done to our natural environment, including water resources (supply, distribution, ownership, quality, glaciers, snow packs), soil degradation and erosion, salinization of water and soil, air pollution, and forest resources. In one way or another, each of these has the well-demonstrated potential to affect quality of life negatively, especially in developing countries.

Arguably, the greatest current environmental danger is global climate change, which has been tied into all of the problems listed in the paragraph above. Dealing with the *causes* of climate change, however, is far beyond the scope or the resources of virtually all development projects. This is a problem caused, and needs to be solved, mainly (but not exclusively) by the highly industrialized countries. Sadly, a recent report of the Intergovernmental Panel on Climate Change predicts that less developed countries, especially those around the equator, will be harder hit by the effects of global climate change than richer nations, and are less equipped to deal with the ramifications.

Development work related to climate change therefore concentrates on adapting to, mitigating, and coping with, the *local* effects of climate change. Examples of such approaches, for example in arid agricultural areas, include various means of keeping moisture in the soil such the use of trickle irrigation instead of open ditch irrigation, leaving thatch on the field as long as possible, low till field preparation, planting drought-resistant seeds, intercropping, and other measures such as afforestation.

» Example: FAO & the Tropical Forestry Action Plan

Deforestation, primarily the conversion of forests to agricultural land, continues at an alarmingly high rate—about 13 million hectares per year. Forest planting, landscape restoration and natural expansion of forests have significantly reduced the net loss of forest area. However, these newly replanted lands do not have the ecological value of older, more biologically diverse forests, and do not provide the same benefits and livelihoods for local communities. The net decrease in forest area over the period 2000-2005 is about 7.3 million hectares per year (an area about the size of Sierra Leone or Panama), down from 8.9 million hectares per year from 1990 to 2000. Still, the current net loss is equivalent to about 200 square kilometers per day. [53])

In response to the high rate of worldwide tropical deforestation, the Food and Agriculture Organization of the United Nations (FAO) in 1985 took on the coordinating role of a global partnership that included the World Bank, the World Resources Institute, the United Nations Development Program, various donor nations, and the governments of countries with tropical forests, in a program called the Tropical Forestry Action Plan (TFAP).

The TFAP provides a strategy for conserving tropical forests and lays out a framework for action by governments and development organizations. Its priority areas are:

- Forestry in land use: action in this area is at the interface between forestry and agriculture and aims at conserving the resource base for agriculture, at integrating forestry into agricultural systems and, in general, at a more rational use of the land.

- Forest-based industrial development: action aims at promoting appropriate forest-based industries by intensifying resource management and development, promoting appropriate raw material harvesting, establishing and managing appropriate forest industries, reducing waste, and developing the marketing of forest industry products.

- Fuel wood and energy: action aims at restoring fuel wood supplies in the countries affected by shortages through global assistance and support for national fuelwood and wood energy programs, development of wood-based energy systems for rural and industrial development, regional training and demonstration, and intensification of research and development.

- Conservation of tropical forest ecosystems: action aims at conserving, managing and utilizing tropical plants and wild animal genetic resources through the development of national networks of protected areas, the planning, management and development of individual protected areas, and research into the management of tropical forests for sustainable production.

- Institutions: action aims at removing the institutional constraints impeding the conservation and wise use of tropical resources by strengthening public forest administrations and related government agencies, integrating forestry concerns into development planning, providing institutional support for private and local organizations, developing professional, technical and vocational training, and improving extension and research.[54]

However[55], because most of this work has been in the planning and policy areas, there has been little progress in reducing actual deforestation. In 1990, several reports critical of the plan were released by the World Rainforest Movement, the World Resources Institute, and by FAO itself through an independent review. This assessment reflects widespread agreement that TFAP has not met its original objectives and needs to be restructured. The new process would be country-driven, not donor-led. The heavy coordinating role now performed by the FAO TFAP unit would be dispersed among all actors in the process, e.g. developing countries, donors, NGOs, other international agencies.

» Example: Reforestation & Nobel Peace Prize

On October 8, 2004 it was announced that the Nobel Peace Prize had been awarded to long-time environmental activist Wangari Maathai, Kenya's deputy environment minister and founder of the Green Belt Movement. She was the first African woman to win the Nobel Peace Prize and the first person to be recognized specifically for environmental activism.

» Example: Mongolia & mining[56]

Mongolia is rich in mineral resources, and has attracted several large international mining companies seeking mainly gold and copper. In addition, a large number of local and regional mining companies and small-scale informal illegal "ninja" mining operations have sprung up over the country. These mining operations, both large and small scale, have contributed to land degradation and to a number of other environmental and health concerns. Mercury and cyanide are used in the extraction of gold from ore.

The worst despoilers of the landscape are probably the smaller local and regional mining companies. The ninja miners usually work in places in which industrial mining has already taken place and, driven by poverty, they have no economic incentive to clean up the sites where they have worked. The biggest environmental concern for the ninja mining communities is their own health and safety through their unprotected handling of mercury and other unsafe practices.

The Mongolian University of Science and Technology (MUST) is working with Saint Mary's University in Halifax to develop interdisciplinary programs which link the geological sciences to environmental management. Through improved academic programming, applied research capacity, and focused community outreach strategies, MUST will act as an intermediary between the communities, the mining companies and appropriate government departments, providing facilitation and interdisciplinary training. The intentions are: (a) to significantly raise awareness in Mongolia of the environmental issues and the risks, and (b) to train geology professionals who can monitor problems and implement solutions. The project goal is to strengthen technical and managerial capacity of those engaged in the mining industry in Mongolia to carry out mining activities in an environmentally and economically sustainable manner.

Because one major rationale for the project is concern about the possibility of community health being endangered by unsafe large-scale and small-scale mining operations, public health professionals—in all three areas of curriculum development, of applied research, and of outreach—will be participating in the project.

Some important readings in the area of human impact on the environment are Rachel Carson's *Silent Spring*[57], the Report of the World Commission on Environment and Development *Our Common Future*[58] (the "Brundtland Commission Report") and, more recently, Al Gore's book and film *An Inconvenient Truth*.

SUSTAINABILITY OF INTENDED RESULTS

It is hoped that our overseas partners will continue to produce, and to enjoy, the results of a project after the project has finished and the Westerners have gone home. Some of the foundations of such sustainability are:

- A strong desire on the part of the intended beneficiaries of the project to continue to receive these benefits, e.g. improved health facilities, improved opportunities for education and training, microcredit for small enterprises

- An increased awareness and appreciation within the country of the significance of the results, e.g. in Mongolia, an increased public awareness of environmental risks associated with mining activities

- Enhanced capacity of the partner institution to support these activities, e.g. skills training, curriculum, outreach, research

- Formal expressions of ongoing support by the leadership of the partner institution for the new capacity and programs created by the project

- Strong buy-in by academic colleagues in the partner institution for the new programs

- Formal expressions of ongoing support by the appropriate government level for the institution

- Existence of government legislation to enable (or to require) the results to be used and to be continued, e.g. regulations for increased government scrutiny of mining operations in Mongolia

- Public pride in what is being achieved, e.g. an increased awareness of the rich pre-Conquest cultural patrimony of Peru through archaeological and anthropological research (see the case *Peru & Andrew Nelson* in Chapter Ten). Increased awareness and pride, in turn, help to build public disapproval of the traditional widespread looting of graves throughout Peru (and other parts of the ancient world) and the consequent destruction of knowledge of their own culture. (An excellent, but horrifying, account of the international illicit antiquities trade is *Stealing History* by Roger Atwood[59].)

- Increased employment created by the project activities, e.g. opportunities for pro-poor tourism activities (hostels, restaurants, guides, guards) following archaeological discoveries

- Increased connections and regular interaction with international counterparts (e.g. Canadian universities) and professional associations.

» Example: Cuba & biomedical engineering

Cuba needs to prepare expert engineers and researchers in biomedical engineering (BME) in order to maintain high standards in public health. This is a challenge for a capital-scarce country like Cuba, as biomedical technology is characterized by constant integration of new scientific knowledge in sophisticated technological systems. A key challenge is maintaining knowledge among faculty and health care personnel. Three Cuban universities were given the responsibility to deliver undergraduate education in BME. The three that were selected (Universidad Central "Marta Abreu" de Las Villas (UCLV), Instituto Superior Politécnico "José Antonio Echeverría" (ISPJAE), and Universidad de Oriente (UO)) partnered with the Institute of Biomedical Engineering at the University of New Brunswick (UNB) in Fredericton and with the Department of Medical Engineering at the Hospital for Sick Children (HSC) in Toronto, in order to carry out this mandate.

There are several indicators of sustainability in this project:

- The project contributes to improved public health, and therefore has the ongoing approval and support of the Cuban government and the public.

- The project makes an important contribution to the research and teaching capacity of the three Cuban universities in an area of high priority.

- The major capacity building technique is "training the trainers" and thus there will be a multiplicative effect.

- The linkages among the three Cuban partners are solid, and are expanding to form further linkages within Cuba, e.g. to other academic disciplines within the three universities, to clinics and hospitals within the Cuban public health system, and to Cuban government ministries and agencies, which strongly support the work of the three universities.

- There is an ongoing international partnership with a major Canadian university, UNB, and with a major Canadian hospital, HSC.

- One of the most important sources of sustainability for continuing Cuban development of biomedical engineering is active involvement in international scholarship, publications and conferences. This will require the encouragement of a culture of regularly preparing papers (in English) for submission to high quality international refereed journals and conferences in the biomedical engineering field, the identification of appropriate journals, coaching in the strategies for getting papers accepted, and assistance with scientific style and with English.

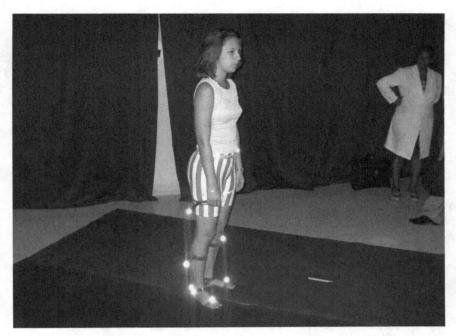

The Movement Analysis Laboratory at the General Hospital in Santiago de Cuba: the motions of the lights when the patient is walking are recorded simultaneously by three cameras in different corners of the room.

INCREASED AWARENESS THROUGH
PUBLIC ADVOCACY AND DEVELOPMENT EDUCATION

Many development projects have a component in which the partners make known publicly what they are doing, and how their work is making a positive difference either locally or elsewhere in the world. There are several reasons for doing this: funding agencies appreciate the recognition they receive for their investment, overseas partners want to increase the sustainability of their achievements by making the results more widely known and understood, Canadian partners in training institutions want to study the processes of successful international cooperation and intervention, the Canadian government and Canadian citizens want to see how tax dollars are being used beneficially.

In the next chapter, *International Development: What Canadians Do,* we see that an impressive number of Canadians have been, and are, involved in international development in a great variety of ways. "Being a good global citizen" is often cited as a characteristic core value that defines us as Canadians.

For this reason, many Canadians want to stay generally informed about what is happening in the developing world, and what are the most pressing areas of need where we can help.

Many Canadians are highly effective public advocates for what needs to done. Among these marvellous individuals are Louise Arbour, a former UN High Commissioner for Human Rights; General Roméo Dallaire, for his valiant attempts to halt the genocide in Rwanda; and Jean Vanier, who established the *L'Arche* shelters for persons with developmental disabilities around the world.[60] One of the most eloquent and effective advocates is Stephen Lewis, a leader in the struggle against the ravages of the HIV/AIDS pandemic in Africa. Lewis' book *Race Against Time* (Anansi Press 2005) is based on The Massey Lecture Series, which he presented across the country. *Race Against Time* became a bestseller in Canada.

» Example: African women & HIV/AIDS[61]

The following is an excerpt from Stephen Lewis' speech to the University of Pennsylvania's Summit on Global Issues in Women's Health, Philadelphia, April 26, 2005:

Why are women so much more vulnerable to the HIV/AIDS epidemic in Africa?

"...because I see the evidence...in the unremitting carnage of women and AIDS...young women, who crave so desperately to live...who can't even get treatment because the men are first in line, or the treatment rolls out at such a paralytic snail's pace...who are part of the 90% of pregnant women who have no access to the prevention of Mother to Child Transmission and so their infants are born positive...who carry the entire burden of care even while they're sick, tending to the family, carrying the water, tilling the fields, looking after the orphans...the women who lose their property, and have no inheritance rights, and no legal or jurisprudential infrastructure which will guarantee those rights...no criminal code which will stop the violence...because I have observed all of that...and am driven to distraction by the recognition that it will continue, I want a kind of revolution in the world's response, not another stab at institutional reform, but a virtual revolution."

In universities and colleges, courses on international development are common, especially in the social sciences, but increasingly in other disciplines. If the institution has a collaboration project that includes visits to Canada by overseas partners, the visitors are often invited to make presentations in the development courses, to visit local service clubs, and to be available for informal discussions with faculty and students.

FINANCIAL ASSISTANCE

Even very small amounts of financial assistance, if invested carefully and sensitively, can make a significant contribution to the stimulation of local economic activity. This assistance can be in various forms, for example, as microcredit (the Grameen Bank[62] is the best known example) and as revolving loan credit.

» Example: Ethiopia & oxen loan revolving credit program

Traditionally, there would be very few oxen in the villages for the plowing. The available oxen would be shared among all the villagers, but the delays in waiting for one's turn could result in a change in the weather, and consequent problems with getting a crop established. There was insufficient money in the village to buy a pair of oxen for each farmer, and so the *Future Forests* project injected enough money into the project to purchase several pairs of oxen at the nearby market. The Partnership Committee was given the money and they selected the farmers to receive a loan to purchase a pair of oxen. The farmer

Oxen purchased using the oxen loan revolving credit program

would use the oxen to create a crop, which they would sell, thus earning enough money to repay the loan in installments. The loan funds would then be allocated to other farmers, who would then purchase their pairs of oxen, and so on. Nobody in the plan defaulted on the loan, in part because their neighbors were watching carefully to ensure that the loan installments were repaid on time, and thus the funds made available on a sustainable basis to other farmers in the community.

This was also a training activity in relation to villagers taking responsibility for the management of money, as well as going to the market and purchasing the oxen. An important part was the selection of the person to be the bookkeeper, which was a responsible and prestigious position. The books were kept meticulously.

An instrument sometimes associated with financial assistance is the *business plan*. Business plans are common in industrialized countries and are essential in making the case for investment decisions in the business sector and in business schools, but are much less well known in other academic disciplines and in rural communities in developing countries. (How to prepare a business plan is presented in Chapter Ten.)

» Example: Ethiopian women & business plan

In the example earlier in this chapter, *Empowerment of rural Ethiopian women*, the women prepared a business plan to accompany their (successful) application for a *Canada Fund* grant.

» Example: Peru & business plan

On May 6, 2002 Andrew Nelson, an Associate Professor of Anthropology, had just returned from a trip to Peru where he wanted to establish a museum of cultural history and an accompanying international bioarchaeological research center. Nelson had successfully gathered all the necessary information and arranged all the required legal agreements while in Peru, and he turned now to fundraising. Nelson understood that, when he approached the private sector for funding, a proper business plan for this venture would be required. Never having previously been involved with such documents, Nelson set out to inform himself about business plans and to prepare one for the Peruvian museum within the next few months. (See the case *Peru & Andrew Nelson* and the material that explains how to prepare a business plan in Chapter Ten.)

The former train station of Pacasmayo, Peru is the site for the proposed museum of cultural history and the accompanying international bioarchaeological research center.

Another type of assistance pertains to countries undergoing the difficult transition from a centrally planned economy to an open market economy:

> ## » Example: LEADER Project & free market business fundamentals

When the Soviet Union collapsed and free markets were getting established, students in the LEADER Project at the University of Western Ontario business school[63] delivered intensive introductory business courses to managers, entrepreneurs and university students in several cities throughout Russia and Eastern Europe. Later, they presented similar courses in Cuba.

LOCAL OWNERSHIP, EQUALITY & ACCOUNTABILITY

Western project managers often say (correctly) to their partners, "This is your project. Tell us what *you* want to do in the project. Tell us what we can do to help you." The concept of local ownership is a powerful one in international development cooperation. In terms of building capacity, of generating self confidence, of stimulating motivation and enthusiasm, of nurturing decision making skills, promotion of local ownership works far better than the older paternalistic donor/recipient model of foreign assistance.

Although the word "recipient" still unfortunately pops up in development discourse, modern thinking promotes full equality between the partners or, even better, having the overseas partner take the lead in the project or program. More precisely, a transition should occur over the multi-year duration of a project. Projects typically begin with a relationship that is usually dominated by the Canadians, and they evolve into a partnership characterized largely by local ownership at the end.

The authors' experience has been that not all Canadian project teams agree that this transition should take place. Some Canadians argue that the partners will not have the ability, the knowledge and/or the motivation to bring a project to a successful end without extensive and constant Canadian involvement and control. We think it is helpful to remember that the Canadians will not be there at all after the end of the project, and thus it is an essential management task to strive from the beginning of the project to help the partners to prepare to carry on after the Canadians go home.

Another factor favoring this transition is that it is relatively expensive to bring a number of Canadians repeatedly to the partner country. Some partners politely make the point that they can find better uses for the money in the later stages of a project than Canadians' travel expenses. Expatriate travel in the second half of a project is not cost-effective when compared to other potential uses of the funds in the partner country.

Some Canadians confess that they really enjoy visiting the partner countries and don't want any diminution in this pleasurable and (in a few cases) ego-stroking experience. Others use the argument that they cannot depend on the partners to manage the project (especially the expenditures) properly, and thus the Canadians will be liable to castigation from AUCC and CIDA.

The transition to local ownership is a demanding management task that begins right at the start of the project, is gradual rather than abrupt, and requires full discussion and agreement involving all the partners. One such management technique is for the Canadians to assure their partners that they do not need to seek prior permission or agreement to carry out activities that will support the agreed-upon outcomes of the project. The partners should not be in fear of the possibility of "failing" if they are truly going to build self-reliance.

However, the need for accountability, especially for funds coming from Canadian taxpayers, results in stringent (some would say excessive) levels of monitoring and reporting. Moreover, contribution agreements for university-to-university collaborative projects, for example, are in the form of legal contracts between the Canadian lead institution and AUCC acting on behalf of CIDA. The developing country partners are not signatories to the contribution agreements. Therefore, if there is a disagreement between the partners in executing the contribution agreement, the Canadian institution legally has to prevail, which is contrary to the concept of local ownership.

(One of the major tools in support of accountability is Results-based Management, which is explained in detail in Chapter Six.)

Another aspect of project ownership is the flow of funds. In university-to-university projects, for example, funds flow from CIDA to AUCC to the lead Canadian partner, who expends the funds on behalf of the project, often with little or no money actually being put in the hands of the partner institution. In the eyes of some overseas partners, because the Canadian institution controls the funds, the Canadian institution effectively is in charge of the project.

On the other hand, some experienced project directors in overseas partner institutions actually *prefer* to have the Canadians looking after the finances in order to avoid problems within their own institutions. They want to preserve the received funds identifiably for the project, and not have them eroded through institutional overhead charges or reallocations. In some situations, an external bank account is set up by the project in the overseas country in order to protect the funds from predation by the host institution.

IMPROVED INFRASTRUCTURE

In this book, infrastructure refers to *physical* infrastructure that needs to be in place so that development can actually proceed, such as transportation facilities, housing, telecommunication networks, water and sanitation. (Human infrastructure is dealt with elsewhere in this chapter in the contexts of capacity building, education and training.)

In 2006, the UN reported[64]

Between 1990 and 2004, sanitation coverage in the developing world increased from 35 to 50 per cent. This meant that 1.2 billion people gained access to sanitation during this period...

The share of people using drinking water from improved sources has continued to rise in the developing world, reaching 80 per cent in 2004, up from 71 per cent in 1990. Growing populations pose a challenge, however, and wide disparities among countries and between rural and urban areas persist. The largest urban-rural disparities are found in parts of sub-Saharan Africa, where city dwellers are twice as likely to have safe water as their rural counterparts

In 2007, for the first time in history, the majority of people will live in urban areas. Throughout most of the developing world, this will result in larger slum populations. Sub-Saharan Africa is the world's most rapidly urbanizing region, and almost all of this growth has been in slums, where new city residents face overcrowding, inadequate housing, and a lack of water and sanitation. In Western Asia, as well, most of the urban growth is occurring in slums. The rapid expansion of urban areas in Southern and Eastern Asia is creating cities of unprecedented size and complexity and new challenges for providing a decent environment for the poor. Northern Africa is the only developing region where the quality of urban life is improving: In this region, the proportion of city dwellers living in slums has decreased by 0.15 per cent annually.

» Example: Rwanda & the African Virtual University

Earlier in this chapter, there was an example *Rebuilding the health sector of Rwanda*, in which the two Rwandan partner institutions were the National University of Rwanda (NUR) in Butare and the Kigali Health Institute (KHI). One of the activities in this project was the development of web-based learning and curriculum development, and therefore a strong telecommunication network was essential. NUR and KHI make use of the African Virtual University (AVU) network.

The AVU was initiated in 1995 by the World Bank. It is a satellite-based distance education project whose objectives are to deliver to countries of Sub-Saharan Africa, university education in the discipline of science and engineering, non-credit continuing education programs and remedial instruction. AVU links 30 learning centers in 15 African countries via the Internet to universities in Europe, Canada, and the United States. As of 2003, the countries participating in AVU's program included Kenya, Tanzania, Zimbabwe, Uganda, Namibia, South Africa, Rwanda, Burundi, Ghana, Benin, Burkina Faso, Mauritania, Niger, Senegal and Ethiopia. The headquarters of AVU are in Nairobi.

One can see large satellite dishes on the campuses on NUR and KHI that provide connections to the AVU. Fiber optic cables laid underground enable Internet connections to be available in the classrooms.

Internet access by satellite connection at the National University of Rwanda

» Example: Peru & *pro-poor* tourism (continued)

Tourism is seen as a vehicle that can bring about positive change in this region. The idea is that local people along the route of the proposed Northern Tourism Circuit could obtain income from food sales, hostels, guiding, guarding, and handicrafts (e.g. carving and weaving). The inputs needed for this project are infrastructure enhancements such as improving the roads and re-opening an airport, training courses for guides, providing security for the archaeological sites, some language training, marketing assistance, loans to providers of food and accommodation.

One of the authors of this book (Keenan) travelled the full length of the Circuit. The total length of this route is 1334 km, of which 607 km is unpaved. The side trips that are needed to visit archaeological sites significantly increase the total mileage. Almost all of these side trips are on unpaved roads. Keenan reported[65]:

> *"The Northern Tourism Circuit is a marvelous place. The Circuit connects an abundance of wonderful archaeological sites, some very good interpretive museums, and areas of breathtaking natural beauty. Tourism facilities range from adequate to very good, including accommodation, restaurants, tour companies, and shopping, all at very modest prices.*

"On the other hand, there is a fundamental problem with travelling the Northern Tourism Circuit: an excessive amount of road travel is required. The unpaved roads vary from "rough and dusty" to "bad" to "appalling". No traveler (other than adventure seekers and some archaeologists) would want to spend seemingly endless days being bumped and jolted, breathing dust, and staring with dismay at the precipitous drop at the edge of the road where it narrows to one lane as it turns a blind corner on the side of a mountain."

» Example: Ethiopia & water

In Africa, it is said, water is life. Often, wells for rural communities are simply holes in the ground that enable humans and animals to share access to underground water. One method of improving the quality of the water supply is to line and to cap the wells with concrete, and to install easy-to-maintain hand pumps. Water coming from the pump is taken first for human consumption and the runoff is channeled into troughs for animals. The water that flows past the animals provides irrigation.

Improved well in the Bette Valley of Ethiopia

» **Example: Ghana & Alison Casey**

Alison Casey[66] was working in Ghana as a Uniterra volunteer in Tamale, Northern Region, Ghana, with the Girls' Education Unit in the Ghana Education Service as a gender advocacy advisor. On June 26, 2007, she sent an email message to a number of friends that included the following two paragraphs:

> *"Things here are going well. We have entered a new era at our house; however…we have no water. For 5 days now, the pump/water station near our house died leaving our neighborhood dry. This morning I bathed with pure-water sachets (500ml bags of drinking water). I am sure I have never been so clean. I totally admire the ability of women here to carry water on their heads. I have tried with a bucket, but I not only lack the strength but the also the skill that is involved in the process. We are very fortunate to have a family behind us who graciously brought us some water yesterday. Answering the call of nature has become somewhat of a feat. At night, we try to go outside, and I am trying to strategically place my visits to establishments with bathrooms…*
>
> *"Up until this week, we have been incredibly blessed with running water most days. Many many people here are not as lucky as we are. I am learning that we cannot take for granted water or electricity…both of which are in short supply here. It is a major problem for many people and many industries here. It is not being helped by a general lack of rain these days. The sky fills with clouds and it feels like rain, but it never seems to come."*

Also with respect to infrastructure, see the case *Nicaragua & Mira Noordermeer* in Chapter Sixteen regarding the provision of low-income housing:

Mira Noordermeer at the house building site in Nicaragua with friends (left to right) Angela, Jacklynn, Angelina and Kimberling (in front with drawing) (Photograph courtesy of Mira Noordermeer)

PROVISION OF APPROPRIATE EQUIPMENT

In the early years of development assistance, some economists lauded the benefits of scale in projects that were large and that used advanced technologies and high capacity equipment. A reaction set in against this thinking, best presented in the classic book *Small is Beautiful* by E. F. Schumacher[67], and subsequently in *Mastering the Machine* by Ian Smillie[68]. These writers called for *appropriate* technologies, *appropriate* equipment, and *appropriate* industries, and they explained what they meant by appropriateness.

The Forest Industries Division of the Food and Agriculture Organization of the United Nations (FAO) provides advice[69] on appropriate forest-based enterprises to developing countries that need to use their forest resources; this activity is part of the Tropical Forestry Action Plan discussed earlier.

In many projects, there will be an opportunity to provide the partner institutions with some new (and appropriate) equipment that will enable them to take a major step forward in their activities. This is a good use of funds, but such donations need to have a comprehensive commitment, including on-site training in the proper use and maintenance of the equipment, training the trainers in order to have a multiplicative effect, a supply of spare parts, maintenance contracts, updating the equipment at appropriate times in the future, and the cost of shipping. We have all seen, unfortunately, pieces of donated equipment not being used because one or more of the above items had not been provided on an ongoing basis.

» Example: Mongolia & mining (continued)

A major step in this project was the purchase, delivery and installation of a polarizing microscope and the associated digital camera and software. This microscope is essential for Mongolian researchers to participate in the international community of geology research and publications, and has brought about a major improvement in the quality of teaching materials. For example, color photographs taken with the polarizing microscope will be incorporated into a new laboratory manual for ore mineralogy and petrography. The manual, with these photographs, will be an outstanding advance over the teaching materials now available to students and lecturers, and will also be of great use to geologists working in this area. In this case, the equipment purchased for the Mongolian partner institution was superior to the equipment possessed by Saint Mary's University, the Canadian partner.

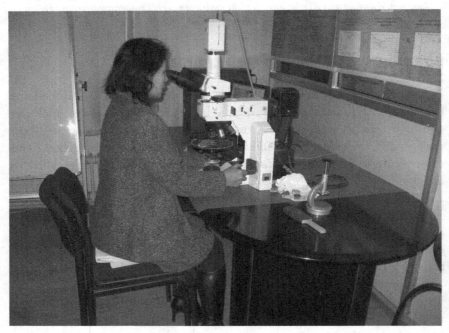

The new polarizing microscope at the Mongolian University of Science and Technology in Ulaanbaatar

An admirable tendency of some Westerners is a desire to donate outdated equipment or books from our own institutions to our partners. We see that this equipment is no longer useful at home, but it is frequently better than what the partners now have. However worthy the intention, there are some problems with this. One, rather delicate, problem is that the partner may not be entirely pleased to receive outdated equipment. In some minds, being the recipient of outdated equipment indicates that the recipient partner is the junior partner in the relationship. Some are even insulted to be accorded "second class" status in a relationship that is supposed to be between equal partners. If the project is intended to build capacity in the partner institution, then the partner should receive at least the same quality of equipment as the Westerners have.

It may happen that, in some instances, there *is* real value in the partner receiving outdated equipment, e.g. undergraduate lab microscopes, but this donation may need to be positioned as being only a temporary measure. Moreover, the equipment has to have a particular relevance to the partner institution—is this equipment essential to what the partner really wants to do, or will it be a distraction?

Another problem is the difficulty and the cost of shipping the equipment and books to the partner. This often arises when the donation is not really part of the project but is an offer made by an individual upon retirement or by a Canadian institution during an upgrading process. Such prospective donors are often indignant when they find that there is no public (e.g. CIDA) money available for shipping their books or equipment to the partner institution.

IMPROVED LANGUAGE SKILLS

One of the indicators of equality between two partners in a collaborative project is that both languages can be used with comfort. In fact, many projects have components of language training for both partners in order to facilitate the relationship. However, although it may be regarded as unbalanced and unfair, the reality is that non-English-speaking partners should be assisted to enhance their English, more than Canadians being encouraged to learn the other language. The major reason for this asymmetrical recommendation is the nature of international scholarship and professional associations. With respect to post-secondary education and research in the partner country, one of the most important sources of sustainability for continued scientific development is active involvement in international scholarship, partnerships, publications and conferences. This will require the nurturing of a culture in the partner institution of regularly preparing papers for submission to high quality English-language international refereed journals and conferences.

An important input to this activity is the mentoring of junior scientists with respect to technical writing in English, in the preparation of proposals, and in project management, and in the complementary areas of identification of appropriate journals, coaching in the strategies for getting papers accepted, assistance with scientific style and with English, and with Results-based Management.

Learning another language, unfortunately, requires very substantial commitments of effort by the learners. Many of the visitors who come to the West have some difficulty with the English language. It is therefore recommended that a significant module of English language training be built into projects for those wishing to travel to North America. It is an open question as to whether this language training should take place in the partner country or here—perhaps initial training in grammar and vocabulary should take place in the home country, followed by immersion conversational training here. The training in the home country can either be funded by the project or claimed as an in-kind contribution by the partner institution.

GOOD GOVERNANCE AND HUMAN RIGHTS

This intended result includes:

- Governance in support of economic development, such as having a fair, simple and transparent framework of regulations governing enterprises, finance and taxation

- Governance in support of human rights, including personal security and safety, access to justice, political freedom, freedom of speech, religious freedom, cultural freedom.

Of supreme importance in creating democratic human rights-respecting stability in a country is the relationship between the civilian police force and the public.

» Example: The Gambia & community-based policing and restorative justice

The relationship between the Gambia Police Force (GPF) and the Gambian public has deteriorated in recent years, and the GPF faces a crisis of confidence in its ability to act in a just and effective manner. Allegations abound that the police regularly shake down drivers for money at police spot checks, are not sufficiently responsive to citizens' problems, give preference to supporters of the ruling political party, and have killed unarmed civilians.

The GPF is trying to improve its badly tarnished image in the country. With help from Mount Saint Vincent University, the Halifax Regional Police Service and the Nova Scotia Restorative Justice Program, the GPF has turned to the principles and practices of community-based policing (CBP) in an attempt to build trust and confidence with the communities. Essentially, community-based policing: (a) engages the communities as partners in preventing crime, and (b) for less serious crimes, lets the existing and traditional structures in the community bring about a resolution of the offence without the permanently damaging effect of the police laying charges and the matter going through the courts. If the problem goes to court, much time and money may be consumed, there may be no effective remedy for the victim, and an ongoing state of hostility can subsequently prevail between the families of the offender and the victim.

The principles and practices of restorative justice (RJ) are part of this process as the means by which attention is paid to finding adequate and appropriate remedies to the damage suffered by the victim, with corresponding accountability and responsibility for the damage and for the remedies on the part of the offender. Restorative justice in The Gambia rests on the traditional centuries-old method of solving problems at the community level. One of the

A police-community meeting concerning cattle rustling at Brikama in The Gambia
(Photograph courtesy Shelagh Abriel)

co-authors (Keenan) had the honor of sitting under a large tree one Sunday beside Karamo Bojang, the *alkalo* (a senior and highly respected hereditary leader in the community) of the village of Tujering, together with the mediation committee, as they promptly settled disputes between community members using a process that provides an appropriate remedy for the victim, and heals the damaged relationship between the offender and the victim.

The struggle for good governance can be hazardous:

» **Example: 81 journalists killed in 2006**

"The number of journalists killed or jailed worldwide has reached its highest level in a decade, with arrests rising as governments seek to control the Internet, an advocacy group said…The survey by Reporters Without Borders, a media-advocacy group, found that 81 journalists were killed last year and more than 140 are behind bars. It was the worst year since 1994, which was marked by the Rwandan genocide, civil war in Algeria and conflict in the former Yugoslavia.

"The report said many governments were seeking to gain more control over the Internet, a popular medium for dissent in less democratic countries and a growing source of news in the U.S.

"At least 60 people are in prison worldwide for posting criticism of their governments online, from 50 in China to four in Vietnam, three in Syria and one each in Tunisia, Libya and Iran."[70]

APPROACHES AND METHODOLOGIES

Because this chapter is so long, it may be useful to repeat the summary that appeared at the beginning of the chapter. Having dealt with desired results in the previous sections, we now move on to the second part of the summary: approaches and methodologies. The chart is repeated here:

Desired Results

- Reduction of extreme poverty and hunger
- Education and training
- Gender equality and empowerment
- Improved health and nutrition
- Combating HIV/AIDS, malaria and other diseases

- Protection of children and women
- Reduced environmental impact
- Sustainability of intended results
- Increased awareness through public advocacy and development education
- Financial assistance
- Local ownership, equality and accountability
- Improved infrastructure
- Provision of appropriate equipment
- Improved language skills
- Good governance and human rights

Approaches and Methodologies

- Listening to your partners
- Building capacity, including research capacity
- Training the trainers
- Getting started properly
- Benchmarking and baselines
- Thinking outside the box
- Choosing the right partners
- Donor coordination and Sector Wide Approaches
- Extending intended results through effective communication
- Management structures, processes and communication
- Results-based Management
- Achieving consensus through collective decision making
- Flexibility and adaptability
- Creating long-term partnerships
- Managing expectations
- Monitoring, evaluation, and mid-term corrections
- Maintaining good links with the Canadian mission in the country

LISTENING TO YOUR PARTNERS

» Example: Ethiopia & listening

Initially, during the days when the Canadian volunteers were running a medical relief camp in northern rural Ethiopia, it was essential to listen and watch very carefully when someone who had no English and was working through interpreters was attempting to describe a situation, a problem, a need. It was necessary to have a great deal of patience, to let the conversation flow fully, and to watch for clues such as body language and speaking tones.

Later, when *Future Forests* was working with the Partnership Committee in the four communities, they held regular (annual or semi-annual) public "update" meetings, at which the villagers talked about their activities, their concerns, their problems, their hopes for the future, in each of the project areas such as water, education, health, oxen loan programs. These meetings were lengthy and loquacious, necessitating interpretation from English to Amharic to Oromigna, and back again from Oromigna to Amharic to English. Of foremost importance was the showing of respect, as well as ensuring that there was enough time to hear all the things that the partners wanted to say (an essential, but "butt-numbing", experience, according to Christine Gilmore, the Administrator of *Future Forests)*.

Future Forests *Administrator Christine Gilmore and villagers in the Bette Valley of Ethiopia*

Another highly useful technique in information gathering and sharing in the villages was the use of Participatory Rural Appraisal (PRA) techniques, as explained in the example *Ethiopia & PRA* later in this chapter.

What is fundamentally important here is that it is essential to understand and appreciate the needs, aspirations, experience and capabilities of your partners. For projects to succeed, we benefit greatly by fully engaging our partners, and by ensuring that their voices are heard and respected.

BUILDING CAPACITY, INCLUDING RESEARCH CAPACITY

The approach of assisting developing countries to build capacity is now one of the prime methodologies in Canadian development cooperation. Many of the examples and cases in this book have been taken from capacity building projects. Capacity building can take place at many locations: within government ministries and agencies, in universities and colleges, in medical clinics, in NGOs, in communities, in the entrepreneurial sector.

When former Canadian Prime Minister Lester Pearson established the International Development Research Centre of Canada (IDRC) in 1970, he viewed the nurturing of national research capability in developing countries as one important road to development. The concept was that Canada could assist developing countries to create their own research abilities in order to solve their problems by themselves, rather than to depend on the more industrialized countries.

» Example: Andean Pact countries & building products[71]

In the 1970s and 1980s, the International Development Research Centre of Canada (IDRC) supported a major collaborative project among the Andean Pact countries of South America (at that time, Venezuela, Colombia, Ecuador, Peru and Bolivia). The goal was to sustainably utilize the forest resources of the subregion as an abundant source of low cost building materials for the urban areas of those five countries. This project strengthened the capabilities of a network of eleven national research institutions to effectively utilize forest resources. The outputs of the project included the training of young researchers, establishing new forest products research laboratories, the production of a body of new research on the properties and utilization of tropical hardwoods, the construction of low-income housing at several sites in the countries, numerous publications including the *Manual de Diseño para Maderas del Grupo Andino*, the building of research capacity in universities and government laboratories in the five countries, and the technological underpinnings for private sector involvement in wood construction.

These led to the establishment of an organization in Lima called *El Centro de Innovación Tecnológica de la Madera (CITEmadera)*. CITEmadera was established, with funding from the governments of Spain and Peru, to provide technical support services to the wood products industry of Peru, including training, publications, visual aids, design services and direct technical assistance. The Centre became the nucleus of a vibrant and growing industrial zone in Lima for a large group of Peruvian entrepreneurs using forest products from their own country.

» Example: Cuba & building capacity in clinical trials for mental health[72]

In Cuba, *el Centro Nacional Coordinador de Ensayos Clínicos (CENCEC)* is the national body that conducts and manages clinical trials for all disciplines. CENCEC is also the institution in Cuba sanctioned to conduct clinical trials for products to be registered on the national pharmaceutical formulary, including drugs for the treatment of mental health. The Department of Psychiatry at Dalhousie University in Halifax, with a funding contribution from CIDA, assisted CENCEC to improve its provision of health care services for the mentally ill and strengthened its production of pharmaceutical products for national use and export.

With respect to the ability of universities to conduct research of potential benefit to the country (as mentioned earlier under *Improved language skills*), one of the most important sources of sustainability for continued scientific development is active involvement in international scholarship, partnerships, publications and conferences. This will require the nurturing of a culture in the partner institution of regularly preparing papers for submission to high quality English-language international refereed journals and conferences. An important input to this activity is the mentoring of junior scientists with respect to technical writing in English, in the preparation of proposals, and in project management, and in the complementary areas of identification of appropriate journals, coaching in the strategies for getting papers accepted, assistance with scientific style and with English, and with Results-based Management.

Another issue is that, in order to build up the permanent scholarly capacity of a partner university, few activities are as important as graduate training in selected other countries. However, most projects cannot afford full scholarships for graduate training, especially at the doctoral level. What may be feasible, however, is to fund research placements of three or four months each for graduate students to go to foreign institutions that have equipment or analytical facilities necessary for their graduate work that are not available in their own country.

TRAINING THE TRAINERS

This is one of the most effective means of building up human infrastructure capacity in a development project, first, because of the multiplicative effect of the training activities and budget, and also because teachers in the partner country are likely to be more effective. Not only do they speak the local language, but they will have a higher sensitivity to the cultural implications of what is being taught.

GETTING STARTED PROPERLY

> **» Example: The Gambia & Don Sawyer[73]**

On November 1, 2005 Don Sawyer of Okanagan College was in Toronto for the International Cooperation Awards ceremony of the Canadian Manufacturers and Exporters Association. A project, of which he was the Canadian Project Director, was a finalist in the awards program. The project was a collaboration between Okanagan College and institutions in The Gambia that had established the West African Rural Development (WARD) Centre. In his speech at the ceremony, Sawyer recounted how WARD got started, as follows.

He explained that WARD had been created to train community development workers from across West Africa, including Sierra Leone, Liberia, Ghana and Nigeria, as well as The Gambia. WARD was to be located on the campus of the Gambia Technical Training Institute (GTTI).

This project had gone extremely well right from the start. At the beginning, Sawyer realized that he needed to seek out a local champion or champions for the project, who would give invaluable advice as to the individuals from their institution who needed to be involved in the project, i.e. to decode all the local politics and animosities, and to help organize the initial two-day inception meeting. He sought help from Mr. Alpha Jallow, who had been a student in a previous project. Jallow possessed energy, intuition, political awareness, understanding of development, desire to bring about beneficial change, and logistical ability—all the skills and abilities essential for leading a successful project.

At the inception meeting, the attendees selected Jallow to be the Gambian Project Director. Jallow remained with the WARD project throughout its duration, and his leadership was a major reason for its success. Sawyer was uncomfortably aware that, if Jallow had left the project before it was completed, the result could have been very different. He therefore wanted to encourage the mentoring of emerging young leaders who could step in if Jallow left. Sawyer saw the necessity of building "bench strength" in a project so that there would be a line of emerging young leaders that would be able to step in if one of the original good leaders left the project.

Sawyer's objective at the inception meeting was to build consensus among the partners and stakeholders in order to maximize commitment of the key players. An excellent cross-section of stakeholder representatives was assembled for the inception meetings. The meetings were very carefully planned so that all issues were thoroughly explained to, and discussed by, all the participants. The persons attending the meetings were presented with a package of materials including a meeting agenda, background on the project, and principles of Results-based Management. Impact, outcomes, outputs and reach (to be explained in Chapter Six) were all discussed, as were monitoring and regionalization considerations. Activities were also examined, and input from the group suggested a number of new activities that needed to be incorporated. Results of the discussions were recorded on more than 30 sheets of flipchart paper and were used as the basis for the revised project agreement with the funding agency.

The inception meeting planning team structured the meetings, including having small groups coming up with different ideas, such as defining the mission statement for the Centre. Sawyer facilitated these discussions, and the group had a lot of fun merging different ideas into a coherent concept. Effective facilitation was crucially important. All decisions were joint decisions. In order to build consensus, collective (rather than individual) decision making was essential. Mutual respect and trust were sought and achieved. At the end of the process, they produced a document that represented real consensus as to who they wanted to be, where they wanted to go, how they wanted to get there. This became the guiding document for the rest of the project.

At this inception meeting, the participants agreed upon a clear goal for the Centre: *to improve the quality of life of West African rural people on a sustainable basis through the increased capacity to educate and train human resources to meet priority needs in the area of rural community development.* Over the six-year life of the project, the project intended to train more than 180 rural development workers in improved community development techniques and facilitation skills and to train a core WARD staff of 12. The vision for WARD was clear: it was expected to become an internationally recognized "center of excellence" in the area of rural community development.

This was a situation where community involvement and local ownership of the project were essential right from the beginning. Sawyer had previously written, "This project cannot be run from Canada", an observation that has proven to be abundantly correct.

BENCHMARKING & BASELINES

It is recommended that a baseline study be carried out at the beginning of a project. This will enable the partners to demonstrate the changes that have been brought about by the project by making a "before and after" comparison.

THINKING OUTSIDE THE BOX

In Chapter Eight, there is a case analysis *Uganda & Shafique Pirani* in which the issue was whether to do something so ambitious and so unprecedented that there was a real risk of the project not getting funded.

CHOOSING THE RIGHT PARTNERS

In the example earlier in this chapter entitled *Rebuilding the health sector of Rwanda*, Dr. David Cechetto reflected on asking either the National University of Rwanda (NUR) and/or the Kigali Health Institute (KHI) to be his Rwandan partner(s). See the case analysis *Rwanda & David Cechetto* in Chapter Eight.

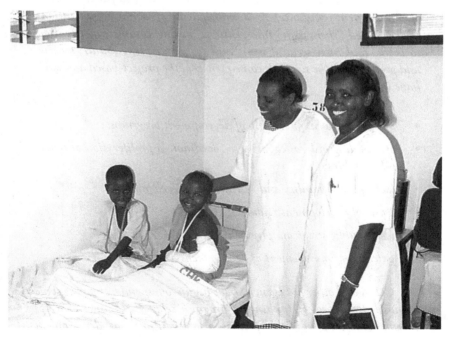

The children's ward at the Kigali Central Hospital. At the far right is Florence Mukakabano, Director of Nursing. (Photograph courtesy of Dr. David Cechetto)

DONOR COORDINATION AND SECTOR WIDE APPROACHES

Continuing the example immediately above:

> *Cechetto was aware that he should check his ideas against the Poverty Reduction Strategy Paper of Rwanda [PRSPs were described in Chapter Two]. He did this, and supplemented his findings with conversations with the World Bank representative in Rwanda, with the President of the National AIDS Commission, with the cabinet minister responsible for the struggle against HIV/AIDS, with the Minister of Health, and with the Minister of Education. Cechetto found that, although there is a great deal of activity in Rwanda in the field of HIV/AIDS—both by Rwandans and by international aid agencies—there was no overlap between his ideas and the activities of others. In fact, the efforts would be complementary.*

According to the Institute on Governance in Ottawa[74]:

> *During the 1990s the project form of aid delivery came under severe attack. The project-based approach was seen as contributing to fragmentation of development assistance, as a multiplicity of donor organizations each pursued "their own" interventions, paying insufficient attention to intra- and inter-sectoral issues and to the recipient country's needs and preferences. The negative consequences of the project-based approach have included:*

> - *inadequate local ownership of development programs;*
> - *overloading of local capacity to coordinate a proliferation of donor relationships;*
> - *lack of sustainability and institutional development;*
> - *waste of development resources;*
> - *weak public sector management;*
> - *patchwork management of development assistance.*

> *CIDA and other aid agencies have begun to respond by moving some resources from project funding to program-related assistance. SWAps [Sector-wide Approaches] represent a mechanism that development agencies are using in order to operationalize the new program-oriented thinking...The central idea of a SWAp is that in a given sector in a*

given developing country, all significant donor interventions should be consistent with an overall sector strategy and sector budget that have been developed under the leadership of the recipient country.

A rough working definition that has gained some acceptance among practitioners is that a SWAp covers a situation where all significant funding for a sector supports a single policy and expenditure program, under Government leadership, adopting common approaches across the sector, and progressing toward relying on Government procedures to disburse and account for all funds.

In its ideal form, a SWAp is based on a developing country's own sector objectives, sector policy and sector program. Instead of providing support to discrete projects within a given sector, donors support the overall sector program. In short, under the ideal model of a SWAp, donors would give up their right to decide which projects to finance, and focus instead on having a constructive voice in the process of developing and implementing a sector policy and program.

The reality, of course, is that virtually all current SWAps fall far short of this ideal. *All are experiencing significant "teething pains." Indeed, at the moment we do not know whether an "ideal" SWAp is an operationally feasible concept. But whether or not the ideal is ever achieved is not the point. The point, rather, is that donors have recognized that* moving in the direction *implied by the ideal SWAp model is a worthwhile undertaking*[75].

EXTENDING INTENDED RESULTS THROUGH EFFECTIVE COMMUNICATION

In addition to management communication (discussed in the section after this one), *development communication* in general is a rich area in which to work, partly because of the great range of techniques and technologies available, partly because of its impressive effectiveness, and partly because this is an area in which the developing country partner can readily take the lead through local sensitivity, inventiveness and adaptability.

» Example: Egypt & extension materials

A baseline study was carried out at the beginning of the project, in which one important issue was the level of literacy. Prior to the project, it was thought that large numbers of the rural population were still illiterate. In the baseline study, the project looked at whether there was at least one person in the family (not necessarily the heads of the household) who could read, and thus they decided to deal with the concept of levels of *household* literacy. They determined that household literacy was high enough that the use of *print* materials was feasible. Therefore various print materials were created in order to get useful information into the hands and into the awareness of villagers in the Nile Delta, including:

- 17 illustrated multi-colored pamphlets intended for rural people on subjects such as nutrition, dealing with pests, raising rabbits and poultry, making pickles and processing apricots

- 16 fact sheets intended for extension workers on subjects such as gender equality

- 4 awareness-raising posters intended for rural people, especially farmers, on optimum spacing of rice rows, production of corn, reduction of insect pests in order to increase milk and meat yields from cattle, and damage from cotton worms

- 10 videos for students and rural people including women, e.g. on maintenance of farm equipment, preparing corn silage, and raising rabbits.

Ironically, at the same time as the project was worrying about basic literacy, Internet cafés were springing up around the country and some younger people were requesting computer-based information. There were pressures and opportunities to disseminate information and to provide a forum for communication via the Internet. Accordingly, extension workers now have access to a network called Vercon—the Virtual Extension & Research Communication Network—including expert systems on wheat and rice, and a forum for the exchange of information and advice among extension workers.

» Example: Cartoons, comics and illustrated novels

Cartoons can be used very effectively, for example, in posters put up in medical and community centers. Comic books can also work well, e.g. *Common Ground*[76] works to reduce ethnic conflict in Indonesia. Since 2003 they have published a comic book series entitled *Gebora* whose leading characters are members of a multi-ethnic football team. Promoting tolerance and nonviolent conflict resolution, the comics are integral to the organization's program of activities in areas vulnerable to violence. They are distributed in Madura and West Kalimantan through a network of co-operating NGOs."

Also, illustrated novels (or "comic books with certain literary pretensions" as a *Globe & Mail* reviewer described them) have become enormously popular as a new literary genre. One outstanding recent illustrated novel (now a film) was *Persepolis,* Marjane Satrapi's memoir of the Iranian revolution.

» Example: Plays and drama

In the film *The Constant Gardener,* which is based on the book of the same name by John le Carré[77], one scene witnesses a public presentation put on by villagers (possibly community activists or public health workers) in Kenya concerning the stigma of HIV/AIDS. This is a bit of drama, combined with music, which enacts how a family reacts when a son is diagnosed as being HIV-positive. The son is initially wracked with guilt, and his friends and family react with scorn, revulsion and fear. After much dialogue about the issues, the son is welcomed back into his family, and is supported by the community.

In The Gambia, in a CIDA-funded project on peer health, a group of young people in a local NGO with acting talent put on brief dramatic skits in schools and in community meetings to illustrate, and provoke discussion, on topics related to peer health. This was a highly effective method of raising consciousness on important issues compared to the less engaging approach of lecturing to the audiences. In fact, it is often much more inoffensive when sensitive topics are raised within the context of a drama presentation rather than in direct discussions. (One is reminded of the role of the court jester in saying things to the king that no one else in the court had the courage to say, the role of the idiot in Dostoyevsky's writings, the madman of Nietzsche, and the fool of Shakespeare.)

Because of its considerable success in the peer health project, the drama troupe was also used to introduce students in school assemblies to the concepts of community policing and restorative justice. Moreover, there were spin-off benefits from the drama troupe's successes. In at least one school (in Farafenni), a student drama club was formed under the energetic and capable leadership of Mr. Bah. During a visit to the school the group was requested (on only a few minutes notice) to devise and present a skit illustrating community-based policing principles. They readily accepted the challenge, and put on a rather sophisticated skit that impeccably illustrated some important aspects of CPB.

*Drama troupe members in The Gambia performing a skit on
community-based policing and restorative justice*

» Example: Community radio

One very effective vehicle for empowerment is community radio. There
are thousands of these facilities throughout the world—in industrialized
countries as well as in less developed nations—and they typically consist of
a single small building and a transmitter. Community participation is a key
characteristic of the operation of these stations.

Programming, especially the generation of local content, is a large task and
a constant challenge. Consequently, there is a temptation to fill air space with
music. Another challenge is balancing local information with information
from elsewhere—from other parts of the country, from government sources
in the country, from other countries in the region, and from other parts of
the world.

The Community Radio Network in India has prepared a guide "How to
set up a Community Radio Station".[78]

The Developing Countries Farm Radio Network[79] is an outstanding
success story of community radio. The DCFRN "...is an Ottawa-based
charitable organization, founded in 1979, that has built on Canada's rich
history in farm radio to provide a unique international development program.

Working with rural radio broadcasters, our goal is poverty reduction and food security for smallholder farmers in low-income countries.

"Our network is comprised of over 290 partners: radio stations and organizations with radio programs, such as communication branches of government agriculture departments, or international agencies with radio projects. We work with community, public and private radio. We also maintain a database of more than 600 organizations that promote sustainable agriculture and rural development in the South. We have radio partners in more than 35 African countries.

"Our core program has two main streams. One develops content for radio programs that are relevant to smallholder farmers. The second provides training and professional development opportunities for our radio partners.

"In the first stream, the Farm Radio Network researches and writes radio scripts. Topics we cover include crop production, environment management, farm and household management, food safety, nutrition, HIV/AIDS and agriculture, children on farms, farm safety, youth in rural areas, farm income, women farmers, and more. We send these scripts, free of charge, in English and French, to our partners in sub-Saharan Africa, where they are adapted to local conditions, translated into hundreds of languages, and broadcast to a potential audience of several hundred million people. These scripts are also available on our website and are sent out electronically to our associates and to other organizations in Africa, Asia and Latin America that support small-scale agriculture and rural development.

"Our primary beneficiaries are smallholder farmers, small plot gardeners and farm laborers—especially women, who provide about 75% of the labor for agriculture in developing countries, and are often excluded from traditional agricultural extension services. Other beneficiaries are their families, and in particular their children, who benefit from better nutrition as a result of improved food production and processing, and better education as a result of improved household income.

"In the second stream, we provide training to develop the skills of rural radio broadcasters so that they can meet the needs of farmers; we promote training resources and opportunities offered by other organizations; and we publish examples of "best practices" of our radio partners."

The World Bank has recognized the value of community radio in empowerment of the poor, informed social engagement, and increased social accountability as building blocks towards good governance and reduction of poverty.[80] "A conducive policy and regulatory environment, access to information, and the means to freely report and comment on issues of local interest are recognized as critical enablers of these values." The World Bank Institute (WBI) is supporting a Bank-wide Grassroots Media Program to strengthen the community radio sector and the climate for public interest media in developing countries. The Bank's work in this area began in early 2000 in Timor-Leste and later expanded as pilot projects into Malawi, Zambia, Ghana and Nigeria. In 2003 and 2004, Ecuador, Peru, Benin, Sri Lanka, Indonesia and Mongolia were added to the list. Two important findings from this early work are:

- The community radio sector depends on a friendly legal and regulatory environment.
- When governments give up control over the airwaves, the resulting "privatization" often does not leave part of the radio spectrum for public interest and community broadcasting.

Based on the results from these pilot studies, the Bank is preparing a Good Practice Guide on the Enabling Environment for Voice and Media, including community broadcasting.

David Dacks, a Canadian who has worked in community radio for many years, recently looked into the future and made these comments to the authors:

"...I think you might want to look at the potential impact of satellite radio and the role of computers for archiving/syndicating content.

"Satellite radio can play an important role in addressing the two points you noted from the World Bank report. Although Worldspace Satellite Radio recently declared bankruptcy, its concepts of the potential deliverables of its medium were interesting. As to the first point, satellite radio is outside of the jurisdiction and infrastructure ownership of governments and government owned utilities, so it is possible to broadcast the same kind of information over a channel without being threatened by local or national governmental reprisals or infrastructure failings. A community radio provider or organization can rent a sliver of satellite radio bandwidth and deliver not just audio content but any type of computer file-pictures, documents etc.

"Tech support and reliability of transmission is greatly improved with satellite radio. The signal is clear even in the middle of the Sahara desert where it may not make sense to establish even a bare-bones microbroadcasting operation with only a fraction of the range and fidelity of satellite. Furthermore, the means of reception need not be specialized receivers, but cell phones which are now/will soon become the handheld computing standard of most of the world. Moreover, a satellite

radio linkup is a two way street-it is also a means of retransmission of cell phone generated text messages, video files, even web pages. Arguably, this could promote literacy as cell phone operating systems are based on entering and following text based commands.

"Granted, satellite radio is not a community-based radio solution, but it is a more straightforward, reliable and potentially cost-effective solution (if a development agency rents a block of bandwidth on a satellite to cover thousands of square kilometers) to the needs addressed by community radio. The downside to dealing with satellite radio providers is that these are large corporations with their inherent interests: profit maximization, accountability to shareholders, consistency of deliverables etc.

"Another benefit to having a computer based system is the ability to archive and syndicate. The ability to customize scripts to local conditions, and translating them into hundreds of languages is enhanced by having content available on demand for download or streaming. While a community radio station could broadcast "the hygiene hour" at 2PM, 4PM and 8PM, it is surely more convenient to have it available 24/7 and to be able to fast forward and rewind through the content to get what one needs. A community radio station could also have a computer based system to "wiki" the knowledge of an area; for instance with regard to gathering info on local agricultural conditions, medical issues, and political adverse situations. Furthermore, this can be syndicated to the rest of the world in nearly real time without the multiple filters of established news gathering organizations.

"I would give more thought to community radio as a two way communication tool and implications for development. Personally, I don't think music broadcasting is a negative on community radio. Storytellers and musicians play an important role throughout the world in promoting cultural consciousness. Music is effective because it allows people to absorb and dance to certain types of messages. I also believe that the day is coming soon when truly local recordings will be possible, and that those recordings could be sold through fair trade music companies like NatGeo/Mondomix music (or if they are text-based or speech-based, through an article archive system like ProQuest) in a fair-trade business model, providing a new means of income for many individuals or communities."[81]

» Example: Cell phones

The use of cell phones is expanding explosively in all parts of the world. The growth is especially great in those countries (and this very much includes developing countries) that did not previously have very much landline infrastructure. These countries were able to leapfrog over the need for landline infrastructure and go directly to cell phones, which are now seen virtually everywhere in the developing world. This has become the preferred method of communication for all age groups and for all economic classes. For example in *A Conversation with Hank Vander Laan* in Chapter Eleven, Mr. Vander Laan recounts this story told to him by a Kenyan friend:

> ...*my dad always used to sell his crops from his little farm to a local entrepreneur who would come around and say "I'll pay you so many shillings for the sorghum and so much for your sweet potatoes" and my dad just sold it to him for that price. But now he text messages "My crop is ready. What do sorghum and sweet potatoes sell for in Nairobi?" And now the guy comes around to buy and says, "I'll buy the sorghum and the sweet potatoes for so many shillings a basket." And my dad says, "Oh, no you don't. I just got this message from my son. He says, 'It sells for that much.' I want this much." He more than doubled their income.*

Another highly promising area is in delivering learning through cell phones.[82] When an audio lesson is received on a cell phone (for example, by a farmer, a herder, a fisher, a business person) the worker can listen to the message, save it for later, or ignore it. Importantly, auditory learning can reach illiterate learners.

» Example: Ethiopia & PRA

Another highly useful technique in information gathering, transmission and sharing (and in participatory assessment, research, planning, and program design) at the village level is the use of Participatory Rural Appraisal (PRA) approaches. Two major references in this field are by Robert Chambers: *Rural Appraisal: Rapid, Relaxed and Participatory*[83] and *Whose Reality Counts? Putting the First Last*[84].

Christine Gilmore had previously been exposed to PRA in a workshop led by Robert Chambers[85]. She was enthusiastic about using PRA as the tool by which *Future Forests* could best learn the wishes and possibilities of the three neighboring communities in Ethiopia (Goda, Arso Amba and Muta Fecha) that wanted to join the project. This took the form of the villagers jointly making a "ground map" of their community using stones, sticks and other materials at hand, arranged on the ground (and later transferred to paper). The process permitted *Future Forests* to learn, in a very graphic way, about population, health, agriculture, water, etc. in the community and the associated problems.

Importantly, PRA enabled the members of the community to take charge of the communication by making their physical portrayal of their villages and to reach consensus on the messages they wanted to give. PRA also gave *FF* the opportunity to "dig down" by asking increasingly detailed questions about the situation that each stick or stone represented, for example, to find out the locations of gardens and of cottage industries, such as weavers and potters. This "aerial view" of the villages was a very effective platform for developing cultural insights as to what men and women typically did each day in the villages.

Chambers makes a distinction between the RRA (Rapid Rural Appraisal) methods developed in the late 1970s and 1980s, and PRA, from the late 1980s and 1990s: RRA is extractive, i.e. information flows from the villagers to the outsiders. PRA is participatory: the information is owned by, and used mainly by, the local people. Obviously, there is much common ground between RRA and PRA, but the objective of PRA is the empowerment of local people leading to sustainable local action and institutions[86]. "What distinguishes much PRA from other approaches is also the use of visual methods, usually with things that are tangible, as with participatory mapping, often by groups. We talk of group-visual synergy. (A bit on this is in the *Whose Reality Counts?* Book.)"[87]

Bernie Gilmore used PRA methods effectively in 1993 in the Ethiopian village of Wake Tiyo[88]. Ground mapping was used here as a vehicle for the villagers to share information about health and nutrition, to formulate what they needed from health officials of the government, and to communicate these requirements to health officials who were present. Gilmore also made effective use of drama as a training tool for malaria control (the actors included ten children who played the role of mosquitoes, complete with paper nose cones as their stingers, who swooped threateningly around the other actors going "buzzz buzzz").

In addition to being an effective means of communication, PRA can also be used as a participatory evaluation process, for such things as programs, seeds, crops, agricultural issues. This is discussed in Chapter Fifteen, *Monitoring and Evaluation*.

MANAGEMENT STRUCTURES, PROCESSES AND COMMUNICATION

» Example: Cuba—Management communication in a multi-partner project

Dalhousie University's Dr. Aldo Chircop and Ms. Pat Rodee were preparing a proposal, along with one other Canadian partner and three (very different)

Cuban universities, for a new project. The partners knew that the effective and harmonious management of this large and disparate group was going to be a challenge. They had to decide, right at the beginning, how to establish a management system, and especially a system of management communication, that would put in place a framework for building consensus and the equitable participation of all partners during the next five years.

What they did is described in the case analysis *Cuba—Aldo Chircop & Pat Rodee* in Chapter Eight.

> **» Example: Latin America & management of international cooperation**

The Inter-American Organization for Higher Education (IOHE) is an association of universities throughout the Americas, in which the member institutions benefit by building linkages and sharing information. One such activity was to increase expertise in the management of international activities. IOHE organized a number of training workshops and published manuals in Spanish, Portuguese, French and English[89] on the management of international university collaboration. Typical participants were those officials at the universities who had responsibility for student exchanges, for collaborative research, and for the internationalization of the campuses.

RESULTS-BASED MANAGEMENT

Chapter Six contains a presentation on Results-based Management.

ACHIEVING CONSENSUS THROUGH COLLECTIVE DECISION MAKING

There were several examples of this earlier in this chapter including *Ethiopia & listening*; *The Gambia & Don Sawyer*; and *Cuba—Management Communication in a Multi-partner Project*.

FLEXIBILITY AND ADAPTABILITY

Having gone through the lengthy process of arriving at consensus and collectively making decisions regarding the content and the structure of the project, it nevertheless is necessary to maintain flexibility and to be open to the need to make changes in response to the changing project environment.

A typical project will occupy much of a decade, considering that the project creation process (described in Chapter Six) could take two years, plus (if the application is successful) another year in setting up the contribution agreement, plus six operational years of the project. The world will have changed substantially during that time period, including the situation in the host country and the individuals who are participating in the project.

A part of the ongoing monitoring of the project should be a consideration of whether changes or fine-tuning of the project plan would be beneficial. Most funding agencies are open to making useful changes in a project, and thus maintaining good ongoing communication with the funding and/or executing agency is essential. These considerations come to a head during the mid-term evaluation of a project (described in Chapter Fifteen), which will explicitly include asking the question as to whether mid-course corrections are needed.

Nimbleness and the ability to respond quickly to unwelcome surprises are highly desirable traits:

» Example: Ethiopia & unwelcome surprises

- The Government of Ethiopia changed, not just from one party to another, but from one cultural group to another, and the programs that the original government was supportive of were looked at with suspicion by the successor government.

- The national currency was revalued, necessitating the budget to be reworked.

- A previously influential member of the community worked assiduously to undermine the work of the project.

- The Ethiopian project manager was thrown in prison briefly on trumped-up charges, thus damaging his reputation with government officials and with villagers.

- An affiliated group had an irresponsible attitude to finance and accountability leading to a surprise at learning they were bankrupt and unable to pay their staff.

Another example of the need for immediate decisions is the case *Nicaragua & Mira Noordermeer* in Chapter Sixteen, in which a sudden health problem threatened to derail an international development activity.

CREATING LONG-TERM PARTNERSHIPS

The eighth (and final) Millennium Development Goal is "Develop a global partnership for development", and the targets are:

- Develop further an open trading and financial system that is rule-based, predictable and non-discriminatory.

- Include a commitment to good governance, development and poverty reduction—nationally and internationally.

- Address the least developed countries' special needs. This includes tariff- and quota-free access for their exports; enhanced debt relief for heavily indebted poor countries; cancellation of official bilateral debt; and more generous official development assistance for countries committed to poverty reduction.

- Address the special needs of landlocked and small island developing states.

- Deal comprehensively with developing countries' debt problems through national and international measures to make debt sustainable in the long term.

- In cooperation with the developing countries, develop decent and productive work for youth.

- In cooperation with pharmaceutical companies, provide access to affordable essential drugs in developing countries.

- In cooperation with the private sector, make available the benefits of new technologies—especially information and communication technologies.[90]

This MDG refers principally to what the industrialized countries should do in order to make possible the productive involvement by developing countries in working towards the other seven MDGs.

The partnerships included in the eighth MDG are all long-term partnerships. In development cooperation, long-term relationships are more effective than short-term partnerships. This observation is borne out by the success of collaborative projects that continued for a decade or more (for example, the wonderful relationship between Ghana and the University of Guelph dating from the 1970s, and the decade of friendship between the *Future Forests* NGO and the farmers of the Bette Valley in Ethiopia.) These relationships result in mutual respect, friendships, and often *surprise* that the Canadians keep coming back year after year.

When talking with Canadians who have taken part in these relationships, one hears comments such as "It's not just a matter of throwing money at them" and "It's important to keep your promises–when you are back in Canada, it's easy to forget that you had promised to write and to send photographs. Such promises are often taken quite seriously by the persons to whom they were made."

MANAGING EXPECTATIONS

It is essential for Canadians to be absolutely candid with their partners about the possibility that a project proposal, on which the two sides have worked together assiduously, may not become funded—frequently the probability of funding is less than 50%. There is often great disappointment, even disillusionment and resentment, on the part of the overseas partner if a proposal is not successful.

Another challenge can occur when the role of the Canadian partner changes. An example, mentioned a number of times in this chapter, is that the Canadian group who helped in the Bette Valley of northern Ethiopia changed from providing emergency relief to development cooperation. In their original role, the Canadians were totally donors, whereas in their subsequent role, they helped the villagers to work towards self reliance and independence. At least at first, this role change was difficult for some of the villagers to understand.

Another frequent perception is that Westerners are wealthy and we therefore have a great deal of our own funds to use in a discretionary manner if our partners make a well-argued request for it. Sometimes the Western partner can do this (for example, using recovered overhead revenues) but, more often, such funds are just not available. Explaining that we don't have funds (or don't have funds *yet*) can be met by skepticism.

MONITORING, EVALUATION, AND MID-TERM CORRECTIONS

Chapter Fifteen of this book deals with monitoring and evaluation of development projects, and coping with the changes that need to made as a result of the evaluation.

» **Example: Mexico-responding to a critical evaluation**

A project entitled *Connecting Campus and Community* was a collaboration involving the University of Calgary, la Universidad Autónoma del Estado de Morelos in Mexico, and the University College of Belize. Approximately halfway through the project, Dr. Eric Dillmann became the Canadian Project Director, replacing the original person in that position. On May 21, 2003, shortly after assuming his new responsibilities, Dillmann had just finished reading the report of the mid-term evaluation of the project. He was surprised and disheartened at the apparent harshness of the criticisms leveled at the project, and he had to decide what to do.

See the case analysis *Mexico & Eric Dillmann* in Chapter Fifteen.

MAINTAINING GOOD LINKS WITH THE CANADIAN MISSION IN THE COUNTRY

There is often an officer situated in the Canadian Embassy (or the Canadian High Commission if the country is a member of the Commonwealth) who has responsibility for development activities funded by the Canadian government in that country. These are predominantly CIDA bilateral activities, but the officials are also involved in CIDA's Partnership Branch activities, such as those of the NGO Division or the UPCD program. It is highly recommended that project directors should take the initiative to build a strong working relationship with these officials, including regularly copying them on reports and announcements. This will have an obvious impact on CIDA's enthusiasm for future project proposals.

It is also recommended that the head of the partner organization send invitations to the Canadian Ambassador (or High Commissioner) and the development officials to visit the project from time to time, and to bring eminent Canadians making official visits to the country to view the project's achievements.

CHAPTER FOUR

INTERNATIONAL DEVELOPMENT: WHAT CANADIANS DO

In Canada we frequently (perhaps *too* frequently) find ourselves drawn into discussions about our national identity. This discussion often starts with someone speculating about how we are different from Americans, and inevitably reaches the point where we start listing the national virtues that we possess (or we like to think that we possess). Near the top of this list, there usually appears "Canada is a good global citizen". When pressed as to what this actually means, we start talking about our role in peacekeeping missions in conflicted countries, our prompt generosity in responding to crises such as the Asian tsunami and the Ethiopian famine, our multiculturalism, the eagerness of many Canadians of all ages to serve as volunteers overseas.

When we list our national heroes, we regularly include Stephen Lewis, a leader in the struggle against the ravages of the HIV/AIDS pandemic in Africa; General Roméo Dallaire, for his valiant attempts to halt the genocide in Rwanda; and Jean Vanier, who established the *L'Arche* shelters for persons with developmental disabilities around the world.[91]

There is indeed a genuine interest by a large number of Westerners to be good global citizens by striving to improve the quality of life in other countries, and this book was written for (and about) those individuals. In this chapter, we look at how some Canadians actually go about doing this.

CANADIANS AND THE UNITED NATIONS

The modern era of international global assistance grew out of the final days of the Second World War with the creation of the United Nations family of organizations:

Canada has been an active and committed participant in the United Nations since its founding in 1945 in San Francisco, where Canada played a key role in the drafting of the Charter. Individual Canadians have played vital roles within the United Nations, and many of the Organization's great accomplishments have had a Canadian dimension. For example, fifty years ago John Humphrey was the principal author of the Universal Declaration of Human Rights; Lester Pearson helped to invent the concept of peacekeeping, winning the Nobel Peace Prize for his efforts to resolve the Suez Crisis of 1956; and Maurice Strong chaired both the 1972 United Nations Conference on the Human Environment, in Stockholm, and the 1992 United Nations Conference on Environment and Development, in Rio de Janeiro, and also served as founding Executive Director of the United Nations Environment Programme. Canadians have occupied key positions within the United Nations System, including the Presidency of the General Assembly (Lester Pearson, in 1952-53). In January 1998, a Canadian, Louise Fréchette, was appointed the first-ever UN Deputy Secretary-General and on July 1, 2004 Madame Justice Louise Arbour became High Commissioner for Human Rights.[92]

The sight of the big blue United Nations flag flying over an assistance operation in some beleaguered part of the world can evoke powerful emotions. One of the authors of this book, Christine Gilmore, was working as a volunteer in an emergency relief camp in northern Ethiopia in 1988 (see the case *Ethiopia & Christine Gilmore* in Chapter Nine). Christine remembers:

The food lines at our cookhouse had been getting longer and longer. More elderly persons, more children. They waited, with the patience of Job, in the heat of the day. But the supply of wood and the supply of grain for the bread bakery were quickly diminishing. We had to start handing out only halves of the flat loaves. We had to grind everything to make flour—grain that had deteriorated and would not otherwise have been used, with some dirt and even weevils being included. I was becoming very concerned as the lines continued to grow.

I became aware of a cracking or whipping sound coming from a great distance down the road. Our camp was on the only road to the north. Very soon I saw some absolutely massive trucks barreling up the road, each with a huge blue United Nations flag mounted on the hood. They were heading for another relief area in the north, and drove fast without stopping. On previous trips up this road they had been shot at and stopped by rebels. The cracking sounds I had heard were the huge flags whipping back and forth with the speed of the trucks. I stood by the side of the road and waved, the only foreign person for miles around. They honked and waved back as they passed in a cloud of dust. When I turned back to the cookhouse, I no longer felt so alone in our quest to help these people.

LESTER BOWLES PEARSON

"Mike" Pearson was Prime Minister of Canada from 1963 to 1968. During his years in office, the government brought about major domestic achievements such as the creation of the Canada Pension Plan, the appointment of a royal commission on bilingualism and biculturalism, the new Maple Leaf flag, and a national medicare system.[93] In spite of these significant domestic accomplishments, however, we probably remember Pearson even more for his *international* vision and successes. He is credited with the invention of multilateral peacekeeping, as mentioned above, and won the Nobel Peace Prize for his efforts to resolve the Suez Crisis of 1956.

In 1970, Pearson led a UN commission that proposed a target of 0.7% of GDP as the amount of money to be devoted to foreign aid by rich nations. Canada has not yet reached this level, but 0.7% remains in front of us as a worthy goal. Having been instrumental in establishing Canada's International Development Research Centre (discussed later in this chapter), Pearson served as the first Chair of the IDRC Board of Governors from its inception in 1970 to his death in 1972.

Pearson understood, better than most, the connection between who we are as Canadians and what we do in the world. He once said:

Foreign policy is merely domestic politics with its hat on.

Christopher Ondaatje and Robert Catherwood, writing in Centennial Year 1967 about Lester Pearson, concluded:

History will remember him not as Canada's centennial Prime Minister but as the most effective person this country has ever contributed to international affairs.[94]

PIERRE ELLIOTT TRUDEAU

Pearson was succeeded as Leader of the Liberal Party and as Prime Minister of Canada by Pierre Elliott Trudeau.[95] Many readers of this book likely have strong feelings—both positive and negative—about the political legacy of Trudeau, but he is often honored as the "Father of Multiculturalism in Canada"[96]. Trudeau's vision was that Canada as a nation rests on pluralistic foundations, beginning with the aboriginal peoples, then with the founding nationalities of English and French, and now including people arriving from all parts of the world. We can now be described as "one country, two languages and many cultures."[97]

Bill C-93, *An Act for the preservation and enhancement of multiculturalism in Canada*, was tabled in the House of Commons on December 1, 1987. The *Canadian Multiculturalism Act* became law on July 21, 1988. This legislation, and the resulting increases in the flow of immigration to Canada, have profoundly changed who we are and our perceptions of our role in the world. We are now a proudly diverse society, with a unique view of our role in the world, as discussed in the next section.

CANADIAN PRIORITIES FOR ASSISTANCE TO INTERNATIONAL DEVELOPMENT: CANADA'S FOREIGN POLICY

Canada's foreign policy, and the priorities for international development cooperation, have evolved over the past two decades, as follows.

In 1995, the Canadian Government's foreign assistance policy was laid out in a document entitled *Canada in the World*. It provided the goal for Canadian Official Development Assistance (ODA):

> *The purpose of Canada's ODA is to support sustainable development in developing countries, in order to reduce poverty and to contribute to a more secure, equitable and prosperous world.*[98]

This goal became the main mandate of the Canadian International Development Agency (CIDA) as the lead organization responsible for Canadian ODA. Based on this mandate, CIDA developed a poverty-reduction strategy that committed the Agency to making poverty reduction a key element of each of its six ODA program priorities:

- basic human needs, to meet the needs of people living in poverty in primary health care, basic education, family planning, nutrition, water and sanitation, and shelter, as well as to respond to emergencies with humanitarian assistance—*Canada in the World* committed the Government to providing 25 percent of its ODA to basic human needs

- gender equality, to support the achievement of equality between women and men to ensure sustainable development

- <u>infrastructure services</u>, to help developing countries deliver environmentally sound infrastructure services—for example, rural electricity and communication—with an emphasis on poorer groups and on building capacity

- <u>human rights, democracy, and good governance</u>, to increase respect for human rights, including children's rights, to support democracy and responsible government, and to strengthen civil society

- <u>private-sector development</u>, to promote sustained and equitable economic growth by supporting private-sector development in developing countries and organizations which are working in micro-enterprise and small business development to promote income generation

- <u>environment</u>, to help developing countries protect their environment and contribute to addressing global and regional environmental issues.

In 2001, CIDA announced its four Social Development Priorities:

- health and nutrition
- basic education
- HIV/AIDS
- child protection

with gender equality as an integral part of all these priority areas.

In 2002, the Minister of Foreign Affairs issued *Canada making a difference in the world: a policy statement on strengthening aid effectiveness*. The Minister wrote:

> *This document outlines the international context for our agenda to strengthen aid effectiveness and the principles that will guide our efforts. These include providing increased attention to the leadership role of developing countries, promoting greater coordination with other donors, and fostering greater coherence in Canada's policies that affect our developing-country partners. In keeping with the principles, this document identifies the framework within which decisions will be made on the geographical and sectoral allocation of CIDA's resources. It also*

identifies changes in tied aid policies designed to reinforce aid effectiveness and the steps we are taking to strengthen CIDA as an institution.

Canada is making a difference in the developing world, and we want to build on our success. We will continue to focus on the four social development priorities established in 2001: health and nutrition, basic education, HIV/AIDS, and protecting children. Promoting gender equality will be an integral part of these programming areas. Further, CIDA will give added emphasis to rural development and agriculture. Recent research indicates the critical importance of these sectors not just for food security, but as an engine for economic growth. In keeping with Prime Minister Jean Chrétien's stated priorities at the G8 Summit, Africa will remain the priority for our work.

The New Partnership for Africa's Development (NEPAD) best captures the nature of this changing relationship. Initiated by African leaders, NEPAD stresses mutual accountability and respect, and the need for developing countries to set their own priorities.

In 2004, CIDA released its *Sustainable Development Action Plan 2004–2006: Enabling Change*, in which the basic structure of development objectives resides in four Key Agency Results:

- economic well-being
- social development
- environmental sustainability
- good governance

which, according to CIDA, are fully in accord with the Millennium Development Goals (described in Chapters Two and Three).

On April 20, 2005 then-Prime Minister Paul Martin released the long-awaited *Canada's International Policy Statement: A Role of Pride and Influence in the World*.[99] Over the previous few years, much effort had gone into reviewing, revising and updating Canada's foreign policy, including the priorities of the federal government for international development. During the public debate leading up to the release of this document, a great diversity of views came forward from the various interested publics, but certain ideas came through repeatedly. These included the following:

- greater coordination is needed among the Government's policies for defence, diplomacy, development, and trade

- in development assistance, Canada should not try to be "all things to all people", but should strive for much more focus and impact.

With respect to international development within *Canada's International Policy Statement*, here are some of the highlights:

- Previously, 146 countries qualified for assistance under criteria adopted by the Canadian International Development Agency (CIDA). In the future, two-thirds of Canada's country-to-country assistance will go to 25 countries, most of which are in Africa: Bangladesh, Benin, Bolivia, Burkina Faso, Cambodia, Cameroon, Ethiopia, Ghana, Guyana, Honduras, Indonesia, Kenya, Malawi, Mali, Mozambique, Nicaragua, Niger, Pakistan, Rwanda, Senegal, Sri Lanka, Tanzania, Ukraine, Vietnam, Zambia.[100] These "Development Partner Countries" were chosen on the basis of greatest need, demonstrated ability to use aid effectively, and current level of Canadian involvement.

(Increased focus on a smaller number of assisted countries also shows up as a major issue in the case *CESO & Gordon Cummings* in Chapter Nine.)

- Canada's contribution to the Millennium Development Goals will focus on governance, private sector development, health, basic education and environmental sustainability, and will systematically incorporate gender equality throughout. Key Initiatives will include:

- additional funding to combat HIV/AIDS, tuberculosis and malaria

- encouraging the implementation of Canada's new generic drug legislation in other countries

- focusing education assistance on improving community access to schools

- increasing the quality of teaching and supporting life skills training

- launching the Canada Investment Fund for Africa to provide risk capital to support growth-generating private sector development

- renewing Canada's Climate Change Development Fund as an important mechanism to help combat the challenges of global warming in developing countries

- The Canada Corps will be established as a key mechanism for providing governance assistance to developing countries, i.e. to develop collaborative partnerships across government, and with non-governmental organizations, the private sector and Canadian citizens; create coherent governance assistance programs with a focus on sharing Canadian expertise in the rule of law and human rights; and create a single portal for Canadians to access international volunteer opportunities.

- The international assistance budget will be doubled (relative to 2001) to over $5 billion by 2010.

- Prime Minister Martin, in introducing *Canada's International Policy Statement*, did not commit to a timetable for meeting the 0.7% of GDP target for foreign aid mentioned earlier, but he said that his government will "work towards the 0.7% mark".

Professor Jeffrey Sachs (identified earlier) responded immediately,[101] urging Martin to join the six countries that have committed to a timetable to meet this target, as well as the five countries that have already achieved this goal.

Rock star and social activist Bono, a Martin admirer, also declared that he was "annoyed" that Martin did not commit to a timetable for reaching the 0.7% target.[102]

One particularly thoughtful commentator in the public debates leading up to the release of the *International Policy Statement* was Jennifer Welsh whose 2004 book, *At Home in the World: Canada's Vision for the 21st Century*[103], undoubtedly had a significant influence on the foreign policy review process. In fact, following the publication of her book, Welsh was asked by Prime Minister Paul Martin to "inject his government's view of Canadian foreign policy with a bold, new vision for the country."[104] Welsh conceives of "Canada as a Model Citizen" and proposed an agenda with four main priorities:

- Reform of international governance: Welsh offers a convincing argument in support of multilateralism and the need for Canada to play a strong role in its reform, principally for the UN system, but also for less formal bodies such as the G20 group of countries.

- Protecting and promoting human rights: In the midst of the "war on terror," Canada can demonstrate how liberty and security can be balanced.

- Ensuring fairness: "alleviating the crippling poverty that grips so many societies around the world" by working towards the Millennium Development Goals. Canada "must increase our financial commitment and improve the way it is dispersed" and "we should assist developing countries in building social infrastructure (education, public health, and a strong legal framework)."

- Preserving our distinctiveness, especially while improving our relationship with the United States.

A few years later, Paul Martin's Liberal government was replaced by a Conservative administration led by Stephen Harper and the region of the world to receive priority shifted from Africa to Latin America, apparently because of the new government's desire to strengthen economic relations with other countries in the Americas:

"As part of its Aid Effectiveness Agenda, the Government of Canada announced in 2009 that it will be focusing 80 percent of bilateral resources in 20 countries of focus. These 20 countries were chosen based on their real needs, their capacity to benefit from aid, and their alignment with Canadian foreign policy priorities. The goal is to make Canada's international assistance more focused, more effective and more accountable. The countries of focus are:

- *Americas: Bolivia - Caribbean Regional Program - Colombia - Haiti - Honduras - Peru*

- *Asia: Afghanistan - Bangladesh - Indonesia - Pakistan - Vietnam*

- *Eastern Europe: Ukraine*

- *North Africa and Middle East: West Bank and Gaza*

- *Sub-Saharan Africa: Ethiopia - Ghana - Mali - Mozambique - Senegal- Sudan - Tanzania"*[105]

GOVERNMENT DEPARTMENTS AND AGENCIES

Many, if not most, of the departments, agencies and Crown corporations of the Government of Canada have international involvements. The department, however, that has the greatest international role is the Department of Foreign Affairs and International Trade (DFAIT)[106].

Leading DFAIT are three Ministers:

- Minister of Foreign Affairs (the senior Minister)
- Minister of International Trade
- Minister of International Cooperation.

With respect to international development, the main ministerial responsibility (after the Prime Minister and the Minister of Foreign Affairs) rests with the Minister of International Cooperation, among whose responsibilities are the Canadian International Development Agency (CIDA) and the International Development Research Centre (IDRC). Also important in development activities abroad are the staff members of Canadian embassies and high commissions.

In fiscal year 2005-2006, the Canadian government spent $3.7 billion on international aid.[107] Of this amount, the following spent:

- CIDA: 78%
- IDRC: 4%
- DFAIT: 8%
- Department of Finance: 10%

CANADIAN INTERNATIONAL DEVELOPMENT AGENCY (CIDA)

CIDA[108] has already been mentioned several times in this book. To recap, CIDA, with headquarters in Gatineau in Quebec, is the lead organization responsible for Canadian Official Development Assistance (ODA). The purpose of Canada's ODA is to support sustainable development in developing countries, in order to reduce poverty and to contribute to a more secure, equitable and prosperous world. As mentioned above, Canadian ODA currently has five priority sectors:

- good governance
- health (with a focus on HIV/AIDS)
- basic education
- private sector development
- environmental sustainability

all implemented with gender equality as a crosscutting theme.

The branches of CIDA of primary interest to a reader seeking support from the Agency are the following. (CIDA's funding programs are described in Chapter Five.)

- Canadian Partnership Branch
- Africa Branch
- Americas Branch
- Asia Branch
- Europe, Middle East and Maghreb Branch.

The Canadian Partnership Branch (CPB):

...is responsible for international cooperation programs with colleges, universities, companies, non-governmental organizations, cooperatives, unions, professional associations and other institutions.

Canadian Partnership Branch's programs are carried out in partnership with those organizations. The Branch's main objective is to help the Agency carry out its mandate of supporting sustainable development and reducing poverty in some of the poorest developing countries in the world.

Partner organizations design and carry out projects that aim at improving quality of life and building the capacities of local private sector and civil society. In turn, the resultant partnerships promote knowledge development and creativity in the voluntary and private sectors, both in Canada and in the developing country.

Canadian Partnership Branch, working with almost 850 partners, currently participates in 1,300 international cooperation programs and projects by offering strategic advice, sharing knowledge, and providing financial support.[109]

Africa Branch, Americas Branch, Asia Branch, and Europe, Middle East and Maghreb Branch are jointly known as the bilateral side of CIDA. They deal with "country-to-country" or "government-to-government", as well as regional, programming in the respective geographic areas.

In the fiscal year 2005-2006, CIDA expended the following on the various regions:[110]

- Sub-Saharan Africa: $1300 million   (47%)
- Asia: 780   (28%)
- Americas: 459   (16%)

- North Africa & Middle East: 129   (5%)
- Eastern Europe: 114   (4%)

In 2005, the then-government's intention was that, by 2010, "Canada will concentrate at least two thirds of its bilateral development assistance on 25 "Development Partner Countries", 14 of which are in Africa".

The situation has changed. As mentioned in the previous section, in 2006 Paul Martin's Liberal government was replaced by a Conservative administration led by Stephen Harper. The region of the world to receive priority shifted from Africa to Latin America, apparently because of the new government's desire to strengthen economic relations with other countries in the Americas:

CIDA has done an enormous amount of good in international development, both through the Canadian Partnership Branch and through the bilateral side. Highlights of the agency's successes appear on its website[111] and are oriented especially towards its considerable achievements in support of the Millennium Development Goals.

Nevertheless, CIDA (or, rather, the Canadian Government's use of CIDA) is not without its critics. One example is Cranford Pratt in his 2000 essay "Alleviating Global Poverty or Enhancing Security: Competing Rationales for Canadian Development Assistance"[112], in which he writes about the continuing debate and uncertainty about how certain parties inside and outside of the federal government tug CIDA among very different international objectives. Another is John Lorinc who, in a November 2004 article in *Saturday Night* entitled *The Best Aid Plans*,[113] refers to CIDA as:

> ...*a politically orphaned, hidebound bureaucracy that spreads itself too thinly, commands little respect internationally and represents an impediment to a development agenda that [then-Prime Minister] Martin himself espouses.*

The debate about the accomplishments, and the proper role of CIDA, continues. The Standing Committee on Foreign Affairs and International Trade of the Senate of Canada released a damning report in February 2007 entitled *Overcoming 40 Years Of Failure: A New Road Map For Sub-Saharan Africa.* The report concluded:

> *Africa is the only continent in the world that has not benefited from the last forty years of significant global growth. It is unacceptable that the average citizen in sub-Saharan Africa has not experienced a real increase in his or her well-being since independence...Slow, unaccountable,*

and poorly-designed development assistance and ineffective foreign aid institutions in Africa, including the Canadian International Development Agency, have also failed to achieve sustained improvements in the quality of life of African citizens.

Within the report's recommendations are the following:

Given the failure of the Canadian International Development Agency (CIDA) in Africa over the past 38 years to make an effective foreign aid difference, the Government of Canada should conduct an immediate review of whether or not this organization should continue to exist in its present non-statutory form. If CIDA is to be abolished, necessary Canadian development staff and decision-making authority should be transferred to the Department of Foreign Affairs and International Trade. If CIDA is to be retained, it should be given a stand-alone statutory mandate incorporating clear objectives against which the performance of the agency can be monitored by the Parliament of Canada.

The Government of Canada should refocus and energize its approach to Africa by:

- *Establishing a new Africa Office. The Africa Office would incorporate international development, international trade and foreign affairs personnel dealing with the African continent and would consult closely with the Department of National Defence. This new office would come under the responsibility of a newly designated Minister for International Development who should be given full status in the federal Cabinet. If Canadian International Development Agency (CIDA) personnel are to be shifted to the Department of Foreign Affairs and International Trade (DFAIT), an Africa Office with a strong mandate should be formed. If CIDA is to be given its own act of Parliament, an Africa Office should be included in this legislation...*

- *Decentralizing a minimum of 80% of the staff within the new Africa Office and decision-making authority, including the distribution of financial resources, to Canadian missions in the field in Africa.*

One of the witnesses in the Senate Committee's hearings was Ian Smillie, Research Coordinator, Partnership Africa Canada, who observed:

CIDA has developed a reputation as one of the slowest bilateral aid agencies in the world. We have more checklists, forms, studies, consultancies and evaluations than any other donor I know. We are pathologically risk averse.

An important book in this context is *Aid and Ebb Tide: A History of CIDA and Canadian Development Assistance* by David R. Morrison:

Aid and Ebb Tide: A History of CIDA and Canadian Development Assistance *examines Canada's mixed record since 1950 in transferring over $50 billion in capital and expertise to developing countries through ODA. It focuses in particular on the Canadian International Development Agency (CIDA), the organization chiefly responsible for delivering Canada's development assistance.* Aid and Ebb Tide *calls for a renewed and reformed Canadian commitment to development co-operation at a time when the gap between the world's richest and poorest has been widening alarmingly and millions are still being born into poverty and human insecurity.*[114]

INTERNATIONAL DEVELOPMENT RESEARCH CENTRE (IDRC)

As mentioned in Chapter Three, when former Prime Minister Lester Pearson established IDRC as a Canadian Crown Corporation in 1970, he viewed the nurturing of national research capability in developing countries as one important route to development. The concept was that Canada could assist developing countries to create their own research abilities in order to solve their problems by themselves, rather than by depending on the more industrialized countries.

IDRC's mission[115] is *empowerment through knowledge.* In carrying out its mission, IDRC provides funds and expert advice to developing-country researchers working to solve critical development problems. IDRC:

- funds applied research by researchers from developing countries on the problems they identify as crucial to their communities. Most projects supported result from direct exchanges between the Centre and developing-country institutions;

- provides expert advice to those researchers;

- builds local capacity in developing countries to undertake research and innovate.

IDRC supports research under the broad themes of:

- environment and natural resource management
- information and communication technologies for development
- innovation, policy and science
- social and economic policy.

These fields of research support the eight Millennium Development Goals[116].

IDRC funds and administers a training and awards program for young Canadians and nationals from developing countries. By supporting academic study and offering opportunities for hands-on experience, IDRC helps countries of the South to provide themselves with a critical mass of trained and experienced researchers and gives a new generation of Canadians an opportunity to participate actively in international development issues.

Through its Canadian partnerships program, IDRC fosters alliances and knowledge-sharing between scientific, academic, and development communities in Canada and the South. IDRC also works in partnership with other donors to increase the resources going to researchers in the South.

IDRC has headquarters in Ottawa, plus six regional offices:

- in Africa: Nairobi, Kenya; Dakar, Senegal; and Cairo, Egypt
- in Asia: New Delhi, India; and Singapore
- in Latin America and the Caribbean: Montevideo, Uruguay.

Guided by a 21-member international Board of Governors, IDRC reports to Parliament through the Minister of Foreign Affairs. IDRC's Parliamentary appropriations were $135.3 million in 2006/07.

The funding programs of IDRC are described in Chapter Five.

CANADIAN EMBASSIES AND HIGH COMMISSIONS

Canada has embassies (and high commissions in Commonwealth countries), as well as consulates and trade offices, in over 270 locations in approximately 180 foreign countries[117]. In the embassies and high commissions, there are one or more staff members responsible for Canada's contributions to development activities in that country, usually through the bilateral side of CIDA. The senior persons in this group usually have "Development" in parentheses after their job titles, e.g. there are a Counsellor (Development) and a First

Secretary (Development) listed in the staff directory of the High Commission of Canada to Kenya in Nairobi[118].

Embassies and high commissions will sometimes have relatively small funds that can be used in the country (e.g. the *Canada Fund*) for activities that are of value to the host country. (See the case *Ethiopia & Christine Gilmore* in Chapter Nine.)

UNIVERSITIES, COLLEGES AND THEIR ASSOCIATIONS

The last two decades have seen fundamental changes in the international attitudes and activities of Canada's universities. Twenty years ago, the typical situation consisted of an individual professor having a personal interest in cooperating with a friend or counterpart in a university in another country. Activities might have included faculty visits in both directions, guest lectures, joint scholarship and publication, and possibly a small student exchange program, usually without much involvement by the central administration.

This situation was followed by the widespread emergence of requests by students for more international exchange and study abroad possibilities; by faculty, students and administrators who wanted to be of service to developing countries; by demands of faculty members for increased support from the central administration for their international initiatives; by an awareness on the part of the scholarly leaders of the university that they had to excel on the global stage if they were to be taken seriously as research institutions.

Most Canadian universities responded positively to these demands by creating administrative units to nurture student exchange and study abroad programs, to provide services to international students on campus, to support international development cooperation, and to enhance international scholarship and research[119]. Administrations typically also started allocating budgetary resources for these activities. Some universities formalized their international commitments by creating strategic plans for the internationalization of their institutions, which affirmed the value of their various forms of international engagement.

CANADIAN UNIVERSITIES AND AUCC

It is evident from the examples presented in Chapter Three, and from the cases contained in the book from Chapter Seven onwards, that Canadian universities are impressively active in international development. A great deal of this activity is assisted by funding from CIDA, both from Partnership Branch and from the bilateral side. Partnership Branch support comes mainly through the University Partnerships in Cooperation and Development (UPCD) program, which is partly administered by the Association of Universities and Colleges of Canada (AUCC)[120].

The UPCD program, as described in detail in Chapter Five, takes the form of collaboration between one or more Canadian universities and one or more higher education institutions in developing countries. The purpose of the collaboration is to build the capacity of the developing country institutions to deal with priority development problems of their countries. (The second phase of the UPCD program has come to a close and a new university partnerships program is being negotiated.)

AUCC represents almost all Canadian public and private not-for-profit universities and university-degree level colleges. Since the inception of the UPCD program in 1994, AUCC has administered well over 100 UPCD projects[121]. Highlights of some of the projects are contained in UPCD Fact Sheets[122].

CANADIAN COLLEGES AND ACCC

Similarly, the Association of Canadian Community Colleges (ACCC)[123] "is the national, voluntary membership organization created in 1972 to represent colleges and institutes to government, business and industry, both in Canada and internationally"[124]. ACCC supports the international activities of its member institutions. *ACCC International*[125], published twice per year, provides current information on its international activities.

CANADIAN BUREAU FOR INTERNATIONAL EDUCATION (CBIE)

CBIE[126] is a national non-governmental organization comprised of 200 colleges, universities, school boards, educational organizations and businesses. A 21-member pan-Canadian Board of Directors governs CBIE, whose activities are managed by a team of professionals located in Ottawa.

CBIE works to:

- Enhance Canada's commitment to and participation in international education—by governments, institutions and other stakeholders

- Expand opportunities for study and work abroad by Canadians

- Increase the number of international students in Canada

- Design and deliver international education projects that emphasize the human element in development and draw on the expertise of Canadian educators

- Build capacity in developing and transitional countries in terms of civil society development, public sector reform and governance
- Export Canadian education around the world including working with international private sectors to establish Canadian offshore institutions.

INTER-AMERICAN ORGANIZATION FOR HIGHER EDUCATION (IOHE)

IOHE[127] is a "non-governmental non-profit organization, the only inter-American university association, decentralized into nine regions and bringing together some 400 institutions of higher education from all over the Americas. This Organization represents about 4 million students, 400,000 professors and 700,000 support staff members, in addition to 20 national or regional associations representing almost 1,900 institutions of higher education in the Americas."

The member institutions of IOHE benefit by building linkages and sharing information. One such activity was to increase expertise in the management of international activities. IOHE organized a number of training workshops and published manuals in Spanish, Portuguese, French and English[128] on the management of international university collaboration. Typical participants were those officials at the universities who had responsibility for student exchanges, for collaborative research, and for the internationalization of the campuses.

NONGOVERNMENTAL ORGANIZATIONS AND FOUNDATIONS

Other than working with Canadian government departments and agencies, or through community colleges, universities and their associations, there is a multitude of not-for-profit organizations through which Canadians can be of benefit to people in developing countries. These are nongovernmental organizations, which include Canadian NGOs, multinational NGOs, and indigenous NGOs.

CANADIAN AND MULTINATIONAL NGOS

Canadian NGOs are non-profit groups that usually have official status as charitable organizations, i.e. donations made to Canadian NGOs are generally deductible from Canadian income tax.

Charity Village has prepared a useful guide, "Starting a Nonprofit or Charity".[129] Also, if a group of individuals is interested in setting up a new NGO, it is the authors' experience that existing NGOs are almost always willing to share their own experiences in getting their organization set up and in getting funded.

The national umbrella organization for Canadian NGOs working in international development is the Canadian Council for International Cooperation (CCIC):

> *The Canadian Council for International Co-operation is a coalition of Canadian voluntary sector organizations working globally to promote and strengthen the role of civil society in efforts to promote peace, defend human rights and to end global poverty and injustice"...The Council comprises about 100 Canadian voluntary sector organizations working to end global poverty.*[130]

Also, there are seven provincial/regional umbrella organizations across Canada:

- Alberta Council for Global Cooperation[131]
- Association Québecoise des Organismes de Coopération Internationale[132]
- Atlantic Council for International Cooperation[133]
- British Colombia Council for International Cooperation[134]
- Manitoba Council for International Cooperation[135]
- Ontario Council for International Cooperation[136]
- Saskatchewan Council for International Cooperation[137]

As an example, the "...Ontario Council for International Cooperation (OCIC) is a coalition of Ontario-based, not-for-profit, voluntary organizations working both in the North and South for global justice. As a Council, OCIC strives to increase the effectiveness and the collective impact of all its members' efforts to promote sustainable, people- centered development in a peaceful and healthy environment. OCIC is committed to principles of fair and equitable cooperation between North and South and promotes a participatory style of education that helps Canadians develop a global perspective and take action for global justice.

"OCIC encourages the development of the Ontario international development and global education sectors and sharing of resources between OCIC members by providing forums for networking, communications and collaborative reflection and action, and facilitating capacity building in public engagement and organizational development."[138]

Some well known Canadian NGOs that are members of one or more of the Councils include:

- Canada World Youth[139]
- Canadian Crossroads International[140]
- Canadian Foodgrains Bank[141]
- Canadian Physicians for Aid & Relief[142]
- CARE Canada[143]
- CUSO[144]
- Engineers Without Borders[145]

...and many more.

Many Canadian NGOs are affiliated with multinational NGOs, for example:

- Aga Khan Foundation Canada[146]
- Canadian Rotary Collaboration for International Development[147]
- Doctors without Borders/ Médecins sans Frontières[148]
- Habitat for Humanity Canada[149]
- Oxfam-Canada[150]
- UNICEF Canada[151]

Within the Canadian NGOs, there is a group, formerly called "Volunteer Sending Organizations", that now goes by the descriptor of Volunteer Cooperation Agencies (VCAs), especially in the context of CIDA's Volunteer Cooperation Program:

VCAs engage Canadians directly by offering them volunteering opportunities, by providing information on development issues, debating international cooperation, and offering people from the developing world an opportunity to speak with Canadians directly on matters of concern[152].

Some VCAs are[153]:

- AFS Interculture Canada[154]
- Aga Khan Foundation Canada[155]
- Canada World Youth (CWY)[156]

- Canadian Centre for International Studies and Cooperation (CECI)[157]
- Canadian Crossroads International (CCI) [158]
- Canadian Executive Service Organization (CESO)[159]
- CUSO[160]
- Engineers without Borders-Canada[161]
- Entraide universitaire mondiale du Canada (ÉUMC)[162]
- Oxfam-Québec[163]
- Solidarité Union Coopération (SUCO)[164]
- Voluntary Service Overseas Canada[165]
- World University Service of Canada (WUSC)[166]
- Youth Challenge International[167]

The VCAs are of particular interest to young persons who want to obtain some initial experience in international development by volunteering for projects overseas (see Chapter Sixteen). Frequently, there will be student chapters of some of the organizations on university campuses.

Some of the funding for Canadian NGOs, as detailed in the next chapter, comes from the Partnership Branch of CIDA, e.g. from the Voluntary Sector Program and the Volunteer Cooperation Program. A list of the Canadian voluntary sector organizations that cooperate with CIDA is on their website[168].

All of the above material deals with Canadian NGOs and multinational NGOs. The third type mentioned at the start of this section is indigenous NGOs–these are in Chapter Nine, *Nongovernmental Organizations*, which discusses further the role of NGOs in international development.

FOUNDATIONS

Several Canadian foundations are also very active in international development. Three of the better known ones are the Stephen Lewis Foundation[169], the Aga Khan Foundation[170] and Calmeadow[171]. A new one is the Little Voice Foundation:

» Example: Ethiopia & Little Voice Foundation

"Our first two projects are located in Addis Ababa, Ethiopia and involve both education and housing. UNICEF estimates that there are as many as 150,000 children living and working on the streets of Ethiopia's capital city. Of that number, maybe 45,000 have families to go home to after their excruciatingly long workday but the rest face a long night on the streets. For those children who have families, they are often the sole provider of the household, many of them also caring for one or more family member who is battling HIV/AIDS. And for those with no shelter the night is spent avoiding rape, robbery or beatings. Education is a luxury very few can afford.

"In February 2006, Little Voice Foundation along with local partners established a small primary school with the goal of offering its 200 seats for free to children from poor families and to those living on the streets. In July 2006, Little Voice Home for Children opened its doors to 30 children for whom the streets have been their only home over the years. The children living at our home are provided with food, clothing, education, health care and a wide range of recreational programs." [172]

PRIVATE SECTOR AND CONSULTANTS

Canada is a trading nation, and thus the commercial sector has innumerable engagements with:

- industrialized countries
- nations in transition from centrally planned economies to open market economies, and
- developing countries.

An enormous amount of trading activity takes place with countries in all three categories.

With respect to development activities, however, the activity is mainly with transition economies and in developing countries. The work is in the form of contracting and consulting assignments for which funding comes principally from CIDA (both Partnership Branch and bilateral) or from one of the multilateral banks, e.g. the Asian Development Bank, the World Bank, the Inter-American Development Bank. Canadian practitioners range in size all the way from a single individual to very small firms like International Project and Protocol Services Inc. [173] to large consulting firms such as Hickling International[174] to giant engineering and construction firms like SNC-Lavalin[175].

(More on this in Chapter Eleven, *The Canadian Private Sector.*)

CANADIAN ENGINEERS IN INTERNATIONAL DEVELOPMENT

There are a good many different ways in which Canadian engineers are involved in international development. Chapter Twelve illustrates their roles...

- as volunteers
- as research partners
- as educators and trainers
- as consultants
- as contractors
- as entrepreneurs
- as Canadian government representatives
- as officials of multilateral organizations
- in emergency assistance and mitigation of loss
- in non-engineering careers.

CHAPTER FIVE

FUNDING FOR DEVELOPMENT

In the chapter following this one, we will begin the process of creating good projects. Before that, however, we need to examine where the funding comes from for international development activities. Associated with the funding are the preferences and restrictions of the funding agencies that will strongly influence, or control, how that money may be used.

Included in the following discussion are major sources of funding for international development. Some of these are available to Canadian development actors and their partners in other countries. The information given below was current at the time of writing, but international funding programs are continually changing, and it is necessary to check for updates on the information presented below before approaching any particular agency. Accordingly, web sites for the agencies are given in the respective endnotes.

CANADIAN GOVERNMENT DEPARTMENTS AND AGENCIES

CANADIAN INTERNATIONAL DEVELOPMENT AGENCY (CIDA)

CIDA is by far the predominant organization in Canada for performing international development, as discussed in Chapter Four, and for providing financial contributions for international development activities by other Canadians. There is an extensive array of support programs available from CIDA, of which the following are some highlights.

UNIVERSITY PARTNERSHIPS IN COOPERATION AND DEVELOPMENT (UPCD)[176]

The UPCD program funds projects between Canadian universities and education and training organizations in developing countries. The goal is to enhance the latter's institutional capacity to develop the human resources to address their countries' most important development needs in sustainable ways. At the same time, partners respond to the needs of local communities in developing countries.

The UPCD program is funded by CIDA[177] through contributions (not grants) provided on a cost-shared basis. The program has two tiers: Tier 1 funds large multi-disciplinary projects to which CIDA contributes up to $3 million over six years; Tier 2 funds smaller and more narrowly focused projects, to which CIDA contributes up to $1 million over six years. Tier 1 projects are managed by CIDA whereas Tier 2 projects are managed by the Association of Universities and Colleges of Canada (AUCC).

Activities involve teams at each of the partner organizations, making them institutional linkages, as opposed to individual grants or a collaboration between two professors. Since its launch in 1994, the UPCD program has funded well over 100 Tier 2 projects throughout the developing world in an array of disciplines including education, natural sciences and the humanities. A list and detailed descriptions of these projects can be found on AUCC's web site[178]. Projects funded through UPCD respond to Canada's Official Development priorities, CIDA's poverty-reduction mandate as well as to the development priorities of developing countries in Asia, Africa, the Middle East and Latin America.

These projects typically include a range of activities, for example: curriculum development, strengthening academic departments and training and further education for professors. The UPCD program does not fund projects based primarily on research. However, some research activities may be included in elements of a project, if they serve to directly strengthen the partner institution and are conducted in order to contribute to development objectives.

The lead Canadian institution is financially responsible for the project. Only institutions that are members of AUCC may apply as the lead institution. Other Canadian organizations may also be involved in the project in a non-lead capacity. This includes higher-education institutions and non-governmental organizations.

All projects also have a developing country partner. Only education and training organizations from countries eligible for Canadian Official Development Assistance (ODA) may participate as partners in the UPCD program. These include universities, colleges, polytechnics, technical institutes, vocational training centers, or other institutions with a clear mandate for postsecondary education or training and/or a government ministry or agency mandated to deliver education and training. The list of countries eligible to receive Canadian assistance can be found on CIDA's web site[179].

In this book, several of the cases, e.g. Uganda & Shafique Pirani in Chapter Eight, utilize UPCD Tier 2 funding.

The second phase of the UPCD program has come to a close and a new university partnerships program is being negotiated.

CANADIAN COLLEGE PARTNERSHIP PROGRAM (CCPP)

Similarly, the CCPP is administered by the Association of Canadian Community Colleges (ACCC), and funds projects developed by community colleges, CEGEPs, and similar institutions, which help build the capacities of educational and training institutions in developing countries. The CCPP supports, on a cost-shared basis, two categories of projects:

- Category I projects (with a maximum CIDA contribution of $800,000) are major development and institution-strengthening projects that often involve policy development, planning, and management of technical and vocational training systems.

- Category II projects (with a maximum CIDA contribution of $400,000) are smaller, more narrowly defined partnership projects that focus on institutional capacity building and poverty reduction for specific communities.

Both categories of projects have a maximum duration of five years.

PARTNERSHIPS FOR TOMORROW (PHASE II) [180]

The Partnerships for Tomorrow Program II is a travel grant mechanism designed to contribute to the democratic and economic reform process in the Balkans and countries of Eastern Europe. The program is funded by CIDA and administered by the Association of Universities and Colleges of Canada.

The program supports small projects, up to a maximum of $10,000, which aim to build and strengthen partnerships and linkages between Canadian organizations and organizations from those countries. These long term relationships will facilitate the capacity development of individuals and organizations in the Balkans and Eastern European region while developing Canadian expertise in working with those countries.

The program funds the direct costs of international travel including economy airfare, a per diem that covers a portion of the cost of accommodations and meals, and local travel (inter-city travel only), to a maximum of $10,000 per project.

The program is open to participants from all sectors including institutions, educational institutions, nongovernmental organizations, professionals, businesses, individuals, youth (ages 18-30) and government (excluding the Canadian federal government). All activities must have a capacity building component and must be compatible with CIDA's programming priorities.

Funds will be awarded to enable recipients to actively participate in the following types of activities:

- institutional linkages
- workshops and conferences
- sector specific training
- professional exchanges
- study tours
- short-term consultancies.

INTERNATIONAL YOUTH INTERNSHIP PROGRAM[181]

CIDA's International Youth Internship Program (IYIP) is an employment program for young Canadian professionals (ages 19 to 30 inclusive) that offers post-secondary graduates the opportunity to gain valuable international work experience. The program is part of the Career Focus stream of the Government of Canada's Youth Employment Strategy which gives young people the tools and experience they need to launch successful careers.

Since IYIP began in 1997, about 4,500 young professionals have participated as CIDA interns, sponsored by more than 190 Canadian organizations and their overseas partners.

Eligible Canadian organizations (including non-governmental organizations, private sector companies and academic institutions active in CIDA-eligible countries) submit proposals for internship projects to CIDA. Once a project is approved, the sponsor organization recruits and selects young professionals for overseas assignments, prepares them for departure and provides them with ongoing job-search support and overseas supervision. On their return to Canada, the sponsor helps its interns re-integrate into Canadian society.

Internships are a minimum six months long and include at least five months working outside Canada. CIDA, the Canadian and overseas organizations and the intern share the cost of each internship. CIDA's contribution to the sponsor organization is in cash or in-kind (for example, training). Participants receive a stipend to help cover their living and travel expenses.

For example, at the time of writing, Engineers without Borders (EWB) offered eight youth internships—four in Ghana, three in Zambia, one in Malawi—to provide engineering support to a wide range of development activities, such as water and sanitation supply, microenterprises, agriculture extension, appropriate technologies.

OTHER CIDA VOLUNTARY SECTOR PROGRAMS[182]

Through its Canadian Partnership Branch's Voluntary Sector, CIDA supports the work of nearly 270 Canadian voluntary organizations. These are cost-shared funding mechanisms that can provide eligible Canadian not-for-profit organizations with support to carry out strategic development programs in developing countries and public engagement activities in Canada. These include, in addition to the programs described above:

- Voluntary Sector Fund
- Innovation Fund
- Stand Alone Public Engagement Fund
- Volunteer Cooperation Program
- Youth Program

OFFICE FOR DEMOCRATIC GOVERNANCE

CIDA's Office for Democratic Governance[183] was created on October 30, 2006, with a specialized mandate to promote freedom and democracy, human rights, the rule of law and open and accountable public institutions in developing countries. The Office has absorbed the work of the Canada Corps. It aims to enhance aid effectiveness by leveraging Canada's comparative advantage and establishing partnerships with key Canadian experts, organizations, institutions and other government departments whose work focuses on democratic governance.

INDUSTRIAL COOPERATION PROGRAM (CIDA-INC)

The Industrial Cooperation Program (CIDA-INC) is a cost-sharing program that provides a financial incentive (a cash contribution) to Canadian companies to start a business or provide training in developing countries or countries in transition to a market economy. CIDA-INC aims to stimulate private sector development and investment in developing countries in order to promote sustainable development and poverty reduction. CIDA-INC is linked to a key CIDA goal, which is to support private sector development in developing or in-transition countries by creating jobs, increasing local capacity, and strengthening local economies. CIDA-INC's financial contribution is provided mainly for studies and training activities. Eligible projects are funded under one of two mechanisms:

- Investment Mechanism: CIDA-INC will fund viability studies and start-up activities by Canadian firms that produce goods or services in an eligible developing country; or

- Professional Services Mechanism: CIDA-INC will fund feasibility studies and implementation by Canadian consulting firms that wish to provide professional advice, or implement and transfer technology for a national or regional infrastructure project. These projects must have funding from the host country government or an international funding agency other than CIDA.

DOING BUSINESS WITH CIDA[184]

CIDA enters into contracts with Canadian individuals and companies for the implementation of some of its programs and projects. Contracting opportunities are listed on MERX[185], an electronic tendering service for a wide variety of business opportunities. To obtain advance information, a prospective contractor can monitor the "Projects at the Planning Stage (Pipeline)"[186] website of CIDA.

INTERNATIONAL DEVELOPMENT RESEARCH CENTRE OF CANADA (IDRC)

The activities and funding mechanisms of IDRC were introduced in Chapters Three and Four. IDRC:

- funds applied research by researchers from developing countries on the problems they identify as crucial to their communities. Most projects supported result from direct exchanges between the Centre and developing-country institutions;

- provides expert advice to those researchers;

- builds local capacity in developing countries to undertake research and innovate.

IDRC supports research under the broad themes of:

- environment and natural resource management
- information and communication technologies for development
- innovation, policy and science
- social and economic policy.

IDRC funds and administers a training and awards program for young Canadians and nationals from developing countries. By supporting academic study and offering opportunities for hands-on experience, IDRC helps countries of the South to provide themselves with a critical mass of trained and experienced researchers and gives a new generation of Canadians an opportunity to participate actively in international development issues.

Through its Canadian partnerships program, IDRC fosters alliances and knowledge-sharing between scientific, academic, and development communities in Canada and the South. IDRC also works in partnership with other donors to increase the resources going to researchers in the South.

ASSOCIATION OF UNIVERSITIES AND COLLEGES OF CANADA (AUCC)

AUCC administers several of CIDA's programs (including some of the ones described above). Because these are subject to change, we refer the reader to AUCC's website: http://www.aucc.ca

FEDERATION OF CANADIAN MUNICIPALITIES (FCM)

FCM is represented internationally by the International Centre for Municipal Development. FCM-ICMD works to help local governments around the world develop their capacity to deliver basic services, promote economic growth and encourage the participation of their citizens. Since 1987, FCM-ICMD has involved more than 200 Canadian municipalities and 1500 municipal experts in municipal development programming with funding from CIDA. FCM has supported initiatives to strengthen local governments and municipal capacity building in approximately 20 countries in Asia, Africa and Latin America. With CIDA support, FCM-ICMD has implemented capacity building programs to support decentralization processes, foster governance and strengthen municipal management. [187]

FOREIGN AFFAIRS AND INTERNATIONAL TRADE CANADA

The Department of Foreign Affairs and International Trade (DFAIT) administers the Human Security Program. The HSP funds projects and undertakes activities that contribute to the evolution of Canada's human security policy. Results and lessons learned are evaluated on an ongoing basis and feed into the annual policy development cycle to strengthen and better promote Canada's human security agenda.[188]

Canadian Embassies and High Commissions will sometimes have relatively small funds that can be used in the country (e.g. the *Canada Fund*) for activities that are of value to the host country.

MULTILATERAL ORGANIZATIONS[189]

Canada is a founding member of most of the multilateral institutions and continues to play an important role on their governing boards. About 40 percent of Canada's Official Development Assistance is channeled through multilateral institutions, which amounts to roughly 4 percent of their funding.

There are five main multilateral funding channels:

- international financial institutions;
- United Nations development system;
- global funds and partnerships;
- Commonwealth and La Francophonie; and
- humanitarian assistance and peace and security.

International Financial Institutions (IFIs) include the World Bank and the International Monetary Fund (IMF); the regional development banks, including the African Development Bank, the Asian Development Bank, the Caribbean Development Bank, the Inter-American Development Bank, the European Bank for Reconstruction and Development; and thematic funds such as the Global Environment Facility and the International Fund for Agricultural Development. These organizations provide financial resources in the form of preferred-market rate loans, interest-free loans, and grants. They also provide analytical and advisory services that support the development programs of developing country members. IFIs are the largest source of development financing in the world, accounting for close to US$44 billion a year.

Canada plays an active role as a member of the boards of governors of these banks and as executive directors, joining with other member countries, to provide policy guidance and approve programs, policies, and projects. Canada also promotes a greater focus on poverty reduction, aid effectiveness, private sector development, and debt relief. Within the federal government, CIDA is the lead agency for most regional development banks and for the International Fund for Agricultural Development. Finance Canada is the lead agency for the IMF, the World Bank, and the European Reconstruction and Development Bank.

The United Nations Development System: the 191-member UN is the only organization that offers universal membership and provides a unique forum for resolving global issues, including socio-economic development and humanitarian assistance. The UN is at the forefront in keeping the Millennium Development Goals on the global agenda. It also plays a critical role in transition and fragile states. CIDA provides funding to a wide range of UN development agencies, but focuses on four core institutions: the United Nations Development Programme (UNDP); the United Nations Population Fund (UNFPA); the United Nations Children's Fund (UNICEF); and the Joint United Nations Programme on HIV/AIDS (UNAIDS). CIDA also supports specialized UN agencies such as the World Health Organization, the Pan-American Health Organization, the Food and Agriculture Organization, and the International Atomic Energy Agency.

Global Funds and Partnerships: CIDA provides financial assistance to international organizations and initiatives that focus on specific issues, including:

- the Micronutrient Initiative, which works to overcome the vitamin and mineral deficiencies that are linked to much of the world's childhood illness and death. It supports and promotes supplementation and food fortification in countries with the highest deficiency rates by providing commodities and technical and operational support;

- the Global Fund to Fight AIDS, Tuberculosis and Malaria, which is a major financing mechanism whose purpose is to attract, manage, and disburse additional resources through a new public-private partnership where donors help countries fight three of the world's most devastating diseases by increasing resources and directing them to areas of greatest need; and

- the Stop TB Partnership, which brings together over 400 international agencies, non-governmental organizations, donors, foundations, and research institutions to ensure that tuberculosis sufferers have access to modern treatment in order to stop transmission, protect vulnerable populations, and reduce the toll of tuberculosis worldwide.

The Commonwealth and La Francophonie are two intergovernmental organizations that promote political dialogue and cooperation among their members. The Commonwealth is an organization of 53 industrialized and developing member states, which share a common history [as former colonies and dominions of Britain] and a democratic, parliamentary heritage. These countries work together on development issues, such as the promotion of democracy, good governance, and human rights, at the governmental and non-governmental level.

La Francophonie is an intergovernmental organization of 63 nations using French as a common language, which promotes education and cultural diversity of Francophones as well as peace, democracy, human rights, and economic cooperation and development. Both are forums for cooperation and dialogue that Canada views as valuable tools in addressing the needs of their developing country members.

In this connection, we should mention the Commonwealth Universities Study Abroad Consortium (CUSAC)[190], to which many Canadian and Commonwealth universities belong in order to foster (and, in the case of LDC Commonwealth countries, fund in part) undergraduate student exchange.

Humanitarian Assistance: CIDA works with the UN system, Canadian non-governmental organizations, and the Red Cross movement to provide appropriate, timely, and effective humanitarian assistance to respond to the needs of conflict and disaster-affected people in developing countries. This includes addressing basic human needs such as protection, food and water, shelter, and medical assistance.

Peace and Security: CIDA also provides support to peacebuilding initiatives, which encourage conflict prevention and resolution and post-conflict reconstruction. CIDA's response to mine-affected countries includes activities through our Mine Action initiative that help build national capacity for mine clearance, mine-risk awareness programs, and the provision of assistance for the care, physical rehabilitation, and social reintegration of landmine victims.

CHARITABLE ORGANIZATIONS AND FOUNDATIONS

At the heart of this group are the individual Canadian citizens who give generously to worthy causes such as emergency relief to countries struck by natural disasters. Others give through their churches, through their service clubs, through their unions (e.g. the Canadian Auto Workers) and, as taxpayers, to the Government of Canada to support relief and development activities on our behalf.

» Example: Rotary International & polio[191]

"In 1979, members of Rotary clubs...were collecting donations for famine relief. Among the pledges were offers of childhood vaccines. Several countries, including Canada, offered polio vaccine in addition to food aid. A Rotary member in the Philippines, where polio was rampant, asked that the vaccine be put to good use. He rallied fellow Rotarians, and lobbied government and international health organizations; soon, six million Filipino children were vaccinated.

"Rotary clubs in five other nations followed suit, and thus was born one of the most successful public health initiatives in history...Rotary clubs have directly contributed more than $600 million—more than any other organization, except the U.S. government...In 1988, more than 350,000 cases of polio were recorded worldwide. By 2001, that number had plummeted to 483 cases, tantalizing close to eradication... The number of infections [crept] back up to 1,185 in 2004, largely due to a fierce anti-vaccine campaign in the Nigerian state of Kano (where radical clerics charged that U.S. officials had laced the vaccine with drugs to render African girls infertile) and the subsequent spread to 16 previously polio-free countries.

"Eradication of polio, though it was not achieved in 2000 as initially planned, and [was not achieved] in 2005, the secondary target, will be achieved sooner rather than later. Rotarians, stubborn lot that they are, will see to it."

The admirable international work of some foundations was introduced in Chapter Four, where mention was made of the Aga Khan Foundation, Calmeadow, the Stephen Lewis Foundation, the Bill and Melinda Gates Foundation, the Little Voice Foundation. The Soros Foundation[192] (and its Open Society Institute) should also be mentioned for its efforts to bring democratic governance and development to countries of the former Soviet Union and, subsequently, to developing countries in other parts of the world.

MICROFINANCE AND REVOLVING CREDIT

The best known proponent of microfinance is Muhammad Yunus, who won the Nobel Peace Prize jointly with the Grameen Bank of Bangladesh, which he established in 1983. The Grameen Bank provides financial services to the poor, including small loans to people who lack collateral. The Bank is reported to have distributed US$6 billion in loans, each on average less than US$200, to 6.7 million customers, most of them women and all of them poor.[193] The Nobel Prize committee[194] specifically linked peace to reducing poverty:

> *Lasting peace cannot be achieved unless large population groups find ways in which to break out of poverty...Microcredit is one such means. Development from below also serves to advance democracy and human rights.*

In its early years, Grameen had several key operational techniques:

- loans were made to individuals but through small groups, who in effect (if not explicitly) had joint liability
- the loans were for business, not consumption
- collection was frequent, usually weekly
- interest charges were significant—the money was not aid, and a fundamental tenet of Grameen is that the poor are creditworthy— but the rates were relatively low (around 20%) ["low" compared to rates charged on the black market].

Grameen restructured in 2001, emphasizing savings (deposits now exceed loans) and relying less on joint liability for groups.

In addition to Grameen, there are now thousands of financial institutions around the world providing financial services to the very poor. One example is the registered Canadian charity Calmeadow[195], which was described in Chapter Four:

» Example: Calmeadow & microfinance

> *"Calmeadow's core belief is founded on the assumption that providing access to affordable, responsive and sustainable financial services to low income self-employed people in underdeveloped regions of the world can make a positive and lasting contribution to their economic and social well being. Our experience, gained from our early participation in a broad*

range of microfinance program initiatives convinced us that the most likely route to massive and near term development of the microfinance sector would come about when the commercial sector became directly engaged.

"Since 1990, we have held the belief that the major opportunity and challenge for this still young component of the financial services sector is found in building robust and financially sustainable institutions that can attract equity capital, commercial debt and deposits. By bringing in market capital, local and international organizations can financially leverage their operations and vastly increase the number of customers they serve.

"To that end, we have actively engaged in the development, fundraising and governance of two regional microfinance funds, ProFund Internacional (Latin America) and AfriCap Microfinance Fund (Africa). In its decade of existence, ProFund held US$22,000,000 in assets and invested in minority positions in twelve institutions in ten different countries. When the closed-end fund was liquidated as mandated by its charter, investee portfolios had grown to a total of over US$800,000,000 and were servicing the financial needs of more than 900,000 small and micro entrepreneurs in Latin America and the Caribbean. Africap currently holds over US$13,000,000 in assets, with investments and/or commitments to microfinance institutions in Egypt, Ghana, Kenya, Nigeria, Mozambique, Senegal, Tanzania and Uganda."[196]

The oxen loan revolving credit program in Ethiopia was described in Chapter Three.

CHAPTER SIX

THE PROJECT CREATION PROCESS AND RESULTS-BASED MANAGEMENT

You now have enough knowledge to start creating good projects. To recap, this is what you already have:

- an informed sensitivity as to what kinds of activities have the potential to improve the quality of life of your partners in other countries,

- an appreciation of your partners' needs and aspirations,

- an awareness that your partners in other countries have knowledge and experiences that are different from your own, but which are complementary to yours,

- a solid grasp of the characteristics and approaches you will want to have in your projects in order that they are likely to be successful,

- information concerning where the money can be obtained to support your ideas, and the requirements of the various funding agencies,

- an introduction to the thought processes needed for effective individual and collective decision making,

- historical knowledge of the array of things that other Canadians have done in international development—this should increase your confidence that you *can* do what you set out to do in international cooperation,

- increasing self-knowledge and an awareness of your own expertise and limitations,

- and, most importantly, you have made a personal commitment to this activity.

Armed with all this, you can now begin to create projects. The process described by the present chapter has proven to be productive and successful for the authors of this book. Without doubt, there are other valid ways to formulate international activities, and it is always useful to examine alternative approaches as you encounter them in order to enrich your skills. Nevertheless, the following four-phase process has proven to work well, and therefore it is offered to you.

- Phase 1 – Preliminary exploration

- Phase 2 – Brainstorming. This is an intentionally chaotic process, ostensibly unstructured, that is intended to elicit all conceivable relevant questions, and to capture all pertinent ideas.

- Phase 3 – Defining the intersection of three things: the needs, aspirations and capabilities of your partners in another country; your own capabilities and interests; and the priorities and financial capacities of funding agencies.

- Phase 4 – Imposing the rigor of Results-based Management to create the structure of the project.

PHASE 1: PRELIMINARY EXPLORATION

The idea of a project has been conceived, and you are exploring whether the idea might be useful to the community being considered, i.e. whether there likely is a valid project that can be developed out of the idea. What is the stimulus for the project? At this stage, you do the preliminary background research, and also explore who your partner or partners in the project should be (both in the partner country and at home). Look into who else is working in this sector in the country. Investigate donor coordination. Refer to the national Poverty Reduction Strategy Paper. Will your project duplicate or overlap the activities of others in the country or, desirably, are they complementary? Who are the stakeholders? Identify everyone who will be involved in this project at home and abroad. Is international collaboration the best way to achieve the desired results, or should the work be done some other way, e.g. an internal NEPAD (The New Partnership for Africa's Development) project in an African country? Carry out a "scouting" mission with your partners. Has there been a needs assessment carried out?

PHASE 2: BRAINSTORMING

This stage is usually highly enjoyable and stimulating. The members of the group doing the project planning typically dedicate a full day to this part of the work, they all agree to shut off all their electronic devices during the session, and they commit to remaining with the group for the entire session. Interruptions and distractions are to be avoided at all costs, and therefore it is helpful to get away from the office and meet at another location.

If your overseas partner or partners have been identified, they must be full participants in the project creation process. In fact, all the key stakeholders and beneficiaries whom you have identified need to participate in the process.

One person acts as the facilitator of the discussions. Either this person or another member of the group records, on flip charts or white boards, all the questions and ideas that the group produces. At this point, there are no bad ideas—all contributions are valid. There are pots of coffee, snacks, several surfaces to write on, and numerous felt markers available in the room. All members of the group are encouraged to write on the boards if they wish, and this is facilitated by having lots of markers lying around in the meeting space.

The facilitator gets the process rolling. She or he then *appears* to play a relatively low key role in the discussions, but interjects questions from time to time designed to make sure that all major aspects of the contemplated project are considered, at least in a preliminary way. Here is a checklist of typical questions and topics that the facilitator may wish the group to consider:

- Whom do we want to help? (Be specific and focused.)

- What aspect of their lives do we want to improve? (Or, more precisely, what aspects of their lives do our partners want to be improved?) How are we going to reduce their poverty? Review the needs assessment if one has already been carried out.

- Is this a development priority in their country? Review the Poverty Reduction Strategy Paper for the country.

- Develop an awareness of the existing knowledge and experience possessed by our partners, and strive to understand their sensitivities and aspirations.

- What capabilities and interests does our organization have that can make a contribution to this development priority? Build awareness both of our expertise and of our limitations.

- Are we going to build capacity in the partner country? How can our organization help to build capacity? (Be specific.)

- How shall we ensure that our contribution is sustainable, rather than being an isolated act of generosity?

- What are the socio-economic, political, gender and cultural contexts of our project?

- How do we interact with all the stakeholders?

- Do we need additional partners in the project, either in Canada or in the partner country? Why?

- How do we go about doing this project? Start with the end point, the *Impact*, and think backwards to the *Activities* and *Inputs*.

- What is the anticipated duration of the project?

- How do we fit the activities into the duration? Can the activities be aggregated into steps?

- Who will carry out each step? Where will it happen? How long will it take? What will each step cost?

- Do the arithmetic to obtain a very rough estimate of the total project cost.

- What funding agencies have mandates that are applicable to this project?

- What financial contributions are potentially available from this agency? How does the estimated total project cost compare with what could be obtained from this agency? If there is a major disconnect at this stage, either consider other funding sources, or modify the project, or both. Iterate on this issue until the estimated total project cost is roughly equal to the money potentially available.

- What is our accumulated track record in international development cooperation in general, and in projects of this type, and in this country in particular?

- How shall we manage the project? Defer to local initiative and local ownership.

- How to establish a system of management communication that will put in place a framework for maintaining consensus and for the equitable participation of all partners.

- Meetings? Decision-making? Advisory roles? Community linkages? Government agencies? Government policy? Publications and publicity?

- How will we know that we have accomplished what we set out to do? (Benchmarking and performance indicators, disaggregated by sex, ethnicity and/or socio-economic class)

- Monitoring and evaluation?

- Anticipated risks – both their potential seriousness and their probability of occurrence?

PHASE 3: DEFINING THE INTERSECTION

In the next part of the project creation process, we narrow the focus on what is possible and desirable by finding the area of overlap of three things:

- the needs, aspirations, priorities and capabilities of our partner organization or community

- the capabilities and interests of the Canadian organization(s), and

- the mandate, priorities and financial capacities of a potential funding agency.

We can display this graphically by the Venn diagram shown below. The shaded area is the intersection of the three components. It is the "common ground" and is the maximum potential scope of the project-it represents those particular needs of the partner that your organization has the capabilities to assist with, and that can potentially be contributed to by a particular funding agency.

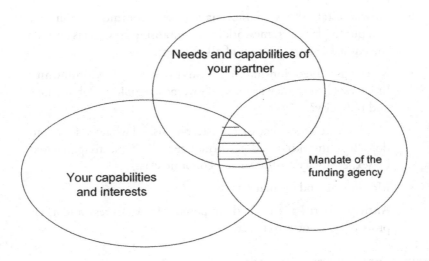

PHASE 4: RESULTS-BASED MANAGEMENT

In Phase 4 of the project creation process, we take all the raw material that was generated in Phases 1 and 2 together with the boundaries that were imposed upon it in Phase 3, and then apply the discipline and the structure of Results-based Management (RBM)[197].

RBM and accountability

Results-based Management is a tool used in the creation, the monitoring, the reporting, and the evaluation of projects. Before RBM, it was common practice to create projects by concentrating on the collection of *activities* that the proponents wanted to carry out. It was a matter of faith that this assemblage of activities would lead directly to the results or to the impact that the proponents were hoping to achieve, especially with regard to projects of international development cooperation. In many cases, especially in the hands of experienced practitioners, the activities did indeed lead to the desired results, but it could be imprecise and unreliable in doing so.

Accordingly, a new approach evolved in which one concentrates on the desired results in the long term, the intermediate term, and the short term, and then devises activities that lead in a direct and logical manner to the results that are being sought. This new approach, which is driven by results rather than by activities, has had a variety of different names and nomenclatures in the past few years, but the most common vocabulary now used in Canada is the one that appears below.

Virtually all funding agencies now require some form of RBM to be used in projects they support, e.g. the United Nations Development Programme, USAID and CIDA. Moreover, the Government of Canada requires RBM to be used in all its programs as a means of ensuring the accountability of government program expenditures to taxpayers.

Most importantly, RBM provides a disciplined approach to the creation, the monitoring, the reporting and the evaluation of projects: Results-based Management ensures that the project designers have carefully thought through all the parts of what they want to do and what they want to achieve.

The RBM basic vocabulary

- Impact: long term results

- Outcomes: intermediate term results (five or six years)

- Outputs: short term results

- Activities: the actions that are actually carried out

- Inputs: the resources (financial and human) needed to conduct the activities

- Beneficiaries (also called "reach" or "beneficiary reach"): those who benefit, directly and indirectly, from the project

- Stakeholders: those who are involved in the project, including providers of resources, participants, advisors and beneficiaries

- Indicators (also called "performance indicators"): evidence that helps you to detect and measure progress towards achieving results at the impact, outcomes and outputs levels

- Risks are possible events or conditions that may impede the progress of the project, assessed in terms of both their potential seriousness and the probability of their occurring.

- Purpose: what you want to achieve by the end of the typically five- to six-year duration of the project (this is essentially the same as the set of outcomes)

Impact is the development objective to which you are making a contribution. You won't achieve it by your project alone within the 5 to 6 year life of the project but, if successful, you will make a solid contribution to it. You will have provided a solid basis upon which your partners can achieve the impact. Here are examples of the intended impacts of projects that the authors have been involved in.

Examples of Impacts:

- Provision of the human resources in biomedical engineering (BME) to sustain high level medical care in three regions spanning most of Cuba and the provision of international education to students, staff, faculty and others within the Canadian partner institutions

- The health sector of Rwanda is rebuilt after the genocide and in the face of the HIV/AIDS pandemic.

- Increased availability of wood as a safe and inexpensive building material for the urban areas of the five Andean Pact countries of South America

Outcomes are specific measurable sustainable institutional or community level results that will be produced by the end of the project. These include new programs or processes that will be continued after the life of the project. In most cases, it is these medium-term results that fulfill the purpose of the project.

Examples of Outcomes:

For each of the three intended impacts in the examples immediately above, here are possible corresponding outcomes (typically, there is one intended impact per project, and there are less than six intended outcomes per impact):

- For the impact *Provision of the human resources in biomedical engineering (BME) to sustain high level medical care in three regions spanning most of Cuba and the provision of international education to students, staff, faculty and others within the Canadian partner institutions,* some corresponding outcomes could be:

  o Strengthened capacity of the three Cuban partner universities to provide education and training to the biomedical engineering professional sector through improved teaching capacity, improved management practices, and an expanded network of contacts outside the universities

  o Establishment of linkages that foster sustainable relationships among the project partners

  o Increased involvement of women in the BME field

o   Enhanced internationalization and strengthened development education of the Canadian partner institutions

- For the impact *The health sector of Rwanda is rebuilt after the genocide and in the face of the HIV/AIDS pandemic*, two outcomes could be:

  o   Increased capacity of the Kigali Health Institute to develop and deliver relevant and current educational programming, particularly in areas related to HIV/AIDS and mental health, including trauma

  o   Improved ability of nursing students and graduates to provide comprehensive and community-based nursing care and counseling to individuals with HIV/AIDS and to women and children experiencing the effects of trauma due to the genocide or sexual violence.

- For the impact *Increased availability of wood as a safe and inexpensive building material for the urban areas of the five Andean Pact countries of South America*, three outcomes could be:

  o   The establishment of a wood products R&D laboratory associated with a university or technical college in each country

  o   A completed inventory of tree species present in the forests of each country

  o   Ten wood products specialists trained to the Master's level at North American or European universities

One of the differences between outcomes and impacts is that outcomes are the sustainable institutional or societal changes that the project has brought about within its five to six-year lifetime, and the impact is what the developing country is able eventually to achieve by itself after the project by making use of the outcomes.

Outputs are the short-term effects of completed activities. Completed activities, in themselves, are not outputs. For example, training is usually called an activity, whereas the output is the new skill or ability achieved by a specific group of people that has resulted from the training.

Outputs are aggregated to produce an outcome.

Activities are the actions to be carried out within the scope of the project. Examples of activities are:

- technical assistance provided by Canadian agriculture experts
- curriculum development and delivery of training programs
- workshops and seminars
- publishing newsletters and pamphlets
- construction of a building to be used as a health center

Example: Activities and Outputs

If, as activities, we develop curriculum and put on a one month training course for 20 Rwandan nurses, the completed activities are the preparation of the curriculum and the completion of a one month training program by 20 Rwandan nurses, but the output is that Rwanda now has a new human resource consisting of 20 nurses who possess an enhanced skill level that can be used directly in hospitals or clinics, or can be used to train other nurses in the country or region.

In *planning* a project, one usually starts by selecting an intended impact, then asks what outcomes are needed to contribute to that impact, then asks what outputs and activities are needed to achieve each outcome, and then asks what resources (human and financial) are needed to enable the activities to be carried out. In contrast, when *executing* a project, we proceed in the opposite direction: the resources are obtained, the activities are carried out, thus producing the outputs, which are aggregated to create the outcomes, and a contribution is thus made towards reaching the impact.

Beneficiaries and reach: Direct beneficiaries are individuals, communities and organizations that benefit at the output and outcome levels. Indirect beneficiaries benefit at the impact level.

Beneficiaries should be identified as completely as possible: boy/girl, man/woman, urban/rural, homeless, victims of conflict, minority ethnic/religious groups, landless, victims of disasters, etc.

Performance Indicators are evidence that helps you to detect and measure progress towards achieving results at the output, outcome and impact levels.

Examples of performance indicators:

- For the <u>output</u> *Twenty Rwandan nurses have been successfully trained to provide care to patients suffering from AIDS*, indicators could be:

  o   Curriculum has been prepared

  o   Nurses have been selected, registered and trained

  o   Nurses have passed examinations based on the course, and diplomas have been awarded to them

  o   Nurses are employed by the Kigali Central Hospital, and are caring for AIDS patients

- For the <u>outcome</u> *Increased involvement of women in the BME field*, indicators could be:

  o   Number of women students enrolled in BME programs

  o   Number of women working in the BME field

  o   Number of women in management positions in the BME field

  o   Women do not perceive that there are biases against them in the BME field

- For the <u>impact</u> *Increased availability of wood as a safe and inexpensive building material...*, indicators could be:

  o   Structural lumber is plentiful and available in markets in cities and towns in the five countries

  o   The available lumber has been classified and graded for construction use

  o   The cost of the lumber is reasonable for most purchasers

  o   Consumers regard structural lumber as being safe to use in their houses and other buildings

Logical Framework Analysis (LFA)

This is a snapshot of the design of a project. In a single chart are the following:

- Purpose
- Budget
- Duration

- Impact
- Outcomes
- Outputs
- Activities
- Performance indicators (for each of impact, outcomes and outputs)
- Beneficiaries (for each of impact, outcomes and outputs)

Example: Create a collaborative project to improve living conditions in four villages in the Bette Valley of Ethiopia. Describe the project by its Logical Framework Analysis (LFA).

Purpose: To establish schools and a clinic and to improve wells for four villages in the Bette Valley of Ethiopia

Budget: $997,000 from the Canadian International Development Agency (CIDA)

Duration: 6 years

Impact: Improved living conditions in four villages in the Bette Valley of Ethiopia

Outcomes:
1. Creation of a school and provision of paid trained teachers in each of the four villages for child education and adult education
2. Putting into operation a regional health clinic with supplies and trained staff provided by the Ethiopian government
3. Improvements to eight wells (lining and capping) and the installation of a hand pump with villagers trained to maintain the pumps

Outputs (three per outcome):
1-1. School building has been constructed complete with electricity, water, sanitation, books, pencils, and desks, and is ready to use.
1-2. Teachers have been hired and trained.

1-3. The four communities have been informed about the new schools.

2-1. A building for the clinic has been obtained and renovated.
2-2. Government of Ethiopia has provided trained staff, furniture, and supplies.
2-3. The four communities have been informed about the new clinic.

3-1. Eight wells have been lined and capped.
3-2. Pumps, spare parts and tools have been delivered to each well site.
3-3. Five persons are trained in well maintenance and repair in each village.

Activities:
1-1a. Organize local community to construct the school and arrange installations of services.
1-1b. Issue a contract for the manufacture and delivery of desks.
1-1c. Purchase a supply of books and pencils.
1-2a. Advertise for teachers, interviews, selection.
1-2b. Sign employment contracts with teachers and start paying them.
1-2c. Train the teachers.
1-3a. Determine the geographic area applicable to each school.
1-3b. Compose the announcement and choose its timing.
1-3c. Choose and use media for advertising – posters, radio, cell phones, direct contact.

2-1a. Find a suitable existing building, and either buy it or lease it.
2-1b. Issue contracts for renovating the building as a clinic, including water, electricity and sanitation
2-2a. Negotiate with the Government of Ethiopia to provide furniture, staff, supplies, and staff accommodation.
2-3a. Determine the geographic area applicable to the clinic.
2-3b. Compose the announcement and choose its timing.

2-3c. Choose and use media for advertising – posters, radio, cell phones, direct contact.

3-1a. Purchase cement, sand, gravel and lumber and plywood for formwork.

3-1b. Organize labour teams to line and cap each well.

3-2a. Purchase and deliver pumps, spare parts and tools to each well site and arrange for their safekeeping.

3-3a. Train five persons in each village to maintain and repair the pumps.

Performance indicator for impact:

There is now a perception in each village that the quality of their lives – specifically, availability of child and adult education, access to health services, and quality of water – has improved.

Performance indicators for outcomes:
1. Children and adults of the four communities have access to primary education.
2. Clinic exists and is in operation serving all people in the four communities who need primary health care.
3. Eight improved wells are operational and are readily repaired by trained villagers when there are problems.

Performance indicators for outputs:
1-1. Four schools, complete with services, furniture and supplies, exist and are in operation.
1-2. An adequate number of teachers have been hired and trained, and are being paid regularly and housed.
1-3. All members of each community are aware of the schools.

2-1. Clinic, complete with services, furniture and supplies, exists and is in operation.
2-2. Properly trained staff have been provided by the Ethiopian government and are being paid regularly and housed.
2-3. All members of each community are aware of the clinic.

3-1. Eight wells have been lined and capped with concrete

3-2. An adequate supply of spare parts, maintenance supplies and tools are in safe storage at each well.

3-3. Five persons in each community are trained to maintain and repair the pumps.

Indirect beneficiaries for impact: populations of the four villages; government officials responsible for education, health and water; people in other villages who are now aware of what is possible

Direct beneficiaries for outcomes and outputs: all members of the four communities who need access to primary education, primary health care, and improved water; school teachers who receive training and employment; technicians who receive training in well maintenance and repair

CHAPTER SEVEN

CASES IN INTERNATIONAL DEVELOPMENT

THE CASE METHOD

We introduced *cases* and the *case method* in Chapter One. To recap, a **case** is a description of an actual situation (a problem, a decision, an opportunity, a challenge, a dilemma) that a real individual in a real organization has recently been confronted with. Readers are invited to put themselves in the shoes of the decision maker to evaluate the information that was available to the decision maker at that moment in time, and with a time frame in which to make a decision. The available information may be relevant or irrelevant, and is often incomplete. Students go though the seven-step process tabulated below, including the presentation and the defence of their decision and plans to groups of their peers.

Seven Steps of the Case Method

1. Accumulate and organize the available information.
2. Establish various potential alternative courses of action.
3. Set criteria for evaluating the various alternatives.
4. Make the decision.
5. Formulate plans for implementing the decision.
6. Establish a system for monitoring and evaluating the results of the work.
7. Convincingly explain and defend the decision and the implementation plans to your peers.

The teaching philosophy behind the case method is that the best way of learning how to dependably make good decisions is to be confronted every day with a wide range of complex decisions that need to be made and defended.[198]

The Harvard Business School is usually credited as being the creator of the modern case method as used in management education. The Richard Ivey School of Business at The University of Western Ontario, however, is the institution most renowned in Canada for the use of this methodology. Ivey, in fact, is the world's second largest producer of field based cases, and maintains an active bibliography of 1500 case titles that are used in business schools and other educational organizations around the world.[199]

According to Ivey,

> *A case is a description of a business situation faced by someone in an organization. Cases contain relevant information about the issue available to the key person in the case, plus background information about the organization. Cases may vary in length from one to more than 40 pages, but normally range between three and 20 pages of text, and one to 10 pages of pictures or exhibits...*
>
> *Cases [are used in education] to enable students to learn about decision making by putting themselves in the shoes of actual managers. Students analyze situations, develop alternatives, choose plans of action and implementation, and communicate and defend their findings. Cases are used to test the understanding of theory, to connect theory with application, and to develop theoretical insight. Cases enable students to learn by doing and teaching each other.[200]*

Cases used in the Harvard Business School and at Ivey (and in this book) are *real*. They are not dreamed up. A case is a description of an actual situation faced by a flesh-and-blood individual in an existing organization (and by extension, by the students). Someone in the organization has signed an official release permitting that case to be used in the classroom and in this book.

In a few (very rare) cases, for a variety of reasons the actual names of one or more individuals, the actual names of organizations, locations or numerical data could not be used, and disguises have had to be employed.

LEARNING AND TEACHING WITH CASES

To illustrate how cases are used in teaching and learning, the case *Ghana & Don Sawyer* is presented in the following paragraphs. This case deals with a tough decision that development worker Don Sawyer suddenly had to make when a meeting with the new manager in Ghana of a collaborative project went bad:

> *The new Ghanaian leader stomped out of the meeting at one point with no indication of when, or even if, he would return. Sawyer's colleague turned to him and said, "Don, I don't think we can work with these guys. I think we should just leave." Sawyer had to decide, and quickly, what to do.*

CASE: GHANA & DON SAWYER[201]

On November 1, 2005 Don Sawyer of Okanagan College was in Toronto for the International Cooperation Awards ceremony of the Canadian Manufacturers and Exporters Association. A project, of which he was the Canadian Project Director, was a finalist in the awards program. The project was a collaboration between Okanagan College and institutions in The Gambia that had established the West African Rural Development Centre (WARD). The Gambian project had gone extremely well right from the start, as detailed in the example *The Gambia & Don Sawyer* in Chapter Three.

Sawyer couldn't help comparing the Gambian project with another West African project (in Ghana), of which he had also been the Canadian Project Director, which had begun so badly.

DON SAWYER

Don Sawyer had been working in West Africa for more than 12 years. In the period 2000 to 2004, he was Director of the International Development Centre at what was then Okanagan University College (OUC) in Salmon Arm, BC. The Centre was devoted to projects in West Africa that emphasized training, institutional capacity building, and curriculum development aimed at improving the skills of community development workers. In this role, Sawyer managed five CIDA-funded projects, including a project located in Ghana and approved in 2000 for the training of managers working in NGOs and other development organizations. He was excited to be doing this because he had previously enjoyed a very successful project with this institutional partner, and had established excellent personal relations with the then-Vice-Chancellor and the faculty of the institution.

A CHANGE OF LEADERSHIP IN GHANA

By the time the Ghana project was approved and final workplans and budgets had been accepted, however, the partner institution had a completely different leadership with a different vision of the project. The new head of the institution in Ghana wanted to renegotiate so that local personnel costs would be covered. In their first face-to-face meeting, Sawyer was taken aback by the new leader—he was uninformed about the project and its history, brusque, and hostile. He was vocal in his disappointment that he was dealing with Sawyer rather than someone of his own rank and curtly dismissed the agreement that his institution had previously come to with OUC. Contrary to UPCD Tier 2 rules, he wanted more money from the project to pay personnel costs, including his own. His vision of the project was completely different from what had already been agreed upon, i.e. he wanted to change it from in-service training programs for development workers and managers throughout the north of the country to essentially a four-year academic degree program in business management at his institution.

A DECISION IS NEEDED

The new Ghanaian leader stomped out of the meeting at one point with no indication of when, or even if, he would return. Sawyer's Canadian colleague turned to him and said, "Don, I don't think we can work with these guys. I think we should just leave." Sawyer had to decide, and quickly, what to do.

At this point, individual students, or groups of students, put themselves in Sawyer's shoes and, either alone or under the guidance of an instructor, work through the seven-step process described above*. In this particular exercise, let us concentrate on Steps 2, 3 and 4 of the process:

---

* If an instructor is involved, she or he might first identify learning objectives of this case, e.g.

- To examine available options when a project is going badly
- To become aware of the vulnerability of development projects to the presence and actions of particular individuals. In this case, the project struggled because of the obstructive actions of a locally powerful administrator (the "big man" syndrome). For readers who are not familiar with this expression in an African context, "big man" is often used to describe an individual with a considerable amount of power or influence, at a national or a local level. "Big man" is not, in itself, a pejorative term—it simply refers to the amount of control the individual exercises. Nevertheless, the term is often found in writings about the actions of individuals who are considered to be impeding change or, in some instances, in creating obstacles to the development of democratic

2. Establish various potential alternative courses of action.
3. Set criteria for evaluating the various alternatives.
4. Make the decision.

Step 2. What alternative courses of action did Sawyer have?

A. Terminate the project.

B. Continue the project, accede to the demands of the new Ghanaian leader, rewrite the project, and reconstruct the budget.

C. Continue the project, resist those demands of the new Ghanaian leader that were impossible or meant abandoning the original project concept, rewrite the project, and reconstruct the budget.

D. Bring OUC's President to the project to meet with the new administration, and get the project activities moving.

E. Ask the funding organization to allow OUC to drop the original partner and find another, more compatible, partner in the same country or region.

Step 3. What criteria should Sawyer apply in deciding among the various alternative courses of action?

1. Sawyer seriously contemplated Alternative A, i.e. to terminate the project. He was aware that, in some difficult circumstances, one very valid option is to shut down the project rather than struggling to accommodate a partner who continues to act in an unreasonable manner. The behaviour displayed by the new Ghanaian leader in the initial meeting did not augur at all well for the future.

2. On the other hand, all of Sawyer's instincts as a development worker were to strive to overcome problems and disagreements in order to have the opportunity to reduce poverty or increase the quality of life in a developing country.

institutions. Descriptions of the "big man syndrome" can be found, for example, in *The Economist* (e.g. the issue of April 8, 2006 on pages 18 and 46) and in the many excellent articles on African issues written by Stephanie Nolen of the *Globe and Mail.*

3. The International Development Centre at OUC had invested enormous time and resources into the project proposal and in negotiating the final agreement. They needed this project, both for the Centre's reputation and for its financial support.

4. The project had to comply with the rules of the funding program, which included, for example, a provision that remuneration cannot be paid to employees of the developing country partner institution, a particularly contentious point in other projects that had experienced this scenario.

5. Having the Canadian institution's President visit the project could help in the short run, but ultimately might undermine the authority and working relationship of the Canadian Project Director with the African partner.

Step 4. What should Sawyer decide to do?

We can construct a chart which displays whether or not each of Sawyer's criteria is satisfied by each potential alternative course of action.

Alternatives / Criteria	End project	Accede & continue	Resist & continue	Bring OUC president	Find new partner
Difficult partner leader	X				X
Project needed by Ghana		X	X	X	X
Project needed by OUC		X	X	X	X
Obey program rules	X		X	X	X
Don't undermine Project Director	X		X		X

The possible course of action with the greatest number of Xs is represented by the column on the far right: "Ask the funding organization to allow OUC to drop the original partner and find another, more compatible, partner in the same country or region". This is the decision that the above analysis would support.

WHAT ACTUALLY HAPPENED?

Sawyer arranged for the OUC President to come to Gambia to meet with the new leader of the partner institution. This satisfied the new leader's vanity, but undermined the authority of the Canadian Project Director. The project was re-written (but remained within the funding agency's rules) and continued. A few years later, the new leader was relieved of his responsibilities and went on to face charges of fraud in the courts of Ghana.

Sawyer is now of the opinion that he should have asked the funding organization to allow OUC to drop the original partner and find another, more compatible, partner in the same country or region, i.e. the course of action in the right column of the above table.

CHAPTER EIGHT

GETTING PROJECTS STARTED PROPERLY

The previous chapter presented a case in which a project got started quite badly. In contrast, this chapter contains three cases that started (and continued) very well. For these three cases, the key success characteristics included:

(a)   carefully choosing one's partners,

(b)   the prolonged and meticulous efforts that the project directors went to in order to build trust and consensus,

(c)   the nature of collective (rather than individual) decision making,

(d)   having the courage to "think outside the box" in which the issue was whether to do something so ambitious that there was a real risk of the project not getting funded.

Finally, after these three cases, there is a summary of the most important activities to be considered when a project is getting started.

CASE ANALYSIS: RWANDA & DAVID CECHETTO[202]

At daybreak on February 26, 2000, University of Western Ontario (UWO) medical professor Dr. David Cechetto took off from Kigali airport. After a distressing week seeing firsthand the impact of the 1994 genocide and the HIV/AIDS pandemic, Cechetto committed himself to dedicate time and energy in accepting a request from the rector of the National University of Rwanda (NUR) to direct a project to help rebuild Rwanda's health sector. Not wasting any time, he began to prepare a proposal for funding while on the plane. His first decision was to determine who his Rwandan partner or partners should be in this project.

STEP 1 – AVAILABLE INFORMATION

Long-standing tensions between the Hutu majority and the Tutsi minority erupted in a bloodbath on April 7, 1994. For the next 100 days, killing squads of extreme Hutus massacred some 800,000 Tutsis and moderate Hutus, using mainly machetes, axes and clubs. Canadian General Roméo Dallaire was commander of the United Nations peacekeeping forces in Rwanda at that time, but he was prevented by the UN bureaucracy from intervening in the genocide. The fighting ended when the Rwandan Patriotic Front army, led by Paul Kagame, who subsequently became president of Rwanda, defeated the Hutu fighters or forced them into exile. President Kagame then had the task of rebuilding an officially unified, but still simmering, country.

Most doctors, in fact most Rwandans with higher education, were Tutsis, and thus the medical sector was literally decimated during the genocide. One of the instruments of the genocide was rape, and this led—intentionally—to a significant increase in the rate of HIV infections. Almost one-third of Rwandan women between the ages of 18 and 35 were HIV-positive. Countless women and children were traumatized by the killings and the rapes.

This is a situation that is well known to most readers through extensive press coverage, the film *Hotel Rwanda*, books such as General Roméo Dallaire's *Shake Hands with the Devil: The Failure of Humanity in Rwanda*, Carol Off's *The Lion, the Fox and the Eagle,* Gil Courtemanche's *A Sunday at the Pool in Kigali*, and media accounts of the work of Stephen Lewis in combating the HIV/AIDS pandemic in Africa.

In mid-1999, a letter from the rector of NUR was received at UWO and forwarded to Cechetto. The rector said that the medical sector in the country had been greatly damaged by the 1994 genocide and, because UWO had an excellent medical school, requested the Canadian university to assist his university to rebuild the medical sector in the country. Cechetto reacted immediately and positively to NUR's request, but knew that he had to gather a great deal of information—both in Canada and in Rwanda—before being able to commit himself fully to this task. He participated in a series of meetings at UWO and in the London community, and travelled to Rwanda to see the situation for himself in February 2000.

Before leaving on his trip to Rwanda, Cechetto had determined, based on advice from UWO's Office of International Research, that the major funding source for international projects to be carried out between training institutions in Canada and in partner countries was CIDA's UPCD program.

The program had two levels: Tier 1 (in which CIDA's contribution was up to $3 million for large programs of cooperation, usually involving a number of partners on one or both sides and which would typically be multidisciplinary) and Tier 2 (in which CIDA's contribution was up to $1 million, for smaller projects of cooperation), both over a five- to six-year duration. Cechetto decided that Tier 2 was the more appropriate program. In investigating the Tier 2 program, he learned that CIDA put priority on *primary* health care, rather than secondary or tertiary health care. This was important, as he also learned during his visit to Rwanda that primary health care was the critical need in the country, and capacity building at this level would be most effective in dealing with Rwanda's immediate health sector problems.

The original letter from the NUR rector implied that cooperation solely in the area of the training of *doctors* was being requested. When Cechetto went to Rwanda, he visited NUR in Butare to talk about the training of doctors, but he quickly became aware of the wide range of other health sector professionals that Rwanda needed, e.g., nurses, traditional birthing assistants, psychologists, nutritionists, community health workers. In this latter context, he met the director and her colleagues of the Kigali Health Institute (KHI), which is the main government-supported training centre for nurses. He also met the president of the National AIDS Commission, members of the Episcopalian Church and representatives of national and international NGOs who were working in the health sector. During his meetings with government ministers and others, Cechetto learned that they preferred UWO to take a broad approach to assistance to the health sector, and certainly to include assistance in the area of HIV/AIDS. Another widespread problem brought to his attention was the psychological trauma brought on by the horrific experiences of the genocide.

STEP 2 – ALTERNATIVE COURSES OF ACTION

Cechetto knew that, to be eligible for UPCD funding, he had to partner with a *training* institution in the health field in Rwanda. There were only two: the medical faculty of NUR and KHI. His alternatives, therefore, were:

A. a partnership solely with NUR;

B. a partnership solely with KHI;

C. a partnership with both NUR and KHI, in which NUR would take the lead Rwandan role;

D. a partnership with both NUR and KHI, in which KHI would take the lead Rwandan role.

Tied into this decision, of course, were the health fields to which each of the Rwandan institutions could contribute. An NUR partnership would be oriented toward the training of doctors, while KHI was the main government-supported training centre for nurses.

STEP 3 – CRITERIA FOR EVALUATING THE ALTERNATIVE COURSES OF ACTION

1. The project had to support activities that were of highest priority to Rwanda. Health issues, specifically the struggle against HIV/AIDS, were repeatedly identified as priority areas for development assistance.
2. The activities had to be within the capabilities and interests of the Rwandan partner(s) and of UWO. Cechetto knew about NUR and KHI, and he knew that UWO had capabilities that would support this approach, i.e., with doctors, nurses, psychologists, psychiatrists, HIV/AIDS specialists, with international experience and aspirations.
3. The proposal had to be fundable. CIDA's official development assistance priorities include *primary* health care. Although the original request from Rwanda was for the training of doctors, Cechetto suspected that the UPCD program would not fund a project centered on doctors, because of the perception that doctors usually were not front-line workers dealing with primary health care.
4. The project should respect the original request for assistance from NUR.

Criterion 4 urged him toward Alternatives A or C, but Criteria 1, 2 and 3 taken together supported Alternative D.

STEP 4 – THE DECISION

He decided on Alternative D, i.e., to partner with both NUR and KHI, with KHI taking the lead Rwandan role. In order to make the best possible contribution in the area of primary health care in Rwanda, he was inclined to concentrate on front-line health workers, i.e., nurses, traditional birthing assistants, doctors, psychologists and others who work at the community level rather than in hospitals. To do this, he needed the skills of doctors, nurses and all health sector practitioners who work at the community level.

STEP 5 – PLANS FOR IMPLEMENTING THE DECISION

Criteria 1, 2 and 3 can be looked at simultaneously by means of the Venn diagram below. The shaded intersection defines the scope of the project.

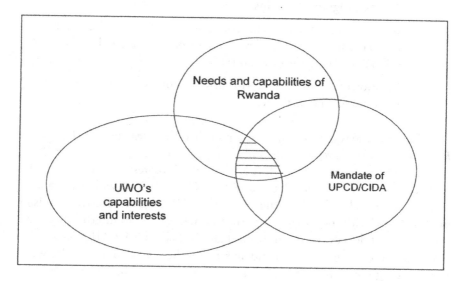

Thinking in terms of the Results-based Management format, Cechetto first articulated the purpose as:

> *To collaboratively rebuild the training programs for health professionals and expand the cadre of health professionals with an emphasis on skills in the prevention and treatment of infectious diseases, particularly HIV/ AIDS, and mental health.*

The expected outcomes were:

- Increased capacity of KHI to develop and deliver relevant and current educational programming, particularly in areas related to HIV/AIDS and mental health, including trauma;

- Improved ability of nursing students and graduates to provide comprehensive and community-based nursing care and counseling to individuals with HIV/AIDS and to women and children experiencing the effects of trauma due to the genocide or sexual violence.

Key activities included:

- Training of all KHI faculty members
- Joint development of curriculum for a four-year bachelor of nursing program at the institute
- Joint development of context-relevant teaching and learning materials, including the development of cases related to HIV/AIDS and mental health and trauma
- Provision of improved access to current information and technical resources for the institute.

Cechetto also was aware that he should check his ideas against the *Poverty Reduction Strategy Paper* of Rwanda. He did this, and supplemented his findings with conversations with the World Bank representative in Rwanda, with the president of the National AIDS Commission, with the cabinet minister responsible for the struggle against HIV/AIDS, with the Minister of Health and with the Minister of Education. Cechetto found that although there is a great deal of activity in Rwanda in the field of HIV/AIDS—both by Rwandans and by international aid agencies—there was no overlap between his emerging ideas and the activities of others. In fact, the efforts would be complementary.[203]

CASE ANALYSIS: CUBA — ALDO CHIRCOP & PAT RODEE[204]

Dalhousie University's Dr. Aldo Chircop and Ms. Pat Rodee were preparing a proposal, along with one other Canadian partner and three (very different) Cuban universities, for a new UPCD Tier 2 project. The partners knew that the effective and harmonious management of this large and disparate group was going to be a challenge. They had to decide, right at the beginning, how to establish a management system, and especially a system of management communication, that would put in place a framework for building consensus and the equitable participation of all partners during the next five years.

BACKGROUND INFORMATION

Cuba needed trained professionals who could respond to three major challenges in its coastal zone:

- pressure to develop the coastal area and its resources for potentially conflicting purposes

- environmental concerns such as coastal erosion and extensive salinization; and

- Cuba's international commitments to contribute to the protection of the sea and coastal environment.

Because of Cuba's relative isolation, however, Cuban universities had not benefited from access to integrated coastal zone management (ICZM) as a means of sustainably developing, managing and conserving its coastal and marine environment.

A long-standing relationship between Dalhousie University and Cuba led to the idea of a collaborative project that also included Saint Mary's University in Canada and three Cuban universities: Universidad de La Habana, Universidad de Cienfuegos and Universidad de Oriente, entitled "Integrated Coastal Zone Management Education in Cuba". The project proposal was eventually approved by UPCD/AUCC and ran from October 1999 to September 2004.

The project's purpose was to build capacity for the training of professionals who plan and manage coastal zone development and use through the establishment of a master's program in integrated coastal zone management shared by the three Cuban universities. The project also aimed to help establish a model for the development of interdisciplinary degree programs in Cuba's higher education system so that individual universities could pool their diverse strengths and address regional and national needs. The expected outcomes included strengthened capacity to deliver ICZM education at three universities; improved skills of current and future government planners and managers in ICZM; and improved and sustained dialogue between Cuban universities and government in areas related to ICZM.

Dr. Aldo Chircop of the Marine & Environmental Law Institute at Dalhousie Law School was the Canadian Project Director, and he worked closely with Ms. Pat Rodee, the Director of Lester Pearson International and the International Liaison Officer of Dalhousie.

COURSE OF ACTION

This case is somewhat different from others in this book because there was only one possible course of action of interest to the project team, i.e. to establish a management system, and especially a system of management communication, that would put in place a framework for building consensus and the equitable participation of all partners during the next five years. The decisions, therefore, dealt with how to accomplish this course of action.

THE DECISIONS, AND IMPLEMENTATION OF THE DECISIONS

- The most fundamental decision was to strive to create an atmosphere of mutual respect and equality among all five partners, regardless of whether they were Cuban or Canadian, and regardless of whether they were large old universities or newer smaller institutions. An essential, and enjoyable, part of this process was to create opportunities (at the beginning of the project and throughout its duration) for a great deal of personal interaction among the project participants using both the Spanish and English languages, and thus to build personal friendships and trust. For example, because the venues for meetings rotated among the various universities, many of the meeting participants stayed in hotels, or in the homes of other participants, and thereby had the chance to socialize and to discuss project-related issues in informal settings in the evenings.

- The three Cuban universities were quite different. Universidad de La Habana is one of the oldest universities in the Americas and is very much larger than the other two institutions. However, La Habana's project coordinator was the highly respected Dra. Maria Elena Ibarra Martín, Director of the Centre for Marine Research. She generously insisted that, regardless of their relative sizes and capabilities, all three Cuban universities were to be treated as equal partners, and were to share equitably in project resources.

- Similarly, in Halifax, the traditional rivalry between Dalhousie and St. Mary's was absent at the level of the respective project participants.The central decision making body was the Project Management Committee (PMC), which had as its members a senior official (Vice-Rectors in the case of Cienfuegos and Oriente) from each of the Cuban universities as well as individuals from the Canadian institutions who were also empowered to make decisions and commitments. Moreover, each PMC member had an alternate, so that continuity and participation would not be lost if a delegate was not able to attend a particular meeting.

- Chircop was formally the Chair of the PMC, but he chose to function as a facilitator of collective decision making, also ensuring that all necessary matters were dealt with during the two-day meetings and that the committee stayed more or less on schedule. The basic concepts were: (a) each person's opinion counts, and (b) consensus is what each member can agree to even if it is not their first choice. Chircop modestly describes his role as the "cabinet secretary" who provides continuity, with the representative of the university where the PMC meeting was being held playing a lead role in the meeting. Dalhousie had had previous good experience with the PMC model, and thus decided to re-create it in this context.

- A key tool for the effective functioning of the PMC was a well-detailed and comprehensive agenda for each meeting with reference materials for the various topics appended to the agenda. Over time, a standard format for the PMC meetings evolved, leading to predictability and continuity of the discussion items. Highlights included progress reports on workshops, review of progress with reference to the work plan, reports of the various project committees, language training progress, budget and finance, AUCC/CIDA reporting requirements, and upcoming activities.

- Pat Rodee kept extensive minutes of the PMC meetings, paying special reference to all action items-what, by whom, and when. This ensured that a good project corporate memory was maintained, and that commitments made by various individuals could be tracked from one meeting to the next.

- Workshops were extensively used in the project. In addition to promoting the goals of the project, they also had a role in project management because, at the end of each workshop, a session was held to summarize and then to deal with follow-up activities–what, by whom, and when. This process led to a higher degree of buying-in to the project by the Cubans, which was essential because the project was gradually being moved out of Canadian hands into being a Cuban project.

- The project was divided into three phases: baselines and program design, curriculum development, and program implementation. This arrangement ensured that the project had a solid planning foundation before implementation began.

- The work plan for the project had been thoroughly and harmoniously developed at an early stage prior to the submission of the proposal, so that strenuous conversations about the project's direction arose only rarely during the project. Largely, the project executed the work plan that had been developed at the beginning.

- They established a Cuban Project Advisory Committee (PAC), which consisted primarily of senior government and university officials, under the direction of Dra. Maria Elena Ibarra Martín. The members of the PAC were external Cuban stakeholders who could provide input to ensure that the program was responding to the needs of those external stakeholders, e.g. the government units who might be sending their staff members to the graduate programs being developed.

- In addition to the PMC and the PAC, there was an extensive group of other committees constituted to deal with specific topics such as the selection of books to be purchased for the library, the equipment committee, and the individual intra-university coordination committees. These committees were usually chaired by Cubans, and all three Cuban universities were fully represented in the memberships and as the chairs of these committees. Every institution had a chance for a leadership role. This mechanism delegated much detailed decision making of this type away from the PMC, which received reports from each of these other committees.

- The project was largely bilingual in Spanish and English. Roughly half of the reports and documents of the project were in English, half in Spanish. The participants had varying levels of competence in the other language, but all participants were free to speak in meetings in the language of their choice. Informal interpretation was available to assist this process.

- Day-to-day communications were extensive, and were facilitated by a very heavy use of phone calls and some faxing. Often, before a Cuba-Canada phone call was to be made, the three Cuban partners would first discuss the matter amongst themselves, and so the Cuban individual who spoke with Canada was representing the views of all three Cuban universities.

- Email listserves were established for groups of individuals who shared an interest in particular topics, e.g. curriculum design for particular courses.

- There was a Project Coordinator, Jorge Angulo Valdes, located at Dalhousie. He was a faculty member at La Habana and had a scholarship to work on a doctorate at Dalhousie. He played a huge role in maintaining frequent and systematic communication among the partners.

- AUCC's UPCD project officer played a key role early in the project by travelling to (and around) Cuba, and explaining clearly and authoritatively what the UPCD/CIDA rules were.

- The close cooperation between Rodee and Chircop meant, effectively, that Chircop was receiving both expert advice and political support from Dalhousie's Central Administration throughout the project, which is essential in UPCD projects.

- Similarly, Chircop and Rodee made a point of maintaining good contacts with the Rectors of the various universities, and with the Canadian Embassy in Havana.

CASE: UGANDA & SHAFIQUE PIRANI[205]

Dr. Shafique Pirani, a Professor in the Department of Orthopaedics at the University of British Columbia, wanted to rid affected children in Uganda of the burden of the clubfoot deformity, and was planning to seek financial support from the UPCD program to help bring this about. He reviewed a number of existing UPCD Tier 2 projects and noted that, typically, they involved one or two partner training institutions and a small number of community-based organizations. Dr. Pirani had the apparently radical idea of wanting to involve *all* of Uganda in the project—all the hospitals, all the community health workers, and all newborn children suffering from clubfoot. He had to decide whether he should attempt such a wide-ranging project using the UPCD program and, if so, how he could achieve his ambitious goal.

AVAILABLE INFORMATION

- Pirani was born in Uganda, and was part of the group expelled by Idi Amin in 1972. He was trained as a doctor in the UK and as an orthopaedic surgeon in Canada, and later decided to specialize in clubfoot. Initially he managed clubfeet surgically and then became aware of the Ponseti Method, which is a nonsurgical treatment involving accurate manipulation of the foot and the successive applications of five plaster casts, followed by four years in a brace. This treatment has been shown to work with remarkable success if initiated on children up to the age of 12 months. For older children, surgery is possible, but is not an ideal solution.

- Clubfoot is a birth defect that is characterized by the bones of a foot being pulled sideways by an imbalance in the muscles and ligaments. A significant proportion of children born every year, especially in the developing world, suffer from clubfoot.

- In 1998, Pirani returned to Uganda, and met a Canadian missionary doctor, Dr. Norgrove Penny, whose practice included operating on large numbers of children with clubfoot. Pirani realized that a simpler and more humane solution would be to employ the Ponseti method on newborns in locations close to where they live.

- In a conversation with a Ugandan mother, Pirani heard about the enormous difference that the correction of clubfoot meant to her young daughter: "Now she can get married. Now she can walk to school. Now she can fetch the firewood. Now she can run after the other children." A conversation with the father of a three year old: "Now I don't have to take my child to the latrine any more. He can stand up without falling into the latrine."

ALTERNATIVE COURSES OF ACTION

A. He could prepare a "typical" UPCD Tier 2 proposal involving one or two partner training institutions and a small number of community-based organizations.

B. He could prepare a "risky" proposal to UPCD that involved *all* of Uganda in the project—all the hospitals, all the community health workers, and all the newborn children suffering from clubfoot.

SUMMARY: GETTING STARTED PROPERLY

- Choose your partner(s) carefully.

- Ensure that the appropriate persons (and skills) at all participating institutions are included in the project, either as participants or as advisors. Make sure there is "bench strength" in the team in case a key person leaves the project.

- Build trust and consensus. Travel to your partner's institution, and go through this painstaking process.

- Update your proposal. Conditions may have changed between the time you originally prepared your proposal for funding and the present. Also, the perceptions, attitudes and focus of the partners sometimes differ between the time when a proposal is being written and the time when a project is about to become operational.

- Set up a management system, and a communication system, that all partners are happy with.

- Prepare a detailed memorandum of agreement between all the partners to make it explicitly clear what are the respective roles, expectations and activities of all the partners, and what each partner agrees to provide in the way of resources. This document is parallel to, and has to be consistent with, the contribution agreement between the funding agency and the lead Canadian partner.

- Set up the Advisory Council for the project.

- Inform the Canadian Embassy or High Commission, and appropriate government officials, in the host country.

- Celebrate and promote, in Canada and in the partner country, the inauguration of the project. Use print and electronic media and web sites. Involve the respective presidents of the participating organizations. Check protocol and customs. Exchange gifts. Seek opportunities to speak to students and service clubs.

- Set up an external bank account in the host country.

- Start the baseline study, including a needs analysis and a gender analysis.

- Check what other organizations in the country are doing in the same field, to ensure compatibility of activities.

- Start language training.

CHAPTER NINE

NONGOVERNMENTAL ORGANIZATIONS

Nongovernmental organizations (NGOs), or "not-for-profit" or "non-profit" organizations, were introduced in Chapter Four. In this book, NGOs include Canadian NGOs, multinational NGOs, and indigenous NGOs. This chapter presents two cases involving two very different Canadian NGOs.

The first one is the case *CESO & Gordon Cummings*. It concerns a crucial moment in the life of the Canadian Executive Service Organization as its President & CEO had to decide whether to make major changes in the international direction of the organization. CESO is one of the Volunteer Cooperation Agencies (formerly "Volunteer Sending Organizations") introduced in Chapter Four.

The second one is the case *Ethiopia & Christine Gilmore*, which describes a grassroots or "kitchen-table" NGO as it was faced with requests for fundamental changes in the project from its partners in the villages in the Bette Valley in northern Ethiopia.

Finally, we present a conversation with Nigel Fisher, President & CEO of UNICEF Canada.

CASE: CESO & GORDON CUMMINGS[206]

During the first week of September 2003, Gordon Cummings, President & CEO of the Canadian Executive Service Organization (CESO) was busy in CESO's Operations Centre in Toronto preparing for a meeting of the Executive Committee of his Board of Directors, which was going to be held on September 27, 2003. He knew that the CESO organization was at a crossroads: CESO could either choose to continue operating as it had for more than three decades, which would probably please most of its staff and its roster of over 3000 volunteers, or it could undergo fundamental strategic changes in order to follow the new directions urged upon it by CIDA, the major funder of its international activities.

CANADIAN EXECUTIVE SERVICE ORGANIZATION

CESO, a Canadian not-for-profit organization of Volunteer Advisors founded in 1967, provided social and economic development assistance in developing nations, in emerging market economies of Eastern Europe and the former Soviet Union, and in Canada, especially in aboriginal communities. There were over 3500 volunteers on its roster, with experience in more than 150 professional, management and technical areas. These volunteers served as trainers, advisors and mentors in about 1500 assignments annually, of which 700 were international and 800 were in Canada. CESO's Volunteer Advisors (VAs) typically (but not necessarily) were retired persons. They carried out assignments of three to 13 weeks, with CESO (with funding support coming mainly from the Canadian government) paying for international travel, and the host organization providing meals, accommodation and local transport. If the assignment lasted more than a month, a spouse's expenses to accompany the volunteer were provided.

CESO's Operations Centre was in Toronto at 700 Bay Street. CESO was represented abroad in 46 countries by what were then called Resident Representatives, who were in effect part time commissioned sales people. Funding for CESO's international services came mainly from CIDA, and from the Department of Indian and Northern Affairs for services to Canada's indigenous peoples, as well as donations from the Canadian private sector and from individuals.

CESO's volunteers had been providing advisory services in an extremely wide range of areas, from baking and accounting to university teaching and social work, in the 46 different countries. A VA typically shared her or his expertise, accumulated over a long career, with counterparts in the client organization. Most assignments were evaluated, and high degrees of satisfaction with the assignments were consistently expressed both by the clients and by the VAs themselves.

CESO was one of what were then called Volunteer Sending Organizations (and are now called Volunteer Cooperation Agencies). Compared to the other eight VCAs (e.g. WUSC, CUSO and CECI), CESO's activities were much more diverse and much less focused in regard to programmatic impact or to geographic coverage. Early indications, however, had already reached CESO that CIDA, the major funder of its international activities, was now looking for more results-based activities and considerably tighter focus in regard both to areas of development assistance and to geographic range.

GORDON CUMMINGS

Cummings had retired in 2001 after an extensive and successful business career. His career highlights included 15 years with Woods Gordon (later Ernst & Young), which he joined in 1969, becoming a Principal in 1971 and a Partner in 1974. In 1984, he became CEO of National Sea Products of Halifax. In 1990, he was asked to join the United Co-operative of Ontario, first as COO then CEO, and led it through five years of restructuring. When the Alberta Wheat Pool was looking for a change in direction in 1995, they approached Mr. Cummings to direct the member-owned enterprise with annual gross revenues of more than $2 billion. He subsequently led negotiations that saw the merger in 1998 of the Alberta and Manitoba pools to create Agricore Cooperative. Cummings was selected as the CEO of the new organization. In 2001 a second merger with United Grain Growers created Agricore United, substantially Canada's largest grain company. That was when Cummings retired (at least, for the first time). When CESO was searching for a new CEO in early 2003, Cummings was invited to apply, in part, because of his track record in bringing about change in organizations. He became President & CEO of CESO on July 14, 2003.

PRIORITIES OF THE CANADIAN INTERNATIONAL DEVELOPMENT AGENCY

The Canadian government's direction in international development had changed with the publication in 2002 of *Strengthening Aid Effectiveness*. This policy document called for CIDA-supported organizations to work in fewer countries and to focus the work in any country on a few sectors in order to maximize the impact of the work.

Moreover, results of the work had to be measurable at the *outcomes* and *impact* levels of Results-based Management, and not just at the *activities* and *outputs* levels. Hints had been received at CESO that CIDA's funding for VSOs that did not make these changes would be reduced.

ALTERNATIVES

As the CEO of CESO, Cummings was facing two alternatives, both of which had attractive and unattractive characteristics. One was the *status quo*, i.e. CESO could continue operating more or less as it had been (with considerable success) for the past few decades. His reading of the organization was that it was, in large measure, averse to change: most managers, staff members and the Volunteer Advisors in its extensive roster seemed to prefer to continue along the existing paths. In fact, the VAs wanted an expanded version of the *status quo* so that more assignments (in a wide range of fields) would become available to them. Cummings suspected that he would be facing substantial opposition and loss of morale if he tried to make fundamental changes. The VAs tended to be older people (their average age was 62), and many appreciated the boost to their self-esteem that came, in their less active years, from being a respected advisor in another country.

If CESO had a single predominant sectoral strength of interest to CIDA, it would be private sector development or economic development. (Over 60% of the work done in the previous four years, both for aboriginal peoples and internationally, had been in the economic development area. In addition, about 2/3rds of the entire roster of volunteers came from the business and economic development sectors.) If CESO's range of activities were to be reduced to the core strength of economic development assistance, many (e.g. educators, health and social workers) would become ineligible for future assignments. Such VAs would be unhappy and critical of Cummings and the CESO organization if this source of personal reinforcement were to be taken from them. Also, as the list of eligible countries shrank, VAs and staff might lose some of their favorite countries, in which they liked to work. Major staff changes would be inevitable in such a transition, with an accompanying potential loss of morale. Cummings would undoubtedly be more popular with his VAs and his staff if he faced down the pressures for change from CIDA, and continued doing things as CESO had always done them.

The other alternative was to fundamentally and strategically change the structure, the management, the fundraising, and the operating parameters of the organization. These new directions would be in line with the evolving priorities of CIDA, and thus would presumably lead to the improved long-term viability of CESO's international operations. Consequently, CESO's Board of Directors was leaning in this direction, and was pushing for a new strategic direction.

Such change would include adopting a much narrower focus on the types of activities undertaken and reducing the number of countries in which CESO would operate. But how would the countries be selected, and how would the activities be determined? How would Cummings have to change the way CESO operated to make it a more business-like results-based organization? Would the changes he was facing in this second alternative enable him to re-define the organization and embark on some new development initiatives? What kind of information and marketing campaign (internally and externally) would he have to produce in order to promote the new directions? How would he deal with those VAs for whom there would be no more assignments? How would he terminate those employees who not longer fit with the new direction? What is actually meant by "private sector development" or "economic development"? Should he try to define these in a narrow sense (e.g. accounting and production management for SMEs) or more broadly (e.g. to include training and literacy)? Should "governance in support of economic development" be included? Should he consider attracting a different type of volunteer onto the CESO roster? Would CESO's fundraising plans be influenced by the changes? How should he organize a strategic planning exercise corresponding to choosing the second alternative?

At the base of these considerations, Cummings had to decide whom he most wanted to satisfy—his staff and his existing volunteers, or his primary funding agency and his Board of Directors.

A DECISION NEEDS TO BE MADE

Cummings weighed the advantages and disadvantages of his two alternatives, and then continued to prepare his presentation to the Executive Committee.

CASE: ETHIOPIA & CHRISTINE GILMORE[207]

On September 7, 1993 Christine Gilmore, the Administrator of a London-based NGO called *Future Forests, Partners in African Community Development*, had just returned from the annual monitoring trip to their project in northern Ethiopia. During the trip, the villagers with whom she met asked her to make fundamental changes to the project. She was now starting to write a proposal to be submitted to the Board of Directors of *Future Forests* for the next phase of the project, and was trying to decide what to do about the wishes of the African villagers.

ETHIOPIA

A country of great antiquity (the remains of "Lucy", a hominid who lived three or four million years ago, were found in the Rift Valley), Ethiopia has always suffered from recurring severe droughts in large portions of the country, and from the resulting famine and widespread displacements of people and their livestock. The Western world remained largely unaware of these repeated tragedies, but the situation changed in 1985 when BBC television cameramen started sending back appalling pictures of the unusually severe drought and famine that struck much of Ethiopia in the mid-1980s, and the resulting countless deaths from starvation. The industrialized world responded with unprecedented generosity through government aid and public fundraising campaigns spurred on, for example, by rock concerts (Bob Geldof and Bandaid). In Canada, many people, mainly but not exclusively associated with the health professions, volunteered to go to Ethiopia for substantial periods of time to serve in the medical relief camps.

One of the medical teams that went over in 1985 comprised Christine's husband Bernie Gilmore of Victoria Hospital, Dr. Jim Gilchrist and others from London, including several nurses. They established a medical relief camp (called "Camp London") in the village of Bette, which was five hours travel by Landcruiser north of the capital, Addis Ababa. The Kinsman Club of Canada provided funds for this mission. Upon their return to London in 1986, this team worked to encourage other community-based teams to go over to follow up. Because of the severity and complexity of the problems to be encountered, Kinsmen recommended that these next teams needed to stay longer than the one- to five-month durations of the original missions, i.e. a year overseas was more appropriate. By 1987, however, the crisis was easing and Kinsmen decided to shut down Camp London. They asked Bernie to return to Ethiopia for a year to bring the project to an orderly closure, and he invited Christine and their three-year-old son Kevin to accompany him.

CHRISTINE GILMORE

When Bernie invited Christine and Kevin to accompany him on his year-long return to Ethiopia in 1987, not having been medically trained Christine seriously wondered what she could contribute. These doubts were quickly erased after she arrived at the relief camp operation in Bette. Christine helped in the medical clinic, organized supplies and storekeeping, drove the truck, and organized construction projects. She also created opportunities for villagers (for women, children and men) in response to the recognition that one definition of poverty or underdevelopment was simply not having any options or opportunities in one's life. And these impediments were linked in large measure to lack of education. So, together with nurse Carol Wallace, Gilmore started providing informal education, sometimes under a tree in Bette, in areas such as health and nutrition. Little charades and simple dramas turned out to be highly useful in these language-challenged exercises. At this point, the transition from a relief operation to rural community development cooperation was, unofficially but effectively, under way.

By April 1988, Camp London had been closed, as were the camps of other donor nations like the Irish and the Danes, and the Gilmore family returned to Canada. This marked the end of a three-year period in which literally hundreds of Canadians had served in Ethiopia.

FUTURE FORESTS

As so often happens, when the emergency eased, and the volunteers returned to Canada, they could not simply pick up their domestic lives where they had left off many months before. For many members of the medical and nursing teams, in particular, the re-entry back to Canadian life was difficult (in fact, every bit as demanding as preparing to go overseas in the first place). Many had trouble adjusting from living in a community in which everything was in desperate scarcity back to Canadian environments of bewildering abundance.

Many had forged wonderful memories and friendships with the Bette villagers. Moreover, they could not shake off the conviction that an enormous amount still needed to be done in Ethiopia. The emphasis had shifted from emergency relief to rural community development cooperation. For this latter purpose, some of the individuals returning to London decided that they needed to create a non-governmental organization, which they did in 1989, and they called it *Future Forests, Partners in African Community Development*. The next step was the conceptualization of a program and the preparation of a first proposal for funding to CIDA, which was successful. In doing this, *FF* decided not to try to become an independent NGO on the ground in Ethiopia but rather to work through an existing and respected highly experienced NGO still operating in a nearby area in Ethiopia, *Save the Children USA*. *FF* and *Save* recruited Ethiopian staff including Tadesse Mesfin as the Bette project manager and two of the translators that the medical staff had previously worked with. Also, the houses and other buildings erected in Camp London during relief time were still there and could be used.

The name *Future Forests* stemmed from the observation that the Bette Valley (like many parts of the country) was completely denuded of trees. Within living memory this had been a richly forested area but, with the drought and the famine, virtually the last remaining resources that villagers had were trees. Wood, i.e. firewood, was the last "currency" that starving people had, and the chopped down remnants of the last trees were piled beside the road to Addis Ababa for sale to passing truckers. The Londoners were therefore struck by the necessity to replenish trees, and this resonated with London's self-description as *The Forest City*. The first proposal to CIDA (in 1989) concentrated on reforestation and agricultural rehabilitation—these topics resulted from the Londoners' direct experience in Ethiopia, but the proposal had very little, if any, input from the Bette villagers or even from *Save*.

Future Forests was governed by a Board of Directors (of which Bernie Gilmore was the Chair), and was operated by an Administrator. Board meetings took place one Saturday morning each month, and there was an Annual General Meeting. Each year there was a three-week monitoring trip to Ethiopia, led by either the Chair or the Administrator and including one or more other Board members (in one case, a representative of Rotary was also included because he was actively raising money for the project). *FF* felt that it was highly desirable for Board members to meet the villagers and to experience the reality of the programs in Bette in order that they may have the knowledge and the sensitivity to function well on the Board. Board members who had been overseas were better enabled to serve as fundraisers; moreover, they became more effective in increasing awareness in the community and in schools of Canada's role in Africa. The preparation of Board members in advance of their first monitoring trip experiences, and dealing with them sympathetically and productively while overseas, were major management tasks for the monitoring trip leader.

THE 1993 MONITORING TRIP

Christine had been only peripherally involved with *FF* during 1989 and 1990, being fully occupied in London with family matters as well as being the new Volunteer Services Coordinator of Victoria Hospital. She later started helping out as the Secretary of *FF* and then, in 1991 she became its Administrator. In 1993, she was asked to lead the annual monitoring trip to Ethiopia, marking the first time she had been back since 1988 and fulfilling her promise at that time to the Bette community to return some day and to continue working with them. The initial grant from CIDA was nearing its end, and so Chris was also asked to make recommendations for a second grant proposal to CIDA based on the findings of the monitoring trip.

In 1991, Christine had been mandated by the Board to implement the program that had been devised in 1989 without very much local African input. She decided in 1993, however, to encourage the process of getting the villagers of Bette to identify their own longer-term development needs. This included, importantly, how the Canadians might work with the villagers in a manner and context very different from relief time.

The 1989 proposal to CIDA had stressed reforestation and agriculture in one village, Bette. In 1991, three other villages in the same area wanted to be involved. The four villages met extensively with Christine and requested many additional activities that eventually grew to include provision of safe water,

water pump maintenance and repair, health, education of children and adults, skills training for economic advancement, electrification, handling money and dealing with banks, gender equity, empowerment of women, an oxen revolving loan program, community gardens, preparing a business plan to obtain a grant to establish a grinding mill, and helping to build bridges to the Ethiopian ministries of health, education and agriculture as the government was increasingly taking control of getting the country back on its feet.

Their overall objective was to help build self-reliance and to move away from the relief mentality when almost everything came from the donor countries.

PARTICIPATORY RURAL APPRAISAL

Christine had previously been exposed to PRA methodology in a workshop led by Robert Chambers[208]. She was enthusiastic about using PRA as the tool by which *Future Forests* could best learn the wishes and possibilities of the three neighboring communities (Goda, Arso Amba and Muta Fecha) that wanted to join the project. This took the form of the villagers jointly making a "ground map" of their community using stones and sticks arranged on the ground (and later transferred to paper). The process permitted *Future Forests* to learn, in a very graphic way, about population, health, agriculture, water, etc. in the community and the associated problems.

Importantly, PRA enabled the members of the community to take charge of the communications by making a physical portrayal of their villages and to reach consensus on the messages they wanted to give. PRA also gave *FF* the opportunity to "dig down" by asking increasingly detailed questions about the situation that each stick or stone represented, for example, to find out the locations of gardens and of cottage industries, such as weavers and potters. This "aerial view" of the villages was a very effective platform for developing cultural insights as to what men and women typically did each day in the villages.

FUNDING

Funding for the work of *Future Forests* came from many sources, but the backbone of the money was a matchable grant from the NGO Division of CIDA's Partnership Branch. In this scheme, CIDA provided two dollars for each one raised by *FF*. The money raised by *FF* came largely from the proceeds of a major gift-wrapping effort throughout the month of December in Galleria Mall in London, which was also an opportunity to raise awareness within the London community. Other donations came from church groups, from Rotary and from individuals. After adding CIDA's 2:1 matching grant, the annual budgets that were made possible were generally in the range of $125,000. However, with an expanded program such as the four villages were requesting, much more money would have to be raised by the *FF* volunteers.

DECISION TO BE MADE

As Christine began to prepare a proposal to the Board of Directors of *Future Forests* for their second grant submission to CIDA, she reflected on all the things she had learned in the PRA exercise in the villages as well as the limitations of their fundraising. She had to decide between (a) continuing the kinds of activities that had already been approved by CIDA in the initial grant, or (b) to expand the program, totally or partially, as requested by the villagers, to justify this major expansion to CIDA, and to devise a plan for increased fundraising in order to support the expansion.

INDIGENOUS NGOS

NGOs established in a developing country are often called "indigenous" or "LDC" or "national" or "local" or "South" NGOs, but these are possibly not the most appropriate labels (especially in the singular form). Our preference would be to call, for example, an NGO that has been established in The Gambia simply a Gambian NGO, just as NGOs established in Canada are Canadian NGOs.

Such NGOs comprise staff and/or volunteers who, usually, are nationals of that country or region. Funding may come from national sources, e.g. philanthropists, religious organizations, service clubs, the private sector, or (ironically for a nongovernmental organization) from government. Some receive funding from other countries or from multilateral organizations.

» Example: The Gambia & ADWAC[209]

ADWAC (the Agency for the Development of Women and Children) is a Gambian NGO based in the North Bank Division of The Gambia. Local staff have been working for more than a decade on programs of integrated rural development to bring about sustainable improvements in rural living conditions, with particular emphasis being placed upon the wellbeing of women and children. ADWAC's Executive Director is Mr. Mamsamba Joof. Mamsamba is reputed to be highly capable, and is one of the primary WARD facilitators.

ADWAC aims at enabling local communities to take an active and leading role in determining their development needs and solutions. ADWAC's vision is to create a better life for women and children in one of the most economically deprived divisions of The Gambia. ADWAC works in the areas of education and advocacy, sustainable agricultural approaches to agro-economic development for women, micro-credit and women's enterprise development, and holistic approaches to mother and child healthcare development.

ADWAC focuses on community development through an 'eco-zone approach' in order to project plan and implement in regional development initiatives that will overcome the effects of environmental degradation as it relates to food security and overall community health and development. ADWAC takes the view that local development issues are inter-related and cannot be addressed in isolation from each other. ADWAC's 'eco-zone approach' is a holistic approach to identifying the needs of local communities while deriving possible solutions for long term sustainability and positive change for communities and their members. This approach takes into account the problems affecting the entire watershed area of the North Bank Division. The 'eco-zone approach' is designed to enhance development planning, coordination and implementation of food security and resources management, and overall participatory development and its sustainability in a number of related areas- healthcare and malarial education, women and children's education and training, HIV/AIDS awareness and education, community resource management and agricultural impacts (food distribution and security and alternative agricultural practices), women's enterprise and income generation schemes, micro-credit and loans, and literacy and adult educational training. ADWAC offers the support of skilled intervention and development workers while promoting the knowledge and participation of community members on the North Bank in the collective development process.

ADWAC works in cooperation with several NGOs and government agencies from industrialized countries, including Gorta of Ireland, Oxfam-USA, Action Aid International The Gambia, Catholic Relief Services, VSO, the US Peace Corps, and with Don Sawyer of Okanagan College (with funding support from CIDA).

Mamsamba Joof, ADWAC's Executive Director, includes the use of case studies in his training programs that are somewhat similar to the cases in this book. One case study deals with proposal writing and is mainly aimed at African development workers tasked (as they nearly all are) with some element of fundraising.

Sawyer also makes use of case studies in his training activities at WARD. One such activity focuses on African adults as individuals with strengths and weaknesses and helps trainees focus on how to accommodate the whole person. An example follows:

» Example: Norbile[210]

Norbile is 23 years old and is the fourth child in a family of eight children. His father, Chimsah, is a subsistence farmer with a very small farm. His fields are small and not very fertile because Chimsah was a settler from another region. He migrated from his home village to his in-laws' village before Norbile was born at the request of Chimsah's father-in-law. Chimsah had married the man's third daughter, and the father-in-law wanted Chimsah nearby to serve him.

During Norbile's infancy he was not fortunate enough to have been vaccinated against the five major childhood diseases, and he contracted polio. The disease made his left leg lame. Norbile has to use a stick to support himself when he walks.

Being physically handicapped, Norbile's parents did not see much of a future for him, and thus he was not sent to the village school nor was he taught any vocational skills that could support him later in life.

At the age of eight, Norbile realized that he was going nowhere. He was the only one of his brothers and sisters who did nothing during the day. They were either taken to the farm by their father or worked with their mother in the fields and hauling water and firewood. Norbile was left alone.

But Norbile knew he had the ability to learn. He also knew that he was clever with his hands. He approached a shoe maker, who was crippled himself, who had a shop near Norbile's home. To Norbile's delight, the shoe maker took him on as an apprentice for no fee.

After four years of apprenticeship, Norbile graduated and began his own shop right in front of the family home. Now Norbile has become quite successful. All four of his brothers have left home for the city in search of greener pastures, and his three sisters have married and left the home. Norbile is the only child left. From shoe making, Norbile is able to help feed both his mother and father. He also provides their clothing and runs all errands for them.

Recently at a village meeting Norbile was elected treasurer of the village development committee—a post many influential villagers vied for. Many in the village see Norbile as an honest, hard working and trustworthy man. Now he is planning to marry one of the daughters of the village chief by the end of the year.

Norbile remains optimistic and hopeful about the future. He says that hard work has gotten him far and will continue to serve him. He would like to expand his business and build a new home for his wife. He would also like to learn basic literacy and bookkeeping so he can manage his business more effectively. He hopes to continue being active in his community and to help develop a new water supply in the village so that the women do not have to carry water so far.

» Example: Training for Transformation

While working in Ethiopia, one of the authors of this book (Gilmore) came across a series of handbooks that proved to be highly effective in training the local community development workers of the NGO. These books consisted of a three-volume set called *Training for Development: A Handbook for Community Workers*. The books were written by Anne Hope and Sally Timble, and published in the 1990s by Mambo Press of Zimbabwe.[211] In 2000 a fourth book joined the series; the four books are currently available from Stylus Publishing.[212]

Using an African Christian perspective, the books address issues and strategies needed to bring about local and national community development and regeneration. The books recognize that the changes that most effectively transform the lives of poor people are those in which they have been active participants, and thus provide "relevant material designed to stimulate interest and debate, including simulations, real life stories, telling statistics, news articles, poetry and drama from local communities".

A CONVERSATION WITH NIGEL FISHER OF UNICEF CANADA

Nigel Fisher, President & CEO of UNICEF Canada since November 1, 2005, has presided over a period of rapid and unprecedented change in the organization's public image and its fundraising approaches. He spoke with Frederick Keenan on November 1, 2007, and began by recounting a startling encounter he had not long after joining UNICEF Canada.

NF: I had been speaking at a dinner for UNICEF at St. Andrews in New Brunswick early in 2006. At the end of my talk I wandered around to press the flesh and talk to people and one, a BMO investment banker, said, "I don't envy you your job. It must be very difficult to represent such a tired brand." I said, "Look, when I finish walking around I'd like to come back and let's talk about it." So I did. And his basic message was, "UNICEF has been around for 50 years in Canada. You don't hear much about it these days. What I know about it is greeting cards and Trick or Treat. My impression is it hasn't changed much but in the meantime your world has changed. How are you getting your message out? How are you going to be getting your message out to the changing philanthropist, the venture capitalist, the younger professionals? Seems to me UNICEF has gotten left behind and there are other edgier," he mentioned the word "edgier", "brands."

FK: Was this the first indication you had that UNICEF Canada needed to make major changes in how the organization is perceived in Canada and in its fundraising?

NF: No, it wasn't. I arrived in UNICEF Canada on the 1st of November 2005. We had just completed what's called a barometer survey of the awareness of Canadians about UNICEF. It came back as something like 98% of Canadians recognize the UNICEF name. Wonderful, wonderful, but you ask them what UNICEF does and it was very fuzzy. So that was one part of my education. I had come from this UNICEF. It's a world leader, around the world it leads for kids. It's recognized for its impact, whether it's in advocacy or whether it's in supporting programs on the ground to reduce child mortality, get girls in school, protect kids from violence. You name it. So we needed to do something to sharpen up the identity of UNICEF and focus it for Canadians.

FK: What did you do about this situation?

NF: I went to the Board and to senior staff and said, "This is what I'm hearing and if this is the case, we have to do something." So we then basically conceptualized what we are. What are we? Well around the world we are the leading organization for children and you can measure that in terms of impact on the actual status of kids that are helped, their wellbeing, their education. You can measure it in terms of the impact we have on leaders to influence them to invest in kids or to commit to goals that will reach kids. You could look at it in terms of our advocacy, how we persuade whole industries like the carpet industry in Bangladesh to come up with a set of self-monitoring standards for child labor. You can go on and on. We are trusted. We're the organization that counterparts call on to coordinate all the others in times of crisis. But Canadians don't know what we do. So we have to turn this around.

One of our strategic goals over the next few years is we have to leverage the leadership qualities and brand that UNICEF have overseas and make sure that Canadians know this about us too. So our brand is leadership. We are not competing with other organizations that are also raising funds for kids. We are differentiating ourselves from them and the differentiation is our global scope, our leadership, our global impact, our global influence, our ability to mobilize and generate results.

So that was one of them. Then, we said, "Well what's the second challenge? We've probably become a little fractured because we tackle Canadians when they're young through Trick or Treat at elementary school and then we basically leave them alone till they're well in their mature giving years. Why don't we take a life cycle approach and let's see how we can reach Canadians at all ages? Not just elementary kids but junior high and high school, universities." We had then, perhaps, 10 university clubs. And then how do we reach younger people in the workforce? We have to be edgier. We have to be smarter. We have to be crisper. For kids at school we have to be more fun etc. And for people who are wealthier, successful, we also have to be attractive too. So we don't want to throw away that aspect of the brand. We want to attract supporters and stakeholders and benefactors who are themselves leaders and influencers and who will see us as the leadership organization that they would like to support.

We also had a consultant who advised on corporate communications who came in and did some work for us. We asked "What is our profile in corporate Canada?" They said, "You don't really have a profile in corporate Canada except for the retail partners you have for the sale of your products. So you also need to tie your desire to link up with leaders in various walks of life with the fact that you don't have a profile. You have to go out and do more research and find out where is the resonance between UNICEF's identity and the brand that these organizations, whether it's what they do or make or whether it's what they like, to support here or overseas. And then develop a strategy."

I also picked up that we'd had certain significant donors, let's say six-figure donors, who we'd really not gone back to and cultivated or thanked systematically. So we were operating in a middle of the road way which didn't reflect to me what the UNICEF brand was. The Board was very excited about this in the sense of re-branding.

So the strategic plan came out and basically identified what we are trying to do. Leverage that global leadership? How do we do it? How do we reach Canadians of all ages? How do we persuade them that we are the organization of first choice? And we also said, "You know, UNICEF, we do so much and why we will continue to support many things. Why don't we take some lead ideas or concepts or campaigns and really emphasize these so that when you ask a Canadian next time, they'll say, 'Oh, yes, UNICEF really makes a difference for kids in emergencies, kids having AIDS education, etc.'"

I had come from an emergency background. Part of this barometer had asked the question, "Who do you associate as being a good organization that responds quickly and effectively in emergency situations?" Top of mind: Red Cross, Doctors Without Borders. They're good organizations but in fact UNICEF, I know from my experience, we're on the ground already. We see problems coming and we're responding on day one.

FK: How did the UNICEF Canada Board react to this?

NF: The Board, at the end of the day, said in terms of where we want to go as an organization in defining our leadership brand, having a whole school relationship with the schools that is not just about fundraising at a certain time of year but an educational relationship all year round, that we want to be edgy and appeal to youngsters in a better way yet, so okay, even though there were some cries of anguish about the loss of the box etc.

And it's interesting, this year, for example, we still produce the box so that people can dress up in it. So it's become now a costume. We have ads out now which say the box has gone online. I've seen them on TV where it starts off with the box but it transmogrifies into a laptop and then transmogrifies into a box on the website. And if you go onto our website, the box is there. The box has now become virtual.

FK: Did you get your Board's approval on that?

NF: I presented it to the Board for their endorsement and got an endorsement. If they hadn't agreed, I don't know what would have happened but anyway, yes, yes, we all agreed to plow through.

FK: How did your management team react to this?

NF: There were some concerns, obviously, because we were taking a risk. I remember we had a management team meeting where for two days we discussed our various strategies but on this one I didn't want to impose it. I wanted buy-in. So I kept on rabbiting away at it and arguing with people until people started to say, "This will work" rather than forcing it because I know that my senior colleague on the marketing side was really concerned. And she had some very good points.

But anyway, at the end of the day, we said, "Okay, let's focus on a couple of countries that would define what we do. And UNICEF was developing a partnership with the Nelson Mandela Foundation and is supporting what's called Schools for Africa in five countries in southern Africa. We decided that we should focus Trick or Treat on fundraising for kids in Rwanda. The program is to provide funds for the repair of schools, upgrading of schools, for teacher training, for production of textbooks and teaching materials and in extreme cases, actual building of buildings, water and sanitation and so on. So we put together a package which described this for schools.

We also said, oh yes, another shocker, because the receipts from the box were going down with less and less kids going out. I also said, "I think we need to drop the box, the 50-year icon." Now, serious internal trauma. But I said, "Look, it's an icon and maybe we could retain its image on our material. Maybe we could eventually think of other ways to use it. For example, in businesses, corporate headquarters where perhaps adults could still donate but as for kids going around to collect with the box, I think we need to drop it. First, it doesn't send a message of leadership. It sends the message that we're the pennies organization and our receipts are going down and the costs are going up.

So we dropped the box and instead put out materials to teachers telling them how they could help kids organize events during the month of October which would be fun but which allow kids also to raise money and get sponsored and so on. So they could do a play in the gym about being a kid in Rwanda. They could go out and get sponsored for doing activities and so on. We had a thermometer shaped like a school. Each time a kid or a class got $20 they could put a brick on their thermometer.

Then we said, "Okay, we still need to hold onto Halloween night". So that's where we went. It was a heck of a rush. We had a real communication challenge to get the message out. We had classic slip-ups, like in Quebec. It was leaked by somebody, I think in a competitive organization, that UNICEF was stopping their Halloween tradition and therefore the other organization could take up the slack.

There was a very vicious interview by one TV station in Quebec: "So UNICEF, you're giving up on kids. You think you're too good now to go out with a box," you know and this kind of thing. So there was a lot of that stuff, plus I would say the overall communication could have been better, could have been better. But we'd taken a big leap of faith to try and cover the country with a new message.

And we sent out, therefore, the new program to schools and we had normally about four and a half thousand schools participating the year before. And I think this year, I'd have to check the figures, but I think last year we had about 3,000 plus. So what it was, that a lot of schools said, "Hm." Some said, "Well we're not sure. Let's wait and see what the program looks like." Other said, "No, we don't want to do this. It's like too much work and so on."

So we went in with many fewer schools and then the program rolled out. I went to speak to school boards, to departments of education. We tried to hit some of the teachers' federations to try and create awareness. Hit and miss because time was short. And then we put out public service announcements [PSAs] and all the other stuff on TV.

When the results came in, we collected just about the same as we had the year before but with fewer schools. The response we got from participating schools was, "We love it. You finally get it. It's educational. It's fun. It's edgy. The kids know why they're doing it. We love it!" But, of course, I mean, less were loving it, but still. So we felt vindicated. That was the Halloween of 2006.

FK: What are you doing this year?

NF: We went into this year saying, "Okay, we're on the right track." This year we said, "Let's go for two countries, Rwanda and Malawi." We got Ben Mulroney to come on board as our Trick or Treat ambassador so I took him out late last year to Malawi so we could take onsite pictures of the before and after schools and then he did, right from Malawi, PSAs, took footage and so on. He's been wonderful. He's been around the country for us, done stuff on TV, radio, live dissertations to schools and so on. And I think this year we've got the message out more.

Our numbers of schools, though, is still a bit down from last year so we are now waiting to see what the financial results are going to be. We feel that we've been much more organized in getting coverage as there has been a lot more coverage of what UNICEF is doing with Trick or Treat in the run up to Halloween night etc. But we still think there are certain things that we have to do.

One, we had paid for the bags ourselves and we said, "We have to get a much stronger corporate partnership and sponsorship for this program." Cadbury Adams came on board so we have a Cadbury Adams sponsorship. They reckon they put in 5 or 6 million into development costs into their participation and advertising campaign to go around the country, and all the candy boxes from Cadbury Adams are branded as schools for Africa and UNICEF.

We had to be careful there. We had to look at their bona fides in terms of chocolate production because there is stuff going around about forced labor of chocolate. UNICEF has a due diligence check where we check any corporate partner before we sign them up. They're also a candy manufacturer so we had to agree with them that this was a strictly off-school relationship and we said, "As we look into the future, we believe we're on the right track but we need to be better and more strategic with our communications." So from now on we're saying, "Okay, over the next year, how are we going to reach out to schools? Schools respond, teachers respond much more positively to a face-to-face communication than they do to either mail or e-mail. We have to get face to face—we have a volunteer core of speakers who go out to schools, we need to strengthen that. We need to get other corporate partners who will sponsor the bags and therefore, we're looking at corporate partners who we think are interested in education, who have the same corporate colors or other interests, you know, like ING for example. ING is already a partner for supporting girls' education in a number of countries and the CEO is an individual supporter so that may be a possibility. We've approached Aeroplan etc. So we've been looking for an Orange Coalition. We're saying bags, environment. Look at all the supermarkets that are now starting to sell bags.

It's solid. We're going to be looking at this too, where are the opportunities? So that's our stage now. We won't know yet how we've performed financially. We haven't recruited the number of schools that we would like to this year because we set a slightly higher target but we think we're on the right track in terms of the message we're sending: that we are not just a partner who wants to raid schools once a year to collect money but we'd like to be a partner that helps kids learn in the process, that helps kids as part of their global education learn that they can make a difference even at their early age. And this is very much a part of our broader approach to schools because one of the other elements of change, as we tried to focus and strengthen our strategy, was to look at what we were doing in the way of learning partnerships with schools. And for years we produced materials on what we call "global education" and we've had speakers who would, in the year, go out to schools and talk about UNICEF's work or children's rights around the world and so on.

But because we've produced the materials, it has always been extracurricular. So, again, a year ago we recruited six professional educators and put one in each of our region offices plus our director here so we now have a team of people all over who have been teachers and their message is different. They're supposed to go to schools, to school boards, departments of education, to teachers, to say, "You want to help your kids become global citizens, aware of social issues, understand social justice, become tolerant, celebrate diversity, not be racist. We have the same goals. We have materials and experience from around the world. How can we work with you to develop materials that are helpful to you as a teacher?" So that we are around the country now, have several things going on: school boards here, faculties of education there, departments of education somewhere else where we are, together with them, in teams, developing curriculum materials focused on these things which will help kids to be better global citizens.

And again, we feel the response from around the country has been so positive that we were actually prepared to go and ask teachers what they need rather than give them what we had. So again, it's part of that process of engagement, a year-round engagement with schools committed to learning with kids, in a sense, on terms that the teachers can deal with.

So we're just waiting now for the financial results but already the Trick or Treat team has presented to us their case for next year. Keep the same theme but we need to even more strongly strengthen our communications and it's everything from going out much earlier in the media and also, interacting much earlier with influences. Going to teachers' conferences, to principals' conferences, to, you name it, to school boards, to departments of education, writing up stories in publications and so on.

FK: What else are you doing?

NF: Trick or Treat, basically the activities are for elementary schools. What we have also developed for high schools but also for universities and the workforce is something we call "Dare to Wear," where people challenge their, like here, in-house people challenge me that if they raise so much I have to wear a costume that they will choose on Halloween evening.

FK: They did that on—was it "22 Minutes?"

NF: Gavin Crawford. He's a "Dare to Wear" guy. He's an ambassador for us too. He's on the "Dare to Wear" thing. Just as we got Rick Mercer on "Spread the Net" on the "Mercer Report." Every week he talks about, there's a challenge we have out to universities. We are doing a campaign with Rick Mercer and Belinda Stronach.

It's called "Spread the Net" but it's basically tackling malaria and the message is you can buy a bed net which is insecticide treated for $10 and that can save a life. Because we've done all the science to show you use bed nets at the community level, at the household level. You can cut the transmission of the disease by 50% and mortality from malaria by 20%. Really amazing results. So we have that program with them and it's "Spread the Net." You buy a net etc.

But I think the insecticide-treated bed nets have really only taken off in the last five or six years. And then I think, let's say 2002, I think there were 5 million distributed around the world. This year 67 million, and we've just in fact issued a report that shows that, in fact, malaria mortality is starting to drop like a bomb because of the use of bed nets. And UNICEF is now the biggest provider, 25 million this last year. And of the new drugs because so many of the mosquitoes are resistant to the older drugs.

But finally, they found that they can soak the net in doses which are not a threat to a child. But the mosquito is killed on contact. It's WHO approved, all the rest of it so we're not reintroducing that old DDT and all that sort of thing.

FK: **You said that when you're dealing with an emergency situation, you have to move quickly. You've said, "We can't wait. We can't do it step by step."**

NF: All the marketers tell you that you have to do your research, you have to do a pilot, it takes time but coming from my background in emergencies, I find it difficult to accept that because my whole life is built on the need for rapid action in life-threatening situations. So when somebody tells me that it takes 18 months to cultivate a new donor, and they're probably right, I say, "It can't take that long." Plus, you know, I can't understand how are we, in this case, going to go out with two messages? In some parts of the country we're saying "drop the box" and in other parts we're continuing the box. How can we have an integrated communication strategy with that? So it seemed to me the research, the survey, had told us this is not really a program that is growing, it's declining. Why hold onto it? Let's go for broke. So, yeah, let's get on with it for God's sake. You know, instead of making a test and then asking questions next year.

I'm not saying I'm always right but that was the motivation.

FK: Will these changes modify the role of your volunteers?

NF: I think there'll be less need to lug sacks of money. I went to a school last year in New Brunswick, where we physically lugged six large cardboard boxes full of coins. I can appreciate that's hernia territory so I think less need for that but still there is coin, but it tends to be toonies and loonies and there are more notes but there are also cheques and online commitments.

We're also asking people to give online making the argument that it is an effective way to continue the tradition and it's less costly. We can now give receipts directly online. It's part of a broader strategy where we're trying to encourage donors to come online if they want to purchase our products, if they want to look at our education materials again. It's all part of that general trend in that this is a highly computer literate country.

But leading up to this, I said, "Well let's look at how we're doing on Trick or Treat." So we surveyed. This is in, end of '05, early '06, bearing in mind that already, at that time, you normally have to have your plans in hand for the next October/ November. So I said, "Okay, let's go out" and we did a quick and dirty survey of some 500 schools I remember. And we asked the basic question, "What do you think of Trick or Treat?" And I'd say the majority response came back, "Well not very exciting. Not educational. The kids don't really know why they're collecting money. It's not much fun. I mean, they go out collecting candies etc."

Especially in the larger urban areas, schools are getting a more and more diverse population, many of whom don't have the Halloween tradition and don't necessarily want to send their kids out in pagan costumes etc. etc.

And then we looked at the costs and basically the cost of collecting pennies was more than 50 cents on the dollar. So back to the drawing board and Fisher being a neophyte marketer, i.e., no experience, said, "Well then let's dump the program and start again." A horrified reaction from our professional marketing development fundraising people, saying, "You can't do that. We've only got nine months left and maybe we could do it on a pilot but to totally turn it around, Canadians will be confused." And they were partly right but anyway ... So I came back and said, "I don't see the point. We don't have the luxury of resources and so on to invest in a pilot and take three years to do this so we are going to do it now." So that was against the express advice of some of my senior colleagues.

FK: **When you brought this idea forward to different parts of the organization, who were the ones most opposed or frightened of it?**

NF: Those who know most about marketing and fundraising were the most concerned and they had a right to be because I have no background in marketing and development and so on, and just sort of came in swinging. So they were very concerned. I didn't know really what I was asking for and didn't know the Canadian market.

FK: **What's your link with Stephen Lewis and the Stephen Lewis Foundation?**

NF: Stephen is a friend. We go back many years. He was the executive director of UNICEF and he started with UNICEF just about the same time as I became director of emergency programs in early '95 after I'd been to Rwanda. And we both shared a deep distress about Rwanda and he went on to lead a postmortem team which looked at how the international community responded. So he became a friend and we worked together closely.

And then I always remember when I left UNICEF in '98, he did my farewell speech saying how glad he was that I was leaving because what a nuisance I was and how bad my puns were-it was very funny. I have enormous respect for that guy. He has so much integrity. He doesn't pull his punches and he has been a critic of UNICEF and also a supporter of UNICEF. I respect him enormously too because I think he's the person who has singlehandedly woken up Canadians to AIDS and its impact around the world. A tremendous guy.

CHAPTER TEN

SMALL ENTERPRISES

Chapter Three contains a substantial amount of information on the benefits of the stimulation of economic activity as a principal means of alleviating poverty, with emphasis on the creation of small enterprises. Some examples were:

- *Egypt & rural women*
- *Peru & pro-poor tourism*
- *Peru & business plan*
- *CESO & economic development*
- *LEADER Project & free market business fundamentals*
- *Ethiopian women & business plan*
- *Andean Pact countries & building products*

As was seen in two of these examples, a useful tool for getting enterprises started is the business plan. Accordingly, the present chapter describes how to prepare a business plan, and then presents a case that is, in effect, an actual business plan that had to be created in support of an enterprise in Peru.

BUSINESS PLANS

In creating an enterprise (of any size), and in attempting to obtain financing for it, it is necessary to prepare a business plan. The preparation of a business plan will serve two essential purposes:

a) The process of writing the plan will force you to think

through for yourself—in unrelenting detail—all aspects of the enterprise. It is the main company document that your employees—and you—use to gauge your company's success and to make decisions about what you should do first, second, or not at all. It will force you to answer four core questions:[213]

o   What service or product does your business provide and what needs does it fill?

o   Who are the potential customers for your product or service and why will they purchase it from you?

o   How will you reach your potential customers?

o   Where will you get the financial resources to start your business?

b)   The plan is needed to convince potential providers of finance (loans, investments, grants) that you have thought through your enterprise carefully, that you have a firm grip on its finances, and that you know how you will repay the funds that are loaned to you.

A typical business plan runs around a dozen pages, and is organized under the following headings:

o   Executive Summary (one or two pages): highlights of the key information contained in the plan. If you are applying for financing, begin by stating the type of financing and the amount you are seeking. The Executive Summary should be concise, and interesting. Write it last.

o   Background: the history and location of the enterprise, and where the idea to create this enterprise came from; start-up plans

o   Product or Service: benefits to be provided to the customers

o   Market Analysis

o   Competitors: strengths and weaknesses of your enterprise with respect to the competition. How does your product or service differ from those of the competition?

o   Management Team: names, biographies and responsibilities of the key managers o   Marketing Plan

- Financial Plan: projections for the next three to five years, including assumptions, balance sheets, income statements, and cash-flow projections

- Exit strategy: if your enterprise hasn't worked, how will you know, and what will you do then?

CASE: PERU & ANDREW NELSON[214]

On May 6, 2002 Dr. Andrew Nelson, an Associate Professor of Anthropology at the University of Western Ontario in London, Ontario had just returned from a trip to Peru where he wanted to establish a museum of cultural history and an accompanying international bioarchaeological research center. Nelson had successfully gathered all the necessary information and arranged all the required legal agreements while in Peru, and he turned now to fundraising. Nelson understood that a proper business plan for this venture would be required when he approached the private sector for funding. Never having previously been involved with such documents, Nelson set out to inform himself about business plans and to prepare one for the Peruvian museum within the next few months.

ANDREW NELSON

Andrew Nelson (together with his wife, Christine Nelson) had been working in Peru for many years, principally in archaeological and ethnohistoric investigations of the Moche culture (approximately 100 AD to 750 AD). Much of this work took place in the Jequetepeque Valley on the northern coast (Exhibit 1). Nelson had excavated skeletal remains in this area, as had a number of other archaeologists from Peru, Germany, the US and Canada. Human remains and artifacts from these graves are required by law to remain in Peru. Nelson, with the active agreement and encouragement of the other researchers, saw great value in bringing all these materials together in one secure research center located in the Jequetepeque Valley where a wide range of comparative analyses could be carried out. These techniques included osteological examination and X-rays (as an indicator of nutrition, status and occupation, for example), mitochondrial DNA testing (to follow mother to daughter linkages), measurements of faces and of imposed cranial modifications (to detect cultural continuities). Nelson understood that the crucial variables here were time and location—much could be learned about the Moche culture and its relationships to other cultures as investigators determined the variation with respect to time and location of the above indicators within a large collection of data.

PERU AND PACASMAYO

North of the capital of Lima on the Panamerican Highway is the attractive and historic coastal city of Pacasmayo (Exhibit 1). In the late 1800s and early 1900s, Pacasmayo was a major Pacific port from which rice, cotton and mineral ores were shipped. The trains from the interior descended on Pacasmayo and travelled out on a kilometre-long pier to transfer their loads to ocean-going ships. Much of the pier still remains, as well as the very attractive British-designed train station, which dates from the 19th Century. The trains stopped coming to Pacasmayo in the 1960s, but the old train station remains.

The station, which had been designated as a historical monument, and the immediately surrounding lands were owned by the Government of Peru through the *Instituto Nacional de Cultura* (INC), but the INC had given the right to use the building to the *Casa de la Cultura de Pacasmayo*, which was a local non-profit organization set up by the late highly respected former mayor of Pacasmayo, Carlos Arbaiza Strohmeier, to nurture community cultural and historic projects.

The INC, the *Casa de la Cultura de Pacasmayo*, and the University of Western Ontario had recently formally agreed to restore the Pacasmayo train station and to use it and its grounds to house a Museum of Cultural History of the Jequetepeque Valley and an integral international Centre for Bioarchaeological Research.

CONCEPT OF THE MUSEUM

The primary objective was to bring together a museum of cultural history and an institute of archaeological research in a single location. This cultural center would celebrate the history and prehistory of the Jequetepeque Valley, reaching out to audiences at the local, national and international levels. The breadth and depth of the Jequetepeque Valley's cultural heritage were well documented in a tremendous wealth of Pre-Columbian archaeological sites, and colonial and 19th century buildings. Thus, it was appropriate that this institution should be housed in a historic building.

The explicit linkage of archaeological research and museum public presentation lay at the heart of the concept. The integration of the research institute with the museum would strengthen both components and would allow the museum to exhibit ongoing developments in the field of archaeology.

This was particularly important in the Jequetepeque Valley where there were at least three major archaeological field projects then active. The integration of the museum with the research institute would provide the institute with a means of directly accessing the interested public. Together, these two components would work to preserve the cultural patrimony of the Jequetepeque Valley, to undertake cutting edge archaeological research, to be active in educating the local school children in the richness of their heritage and to present the rich tapestry of the cultural history of the Jequetepeque Valley to the national and international tourist public.

THE NORTHERN TOURISM CIRCUIT

Tourism was one of the most important contributors to the economy of Peru—both to the national economy and to the economies of individual communities that were fortunate enough to attract tourists—but over 80% of tourists restricted their visits to the capital Lima and to the famous Inca cities of Cuzco and Machu Picchu in the southern highlands. Relatively ignored were the no less fascinating areas of the northern coast and highlands. This is the land of the Moche and other cultures that preceded the Incas of Cuzco and Machu Picchu. These were the cultures whose pottery and textiles kept appearing in the pages of *National Geographic*. This is where the *Lord of Sipán* was discovered near Chiclayo, and where the huge structures of the *Huaca de la Luna* and the *Huaca del Sol,* and the enormous ancient ruined city of *Chan Chan* close to Trujillo, were found.

Because of the rich tourism potential of the north of Peru (and also because the stonework of Machu Picchu was deteriorating under the onslaught of hundreds and hundreds of visitors each day), the British Embassy in Peru had commissioned a study of the tourism potential of the north. That work had just been completed and a detailed plan for the Northern Tourism Circuit (Exhibit 2) of Peru had been prepared. Nelson was delighted to learn that the Pacasmayo Museum had been formally included as a component of the Northern Tourism Circuit of Peru.

ROLES OF THE NORTHERN TOURISM CIRCUIT
AND THE MUSEUM IN THE DEVELOPMENT OF THE REGION

The Northern Tourism Circuit was a *pro-poor* international development concept. Tourism was seen as a vehicle that could bring about positive change in this region. The idea is that local people along the route of the Circuit could obtain income from food sales, hostels, guiding, guarding, and handicrafts, e.g. carving and weaving. The inputs needed for this project were infrastructure enhancements such as improving the roads and re-opening an airport, training courses for guides, providing security for the archaeological sites, some language training, marketing assistance, and loans to providers of food and accommodation.

Nelson, whose father was born in Peru, led teams that contained many indigenous workers, some of whom were probably descendants of the Moche. As they excavated skeletal remains and artifacts from ancient graves in this area, Nelson realized that the indigenous workers were highly curious about these discoveries and quite proud of their pre-European cultural heritage. The Nelsons understood that awareness of the cultural patrimony of indigenous peoples was a valuable aspect of development through increasing self-confidence, and had resolved to help create a museum that would celebrate their heritage.

One of the elements of sustainability in development is public pride in what is being achieved: in this case, an increased awareness of the rich pre-Conquest cultural patrimony of Peru through archaeological and anthropological research. Increased awareness and pride, in turn, would help to build public disapproval of the traditional widespread looting of graves throughout Peru and the consequent destruction of knowledge of their own culture. (An excellent, but horrifying, account of the international illicit antiquities trade is *Stealing History* by Roger Atwood.)

BUSINESS PLAN

To help obtain the funding in order to make the museum concept into a reality, Nelson then informed himself about business plans. In summary, he learned the things that are in Exhibit 3. He then set out to gather the information he needed to write the plan, as follows.

MARKET ANALYSIS

A recent analysis of tourism in Peru had documented that tourism was growing, and was having an increasingly notable impact on the economy of this country. Between 1990 and 1997 the number of three star hotels (such as those in Pacasmayo) had increased by 120%. Since 1984 the number of people directly employed by hotels and restaurants had increased by 24%. In 1998, 832,635 tourists entered Peru, a number that increased to an estimated 955,584 in 1999 and to 1,009,791 in 2001. The average tourist stayed 14 days in Peru, spending approximately $US100 a day. Thus, the total influx of money to Peru through tourism in 1999 was more than $US1.2 billion.

Tourists came to Peru to enjoy the cultural and natural resources of this country. An estimated 90.9% of tourists visited archaeological sites, 74.6%

visited museums and 66.7% visited churches and colonial mansions. 44.9% of tourists came to walk in the mountains and 32.8% came to buy textiles and other artisanal products. Thus, the Jequetepeque Valley and its surroundings had all the important attributes that drew tourists to Peru.

However, it was clear that most tourists (84%) came to Peru to visit Machu Picchu and the Cuzco area. In a summary table of regions visited including Lima, Cuzco, Arequipa and so on, the North Coast did not even rate its own row on the table (it was included with "other sites"). In 1998 only 6.4% of tourists coming to Peru visited the site of Chan Chan, 2.5% came as far as Huaca Rajada and only 0.9% visited Túcume. In addition to Túcume and the Jequetepeque Valley, the site of Sipán (featured in *National Geographic*) had tremendous potential to draw people to the north.

Nelson felt that the timing of this initiative was very important, for several reasons. First, the past several years of archaeological field research in the Jequetepeque Valley had been quite productive, and Nelson and his colleagues were piecing together a very detailed picture of the prehistory of the Valley. Second, there was an increased focus on tourism as a component of economic development, as indicated by a recent Japanese International Cooperation Agency (JICA) report on the Tourist Corridor from Trujillo to Chiclayo (Exhibit 1). Third, an article had appeared in the August 2000 issue of the journal *Iconos* (co-authored by A. Nelson, C. Nelson, L.J. Castillo and C. Mackey), highlighting the importance of osteoarchaeological research in the Jequetepeque Valley. Finally, another article had appeared in the March 2001 issue of *National Geographic*, documenting the recent finds from Dos Cabezas. *National Geographic* reached an audience of some 11 million readers. The publication of this article was expected to generate huge interest in this area.

Nelson concluded that there was considerable room for growth in archaeologically oriented tourism on the North Coast of Peru. Furthermore, he predicted, this growth *will* happen because of the rapidly growing interest in the region, and because of the establishment of the Northern Tourism Circuit of Peru, of which the Pacasmayo Museum was an integral part.

The international tourism industry of Peru was highly developed. As stated above, tourism was one of the most important contributors to the economy of Peru, but over 80% of tourists restricted their visits to the capital Lima and to the famous cities of Cuzco and Machu Picchu in the southern highlands. Nelson obtained the following tourism data.

- The total numbers of international tourists were:
  1997: 746,599
  1998: 832,635

2001: 1,009,791

- Percentage of total tourists who visited archaeological sites = 90.9%

- Percentages of tourists who visited relevant archaeological sites on the North Coast:

Túcume:	0.9%
Sipán:	2.5%
Chan Chan:	6.4%
Huaca de la Luna:	5.1%

- Percentage of international tourists who visited museums = 75%

- Percentage of international tourists who visited museums in the north = 1%

Nelson estimated that the percentage of international tourists who would visit museums in the north after the Northern Tourism Circuit had been established and marketed was 10%. For planning purposes, however, Nelson felt it would be prudent and conservative to select a number closer to the present situation, i.e. 1% of the 1,000,000 international visitors, or 10,000 visitors per year. Distributed evenly over a 200-day period, this represented 50 visitors per day, which would certainly not overtax the capacity of the museum.

Compared to ticket prices at existing medium size museums in Peru, Nelson felt that US$ 3.00 was reasonable and on the low side. Because one purpose of the museum was to enhance the pride of Peruvians in their cultural heritage, he felt that the price of a ticket should be low enough not to be a deterrent to attendance, and $3.00 appeared to be low enough for that purpose. Therefore, the estimated annual revenue from ticket sales to adult visitors was US$ 30,000.

The population of the Municipality of Pacasmayo was 30,000; the population of the Province of Pacasmayo & Chepen was roughly 160,000 people. Nelson estimated that the number of student visitors would be 2000 per year. At US$ 0.50 per ticket, this would yield $ 1000. Therefore, the estimated annual revenue from ticket sales to students was US$ 1000.

OTHER ATTRACTIONS AND MUSEUMS IN THE AREA

Nelson visited a number of similar museums in northern Peru to see first hand what issues they were facing, and thus to benefit from their experiences in drawing up his business plan. He therefore made the following four visits.

A) El Museo Leymebamba

This outstanding museum and research center (Exhibit 2: on the east side of the Circuit, spelled Leimebamba) had many similarities to the type of institution that Nelson was trying to create in Pacasmayo. It had been established in 1999 in response to a rescue archaeology operation carried out in 1997 at the nearby *Laguna de los Cóndores*. This was a major burial site of the Chachapoya and Inca cultures. After fierce resistance, the Chachapoya were eventually defeated and occupied by the Inca Empire in the 15th century. Many elaborate tombs in the area of *la Laguna de los Cóndores* containing Chachapoya and Inca graves were discovered a few years ago to have been devastated by grave robbers, and a rescue operation was mounted to retrieve as much as possible of the mummies and artifacts from these ransacked sites. (The reader may have seen the documentary on this operation on the Discovery Channel.) The extensive recovered material was moved by horseback to the nearby town of Leymebamba to receive temporary shelter in a house. Then, with financial support from the government of Austria and private donors, the present center was established to preserve, display and study the recovered mummies and artifacts.

B) Kuélap

This forbidding, and highly fortified, Chachapoya site (Exhibit 2: on the east side of the Circuit north of Leimebamba) occupying a five-hectare mountaintop plateau was conquered by the Incas in the early 15th century after a long and drawn out battle. On one side were steep precipices; on the other were massive stone walls with only three very narrow (the width of a single person) steeply ascending entrances. Within the walls were some 400 round stone houses that would have had thatch roofs. The site had been partially cleared—there was a path cut through the underbrush to guide visitors with explanatory signs in Spanish and English. The ruins were still covered with trees, similar to Angkor Wat in Cambodia. Decorative stonework was evident on higher status houses.

There was a small, but good, interpretive center on the site, as well as some food and gift services. Some time previously, the site received 4000 visitors in one year, but the number had dropped off because of an adverse tourism image due to a local disastrous plane crash in the cloudy mountains, strikes and blockages of roads, and renewed activity by the *Sendero Luminoso* terrorists.

C) Chachapoyas

Leymebamba and Kuélap lie within the region of Chachapoyas, in the province of Amazonas in northeastern Peru. The city of Chachapoyas (Exhibit 2: on the east side of the Circuit north of Kuélap) was the main center for enterprises providing the logistics for tourism in the region. There were about half a dozen such companies, usually located on or near the *Plaza de Armas* of the city. Typically, they acted on behalf of larger tourism firms and provided services such as transporting visitors from the airport in Chiclayo into the towns, providing guided tours to Kuélap and other sites, horse trekking into *Laguna de los Cóndores*, encouraging the construction of guest houses, stimulating the work of local artisans (usually women) and the organization of shops to sell rugs, carvings, shawls, jewellery, etc. to tourists.

Nelson met with the owner of Chachapoyas Tours, who explained to him in considerable detail how the local tour companies operate. He was pleasantly surprised to learn that many of these companies also acted as non-governmental or non-profit organizations to help the local communities in a variety of ways.

The major drawback that prevented increased tourist flow into the Chachapoyas area was access. Kuélap was unquestionably a spectacular site, which has been described as "the next Machu Picchu", and would certainly be the central attraction of the Northern Tourism Circuit. However, it was very difficult to get there.

D) Site Museum of Túcume

This successful and attractive institution on the coast was, again, of the type Nelson proposed to create at Pacasmayo. It was located at a major archaeological site, *los Pirámides de Túcume* (Exhibit 2: on the west side of the Circuit just north of Chiclayo), and was principally an interpretive center and museum to accompany the archaeological site. It received some 20,000 visitors (foreigners and nationals combined) each year. Its visitor facilities included, in addition to the interpretive center and museum, a restaurant and other food services, a bookstore and gift shop, and campsites. It charged 7 soles (CDN$ 2.80) admission to adults, either national or international. Importantly, it had general purpose rooms in which researchers could examine the skeletons and artifacts recovered from the site. The majority of the site had been constructed by the Lambayeque culture, but it had also been occupied by the later Chimú and Inca. It spanned the period 1200 AD to the Spanish conquest.

MANAGEMENT

A) Ownership and Operating Authority

There were three major parties to this project: the *Instituto Nacional de Cultura* (INC), the *Casa de la Cultura* (*la Casa*), and the University of Western Ontario (UWO). The INC is the national authority mandated to protect, conserve and promote the national patrimony of Peru. *La Casa* is a legally constituted civil association, registered in October 1965, which exists to promote culture (in all its forms) in Pacasmayo. UWO is a public institution created in 1878 that is dedicated to the advancement of learning through teaching and research and to the discovery and application of knowledge.

The railway station building and the immediately adjacent lands were owned by the Government of Peru through the INC. By means of a *Decreto Supremo* [Supreme Decree], the use of the building had been granted to the *Casa* for an indefinite period of time. Through a *Convenio de Cooperación Interinstitutional* [Inter-institutional Cooperation Agreement] signed on July 16, 2002 the INC, the *Casa* and the University of Western Ontario agreed that the *Casa* had the authority to operate a Museum of Cultural History of the Jequetepeque Valley in the railway station. The Museum would include a Bioarchaeological Research Centre. The *Convenio* had a duration of five years and was renewable. UWO was given executive authority for the Bioarchaeological Research Centre, reporting to the Museum Director. The Museum Director reports to the Board of Directors of the Museum.

B) Board of Directors

The Board of Directors of the Museum was the Board of Directors of the *Casa*. The Chair of the Board of Directors of the Museum was the Chair of the Board of Directors of the *Casa*.

C) Officers

The Chief Executive Officer of the Museum was the Museum Director. The Museum Director reported to the Board and was counseled by an Advisory Committee. Reporting to the Museum Director were:

- the Associate Director (responsible for the day-to-day operation of the Museum) and staff that included security, cleaning and maintenance, marketing and sales, guides and docents and other volunteers. The Associate Director was also responsible for the operation of a gift shop (the gift shop would be an outlet for replicas made locally of pottery found in the valley) and a food services in or adjacent to the Museum; and

- the Director of the Bioarchaeological Research Centre, Dr. Andrew Nelson of UWO.

The five key members of the Management Team, therefore, were:
- Chair of the Board of Directors
- Museum Director & CEO
- Associate Director
- Director of the Bioarchaeological Research Centre (Nelson)
- Chair of the Advisory Committee.

The Museum Director, the Associate Director and the Chair of the Advisory Committee had not yet been chosen by the Board of Directors, but they would have the following characteristics:

- Museum Director: citizen of Peru, demonstrated abilities as administrator, museologist or archaeologist, communicator
- Associate Director: citizen of Peru, demonstrated ability as a museum administrator and curator
- Chair of the Advisory Committee: citizen of Peru, widely respected in the field of Peruvian anthropology, experienced in the operation of museums, well connected with the INC and the scientific community, and an effective communicator (a specific individual had been targeted for this important position, but it was premature to announce his name).

The desired characteristics of the Museum Director and the Associate Director could be different from the ones stated, at the discretion of the Board, but they would be chosen to be complementary to ensure combined expertise in administration, archaeology, museology and communication.

The post of Museum Director did not need to be a full-time position. If fact, there may have been real value in considering someone for the post who was already the director of another museum in Peru and who was capable of taking on both positions, each on a part-time basis. For financial reasons, this could be a very attractive option for both the Pacasmayo Museum and the other museum.

MARKETING PLAN

Nelson decided that marketing should take place at three geographical levels and to three major groups of potential visitors, as follows:

- Local marketing: educational outreach to inform local children about the rich historic and prehistoric record in their area; local festivals and fiestas; and local radio and television

- National marketing: to Peruvian travel agents; through signage on the Panamerican and Cajamarca highways; through collaboration networks with museums in Peru

- International marketing: to international media already interested in Peru; through inclusion in the existing international marketing efforts of the Peruvian government

- Groups of potential visitors: "soft adventure" travelers, the academic market, inclusion in archaeological tours, special interest groups such as surfing/windsurfing networks, steam engine enthusiasts.

FINANCIAL PLAN

There were four budgets:

- capital budget for restoration of the building
- capital budget for the museography installations
- operating budget of the museum
- operating budget of the research center

A) Capital Budget for Restoration of the Building

Nelson worked with the architectural firm CITEmadera to prepare designs and drawings of the restored building and a detailed budget. CITEmadera's estimate was US$ 180,000.

B) Capital Budget for the Museography Installations

Nelson's estimate was US$ 220,000.

C) Operating Budget of the Museum

The operating budget was to be a balanced budget. He estimated the expenses (in summary) to be:

- Salaries & wages   US$ 37,440
- Operating   US$ 18,374

D) Operating Budget of the Research Centre

The operating budget of the research center would be largely separate from the operating budget of the museum, and would be drawn up annually by the Director of the research center in consultation with the members of the Advisory Committee.

Housekeeping costs of the Research Centre such as cleaning, maintenance, security, insurance and utilities would, however, be included in the Operating Budget of the Museum.

The Operating Budget of the Research Centre would be a balanced budget and would be based on the specific funded research activities to be carried out by Peruvian and international researchers who had been accredited by the Advisory Committee and given permission to work in the Centre in that fiscal year by the Director of the Research Centre.

At least at the beginning, it was expected that the Research Centre would operate only in the usual field season of the international researchers, i.e. May – August. The Research Director would be present during most of that time. This would enable the national researchers to work side-by-side with the scientists from other countries during that time.

NELSON'S TASKS

Nelson set out to write a business plan for the museum and the accompanying research center. He could use much of the information in the case above, but he also had to assess the nature of the competition, if any, to his concept, and he had to draw up an operating budget for the museum (budget C above).

» **Exhibit 1: NORTH COAST OF PERU** (Map reprinted courtesy of Don McClelland)

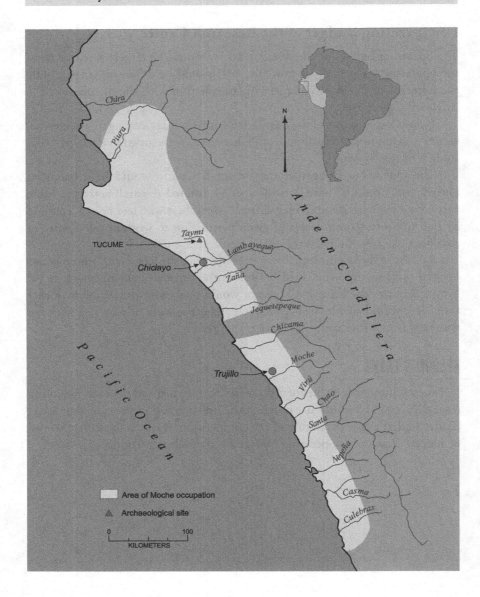

» Exhibit 2: NORTHERN TOURISM CIRCUIT OF PERU

» Exhibit 3: BUSINESS PLANS

For creating and obtaining financing for virtually any type and size of enterprise, a business plan is essential. In addition to the obvious purpose of providing persuasive information to providers of finance (grants, loans or investments), a business plan forces its writer to think through, in relenting detail, all the features of the enterprise.

A typical business plan runs around a dozen pages, and is usually organized under the following headings:

- Executive Summary (one or two pages): highlights of the key information contained in the plan. The type of financing and the amount being sought should be stated first. The Executive Summary should be concise and interesting. It should be written last.

- Background: the source of the concept to create the enterprise, history, location

- Product or Service: what are the features and benefits for the intended purchasers

- Analysis of the Market

- Competition: strengths and weaknesses of your enterprise with respect to the competition. How does your product or service differ from those of the competition? How will you overcome competition?

- Management Team: names, biographies and responsibilities of the key managers

- Marketing Plan: to whom, when, where, how much

- Financial Plan: projections for the next three to five years, including assumptions, balance sheets, income statements, and cash-flow projections

CHAPTER ELEVEN

THE CANADIAN PRIVATE SECTOR

This topic was introduced in Chapter Four. To recap: Canada is a trading nation, and thus the commercial sector has innumerable engagements with:

- industrialized countries
- nations in transition from centrally planned economies to open market economies, and
- developing countries with emerging markets.

An enormous amount of trading activity takes place with countries in all three categories. With respect to *development* activities, however, the activity is with transition economies and developing countries. Much of the work is in the form of contracting and consulting assignments for which funding comes principally from CIDA (both Partnership Branch and bilateral) or from one of the multilateral banks, e.g. the Asian Development Bank, the World Bank, the Inter-American Development Bank. Canadian practitioners range in size all the way from a single individual to very small firms (like that of the authors, International Project and Protocol Services Inc.[215]) to large consulting firms such as Hickling International[216] to giant engineering and construction firms like SNC-Lavalin[217].

» Example: SNC-Lavalin

Founded in 1911, SNC-Lavalin has been active internationally for nearly 40 years, establishing a multicultural network that spans every continent. The

SNC-Lavalin companies have offices across Canada and in 30 other countries around the world and are currently working in some 100 countries.[218]

In an article about SNC-Lavalin and its CEO Jacques Lamarre in the *Globe and Mail* on August 26, 2006[219], *Report on Business* writer Konrad Yakabuski had this to say:

> *"Many of the countries where SNC-Lavalin is active, from Libya and Algeria to Saudi Arabia and India, score dismally on Transparency International's Corruption Perceptions Index, the leading indicator when it comes to public sector ethics. But Mr. Lamarre, without sacrificing his or SNC-Lavalin's integrity, believes it essential to engage developing countries, democratic or not. It is a key step to 'normalizing' internal politics and, in the end, benefits business and citizens alike."*

FUNDING

Chapter Five dealt at length with sources of funding for international development, including the following that are of particular interest to the Canadian private sector.

- Industrial Cooperation Program (CIDA-INC)[220]
- Doing Business with CIDA[221]
- CIDA's Private Sector Directorate[222]
- Export Development Canada
- International Financial Institutions
- Program for Export Market Development (PEMD)

COPING WITH CORRUPTION

There is no end of anecdotes—real or apocryphal—about corruption in international development, and Canadian companies working overseas will need to take a proactive informed position on this issue before getting started.

» Example: Transparency International

In the example earlier in this chapter about SNC-Lavalin, there was mention of Transparency International's Corruption Perceptions Index.

"Transparency International is a global network including more than 90 locally established national chapters and chapters-in-formation. These bodies fight corruption in the national arena in a number of ways. They bring together relevant players from government, civil society, business and the media to promote transparency in elections, in public administration, in procurement and in business. TI's global network of chapters and contacts also use advocacy campaigns to lobby governments to implement anti-corruption reforms."[223]

TI publishes two interesting indices:

- Corruption Perceptions Index: "CPI Score relates to perceptions of the degree of corruption as seen by business people and country analysts, and ranges between 10 (highly clean) and 0 (highly corrupt)." In 2006, the top five in a list of 163 countries were Finland, Iceland, New Zealand, Denmark, Singapore. (Canada ranked 14th.) At the other end of the list (reading from the bottom upwards) were Haiti, Myanmar, Iraq, Guinea, Sudan.

- Bribe Payers Index: "The BPI is a ranking of 30 of the leading exporting countries according to the propensity of firms with headquarters within their borders to bribe when operating abroad." In 2006, the top five (least likely to bribe) were Switzerland, Sweden, Australia, Austria, Canada. At the other end of the list (reading from the bottom upwards) were India, China, Russia, Turkey, Taiwan.

» Example: The World Bank's struggles against corruption

In recent years, the Bank has committed to combat corruption in its operations and internally:

"To reduce the corrosive impact of corruption in a sustainable way, it is important to go beyond the symptoms to tackle the causes of corruption. Since 1996, the World Bank has supported more than 600 anticorruption programs and governance initiatives developed by its member countries."[224]

In this general context a fascinating, but chilling, book is *Confessions of an Economic Hit Man* by John Perkins. Perkins describes his career in the 1970s and 80s working for a large US consulting firm as an "economic hit man". The book begins:

Economic hit men (EHMs) are highly paid professionals who cheat countries around the globe out of trillions of dollars. They funnel money from the World Bank, the U.S. Agency for International Development (USAID), and other foreign "aid" organizations into the coffers of huge corporations and the pockets of a few wealthy families who control the planet's resources. Their tools include fraudulent financial reports, rigged elections, payoffs, extortion, sex, and murder. They play a game as old as empire, but one that has taken on new and terrifying dimensions during this time of globalization. I should know; I was an EHM.[225]

INTERCULTURAL EFFECTIVENESS IN INTERNATIONAL BUSINESS

In Chapter Seventeen, *Preparing Yourself for International Assignments*, we will talk about the Centre for Intercultural Learning[226] (CIL) of the Canadian Foreign Service Institute of the Department of Foreign Affairs and International Trade (DFAIT). CIL notes that performance improvement in intercultural effectiveness is needed both for individuals and for organizations (such as companies and government agencies).

With respect to individuals, one of CIL's programs is the provision of a three-day workshop entitled the *Pre-departure Course in Intercultural Effectiveness* to persons who are about to go overseas on CIDA-funded projects, e.g. many of CIDA's International Interns participate in this program, as well as CESO Volunteer Advisors and people involved in UPCD projects. The characteristics of an "Interculturally Effective Person" are discussed in Chapter Seventeen.

With respect to organizations, in its publication *International Projects: Some Lessons on Avoiding Failure and Maximizing Success*[227], CIL proposes "Ten Keys to Becoming an Internationally Effective Organization":

- Examine and prioritize your motives and strategic objectives. Are they consistent with those of a partner organization so that a cooperative, win-win relationship is likely?

- Select partner organizations that have compatible or complementary competencies, management practices, and organizational cultures.

- Be clear on and ensure agreement with partners on operational goals and performance targets.

- Be realistic in setting objectives and performance targets.

- Have clear and unambiguous governance mechanisms and definitions of the roles and responsibilities of the partner organizations and the middle and senior project managers.

- Consult and build consensus. Seek out the views of local partners and stakeholders in the community and try to integrate the best of the management traditions of the host country as much as is possible, consistent with corporate or project goals.

- Ensure the commitment of senior management at headquarters by having a project champion and providing services to ease the life of expatriates.

- Constantly assess the sociopolitical and economic environment of the project, weighing its feasibility in the first place, making ongoing adjustments during implementation, and having programs to consult with and influence local and international stakeholders and build community support.

- Recognize the importance culture will have on project management, and select and train personnel to be culturally sensitive and effective collaborators with people of another culture.

- Trust your partners until proven wrong.

INTELLECTUAL PROPERTY[228]

When Canadian companies or Canadian universities are working with partners in other countries, one possible area of concern is intellectual property (IP)–who owns the IP, how is IP to be shared among the partners (if at all), what are the international protocols regarding IP, how can IP be protected and, if disagreements arise, how are disputes to be resolved. This is a potentially serious issue because: (a) allegations abound that not all countries have the same ethical or commercial standards with regard to respect for IP; (b) there is often a considerable amount of money involved; and (c) the laws and legal precedents vary from one jurisdiction to another. There is also the presumption that protection through patents or other means is intended to provide a permanent level of support.

Intellectual property consists of products of the creative processes. They are expressions of thought in the form of, for example, musical compositions, novel devices and mechanisms, industrial designs, works of art, publications, trade secrets (e.g. the Coca-Cola recipe), institutional "know-how", and software algorithms. (The "thought" itself is not protectable by statute).

Means of protecting IP include statutory protection through patents, copyrights, trademarks and industrial designs. Patents (usually on products, processes, novel devices and mechanisms) make a public disclosure of the invention so that the patent holder can seek recourse in appropriate courts if anyone else uses that technology without permission (i.e. the concept of "infringement"), within the lifetime of the patent and within the geographic area of applicability of the patent. Copyrights generally apply to published books and articles, artistic works, musical compositions and more recently, software algorithms. Trademarks pertain to marks, logos and expressions, for example, the "Golden Arches" of McDonalds or the multi-colored, waving flag of Microsoft.

Countries that take the protection of IP seriously are members of relevant international organizations, e.g. the World Intellectual Property Organization (WIPO), and are signatories to international agreements and protocols concerning IP. The Berne Convention applies to copyrights, so that copyright protection for an author is substantially the same in all signatory countries, as there are differing time frames for such protection. As an example, the United States provides for protection for 70 years following death (the "Sonny Bono" amendment) whereas most countries extend for only an additional 50 years. The Patent Cooperation Treaty (PCT) provides a framework for choosing the geographical scope of a patent, i.e. the countries in which a patent holder can seek recourse if the IP in a patent is being used without a licensing agreement being in place, provided such countries have been selected as part of the election by the patent holder at the point of the definitive 'national phase'. (Otherwise, if the patent is not statutorily protected, any infringement as alleged would likely be fought as a tort action, i.e. a nuisance, or as an infringement action upon the products being imported into a protected country as "grey goods".) Therefore, it is prudent that patent protection be obtained in all countries where potential markets exist or where manufacturing of the product might occur.

Some scenarios concerning IP that could conceivably occur in international cooperation activities include the following:

- Researchers in a Canadian university collaborate with counterparts in another country, and they jointly create new knowledge.

- Canadian holders of IP are willing to licence their technology to entrepreneurs in another country who wish to market products based on that technology in their country or other geographic region.

- Textbooks published in North America have a potential market in another country.

With reference to the first scenario, it would be common for the two sides to sign a confidentiality agreement (or memorandum of understanding) at the beginning of their discussions. This would apply to all knowledge held by the parties that has not already been made public (e.g. in patents and scientific publications)—what is already possessed by each side remains the property (i.e. proprietary information) of that side. It then goes on to deal with the future fruits of that collaboration, which could be held jointly by the partners or in some other manner as agreed upon. In the majority of cases of collaboration between universities, however, the driving force is the excitement of creating and disseminating new knowledge—making money from dissemination of that knowledge is oftentimes a secondary consideration.

With respect to the second scenario, a comprehensive contract would be drawn up that would include a confidentiality agreement as discussed in the paragraph above, as well as the details of how the second party would use the IP possessed by the first party. The risk here for the Canadian partner is that the relationship is contract-driven rather than being statutorily protected. Whose law governs? How well does the court system in the partner country function in regard to IP? Is corruption a potential problem? Could "reverse engineering" or a "work-around" take place, in which the foreign partner explores the IP and modifies it sufficiently so that a revised product doesn't infringe the patent? Can the licensee be prohibited from challenging the validity of the patent as issued and licensed? The agreement will likely cover these kinds of issues, through the creation of various strategies to ensure payment or recovery of the anticipated consideration. If the partner agrees to make payments, e.g. of royalties under a licencing agreement, how can this be enforced at a distance of several thousand miles? Clearly, a level of trust has to exist to make the contract perform satisfactorily to both sides.

In addition to commercial business risks, there are obvious cultural risks, especially in the use of language—nuances, traditions, courtesies, lack of corresponding words in the two languages. Which party is authorized to translate? Which language version takes precedence?

With respect to the third scenario above, either the author or the publisher will hold the copyright on the book (or on a published article) and will have protection as afforded by those countries that are signatories to the Berne Convention.

A CONVERSATION WITH HANK VANDER LAAN OF TROJAN TECHNOLOGIES

Hank Vander Laan is the founder, former CEO, former Chair of the Board, and now Senior Advisor to Trojan Technologies Inc. Headquartered in London, Ontario, the company also has offices in the UK, Germany, Netherlands, Spain, and the US. The company, beginning in 1976, recognized the benefits of ultraviolet (UV) light as a safer, more environmentally friendly alternative to chemical water treatment. Trojan developed UV systems for municipal wastewater and drinking water treatment, and then expanded into environmental contaminant treatment, industrial/commercial/pharmaceutical applications, and consumer water purification systems. Trojan has supplied more than 4000 municipal UV disinfection facilities operating in over 50 countries. Many of these applications are located in developing countries.

Now 70 years old, Hank Vander Laan looks back on what he has come to understand about the process of international development cooperation, especially water resources and water quality. Mr. Vander Laan spoke with Frederick Keenan on Wednesday, February 20th, 2008.

FK: **Trojan Technologies has, over the last three decades, created some very fine equipment and systems for improving the cleanliness of water. Would it not be beneficial for developing countries simply to obtain and to use the technological solutions that are working well in North America and in Europe?**

HVL: The solutions are not obvious. In the evolution of our thinking here at Trojan about working in less developed countries, for example in Kenya, we have come to the point where we do not go in there with some triumphalistic ideas and think, "Well, we have all the answers. All you need to do is throw a little bit of technology at it." It just doesn't work. And so we need to be more thoughtful about it than that.

I think that has certainly been our experience from having worked in 40-some countries for the past 25 years or so. We always found that even in the developed nations you can't necessarily use the same formula for Europe that you do for Asia as you do for South America or that you do in other places. And we always learned, sometimes by making a lot of mistakes, that we needed to go back and rethink our strategies in those markets too.

We found, for example, that in Japan you need to be more sensitive about building relationships than you do in North America. If you work in California, you need to be highly sensitive to their absolute demand for the highest environmental standards that you don't find anywhere else. And if you go to places in South America there is a totally different set of rules there again, too. So it's complex but that's what makes business a challenge. Not only a challenge, it makes it a lot of fun.

But it requires, I think on the whole, a predisposition to learn, to go in and to realize that you only have a very small piece of the puzzle when you walk in, and the piece that you have might not necessarily fit with its current form into that puzzle. It requires you to size up a more holistic view of the challenges that you're faced with. And then determine-and this typically takes place through a lot of interaction at the local level-the economic realities in those countries, the economic realities of the institutions that you're trying to serve, the legislative framework that you're working in, the priorities that regulatory agencies might have and, if the priority is in another direction because there's a greater need, you might find that in the short term there is no market for what you're trying to do with your products. And therefore you need to say to yourself, "How can I participate in building a role for us going forward that indeed is sustainable?" I've seen too many people right away saying, "Well we have the solution. We are convinced it's going to fit. Let's open an office staff and build all kinds of overhead" and find two years later they still haven't solved anything and it's all because they haven't been sensitive to the fact that their piece of the puzzle didn't fit, and they had not figured out that there was a huge barrier to that market that was built into their technology or into their approach.

FK: **How do you educate a person to be sensitive to this way of thinking, to realize that what they had was just one piece of the needs which may or may not even be wanted or can be adapted to a need? How would a Canadian engineer prepare herself or himself to think in this way? What sort of education would a person need to think this way?**

HVL: There are probably several answers to that question but let me, from my own experience, sort of share what works most of the time, not all of the time, for me personally and for us corporately. First of all, you had better be knowledgeable about the cultures and about the economics of that country. You had better, if you're working in a field like ours that is highly regulated, be beware of the legislation and the dynamics of the changes in legislation on a going-forward basis.

The financial capacity of those countries, the priorities that they have in those countries, and all of that. You need to do your homework, in other words. That's before you even get on a plane to go and visit. Some of the things that work well for me (but not always) are, for example, that Canada has trade commissions throughout the world. I tapped into that network a lot and I found some of them really well on top of things and others not so well on top. So you've got to be able to sort out which ones are going to help you and which ones won't be able to help you, in fact, could potentially mislead you because they're not well informed either. So it's like the blind leading the blind. So that can be very dangerous. That's why it's important for you to become knowledgeable about the local situation.

And then, in our case, to visit and discuss with people in the water treatment business, to spend time with the regulatory people-quite often in less developed countries a lot of the expertise lies within academic institutions-to make good connections at the local universities and national universities, to visit with the various ministries that are charged with the responsibility of providing quality water, to talk to the people that are in the business of selling water, people that are in the business of delivering water such as a local water company or a municipality, or dealing with some of the manufacturers in the food and beverage industry who are really concerned about the quality of the water. And to talk to some of the people who supply technology for water treatment. And to develop a well integrated holistic picture. Certainly you want to be aware of the economics, be culturally aware of what's of high priority. You need to become aware of the differences in infrastructure because infrastructure, especially in developing nations, is not anywhere near the same as what we have in the western world. So what works here, most of the time, won't work there.

So don't get hung up about trying to sell your standard solution because the standard solution that fits here in all likelihood won't fit there and that means you need to think about how to adapt your technology so you can fit it into the puzzle there in a sustainable, affordable way.

FK: **With respect to the supply of clean water in African communities, can a common approach be applied to all situations? If someone says to you, "Aren't all poor African countries more or less the same? Don't they have the same kinds of problems in regard to water resources and water quality?" What would you say to them?**

HVL: Yeah. That's not true at all. For example, if you go to places like Nairobi and most African countries you find that an infrastructure was put in place during the colonial years to serve the primarily white colonial population. And they built infrastructures like the Europeans did. And you go to Nairobi and you see a water treatment plant that was state of the art in the 1930s, and provided quality water that was safe to drink for about 350,000 people. Came independence, all of the African people were allowed to move into the city and the city exploded from 350,000 in the 1960s to 3½ million today. The infrastructure could not expand with that kind of population, that explosion, and there were not the resources even to do it if you wanted to do it. But people needed water, so what do you do? You know, you tap into a water line that's going by your street somewhere. And so you go to Nairobi or any city in Africa, all these systems are severely compromised to the degree that the water that was delivered and used to be safe is no longer safe. And so these centralized water systems in Africa just don't work anymore. It's just not a viable option. So you need to come up with a totally different solution than what they used to give. They used to give to the privileged white population a typical western world solution that we are all familiar with, but it's no longer the case in the year 2008.

FK: **If you don't have a centralized system, what's the alternative?**

HVL: The alternative, we're still in the process of figuring that out. We've been trying to figure this out for the past three years and we think we're coming to a somewhat reasonable conclusion as to what that might look like. It certainly would be decentralized as opposed to centralized, but you also need to realize that there's probably within the decentralized model at least half a dozen, if not a dozen, submodels. For example, there are those who are still connected to the main water system or they receive compromised quality of water. So that would be one market-primarily the higher income level people, whether they're black or white.

Then you have other markets that are enclaves within the city-that's another group. Then you have people who moved into the *kiberas* (the slums) of Africa, who buy their water from tankers being pulled by tractors. And you have absolutely no idea what the quality of that water is. And you have kiosks where enterprising people in the slums sell water from a line they tapped into somewhere. Nobody really knows where its origins are, but they deliver water and you can buy your water in gerrycans and pay for it. And that's another market. And it goes on and on. So there's a huge diversity of the way water is delivered.

FK: **Is it up to the more industrialized nations to work out what the solutions are or should the problem and the solutions be owned by the people who live in the country?**

HVL: Yeah, Fred, that's an absolutely key question. As I mentioned to you before, I read this little book that Dr. George Kinote wrote called *Hope for Africa*. What really fascinated me about his book is that he said, "We Africans need to own the problem first of all. If we don't want to own it nobody will solve it, throw billions and billions at it and we don't buy into the fact that we have a problem so we're not going to make it work. We'll find places to put that money if you give it to us. We have, and we will, but it creates a host of other problems and the money's not well spent.

"Secondly, once we own the problem, it will motivate us to design our own solution that is appropriate to our situation because we understand our problems and we can design the appropriate solutions.

"And thirdly," George Kinote wrote, "we want to execute the solution. Once we have the strategy in place and the plans, because of our limited resources, we would go to potential partners to help us execute those plans, for financing, perhaps for certain technical expertise, for marketing expertise and something that we could eventually make indigenous to our own economy. But during these initial periods we would certainly ask for those kinds of resources. But now we could show people a plan, we could demonstrate that we own the problem.

"Also, we could show our capabilities in designing a solution. And if you buy into that, you can then request from us, and you must demand from us transparency. If there's transparency, then any resources that are given to those solutions will help us, and will help the partner to hold us accountable, and by holding us accountable, it will also, at the same time, hopefully, get us out of the vicious circle of corruption and abuse of those resources."

FK: Is there a role for westerners in cooperating with the nationals of the country in developing solutions and implementing them? You talked about partners for them, marketing and technology and some other areas-are we talking about African partners or western partners or both?

HVL: There's a lot of capital in Africa. When you go to the cities there you see all kinds of projects that certainly match or exceed what we do in Toronto or in Montreal or in London, Ontario. You've seen those projects there and a lot of that is financed locally. And so there are significant resources there and those would be the first to tap into.

There's a role, obviously, for westerners. We live in a global world, and Africa certainly and other underdeveloped nations are part of that, but I do think we need to look at these issues not as projects. You know, projects have a way of getting a life of their own and there's a lot of vested interest to keep projects going because, you know, you solve one problem then your job is done but you need to find another project. So you don't want to have an integrated solution as a consultant. As a consultant you like to be able to repeat over and over again the same project because that's good for your consulting business. So projects are extremely inefficient. Unless they're one of a kind. If they're one of a kind, then you can do a project but you don't want to, for example, re-engineer or redesign or develop a business plan for each repetitive model. So it needs to become integral to the local economy and it needs to be indigenized and it needs to become a way of life, really. A natural evolution takes place where of course you pick up on what you've learned and you can now apply it to the next and to the next and to the next. And I think there's a role for westerners, but the primary role is for the Africans themselves.

FK: How does Trojan work in this framework? Do you contact them and ask to join the conversation with them, or do they contact you?

HVL: Well, delightfully, some of both is happening. But don't forget there's a bad history probably somewhat equivalent to what we have even in Canada, their own First Nations people, all right? And so you find 200 years later we have not been able to solve our own local issues, and so how well equipped are we then to help others if we can't even do it in our own back yard? You know, we find a lot of it is all about governance and policy and a governance model that's all embracing and has a strong local ownership. And not only an ownership but it has a significant degree of local leadership. And you always have to ask yourself if local leadership isn't present, why is that? Is that because people have not bought into the solutions that you think might be appropriate? Have you not engaged people? And giving more of the same experience as they experienced during the colonial periods. So there's a real opportunity, if you wish to take advantage of that opportunity, to become very paternalistic and self-serving and to feel good at nights because you provided clean water to a thousand people. Makes you feel good but if it's a project, it will stop there and the other 900 million people won't benefit from your project because it does not have an integrated solution that is owned by those whom you're trying to serve.

So you have to decide. If you think it's about you, I suggest you won't succeed, and you're probably better off to stay home.

FK: I'd like to come back to NGOs. For example, during the time of the terrible drought and famine in Ethiopia, a

deluge of NGOs came in and, by and large, they did a lot of good work. But a lot of them didn't go home afterwards. They became a power onto themselves and eventually the Ethiopian government threw them out. The government referred to them as "cowboys" who would ride around in their white Toyota Landcruisers. They wouldn't let the government know what they were doing and they certainly wouldn't give away any control. The role of NGOs became very distorted and corrupted in that case. What are your views on the role of NGOs in doing good internationally?

HVL: It's always dangerous to overgeneralize here but let me give you kind of my 30,000 foot take on it. Having been on the board of an NGO, I have some experience with what works well, and what does not work well. One of the problems that I see, is that NGOs have become a business where people have a vested interest, for those NGOs are not well governed in this—some NGOs are a person with a briefcase and a laptop who have made Africa, in this instance, their emotional playground. And now with modern communications somebody comes in with a digital camera and sends—at every corner you can take a heartbreaking picture, on every street corner or in a local slum, a heartbreaking picture of children that are in great need and send it back home and "send me $4,000 and I will solve their problem." And that's almost on an instantaneous basis. I've seen personally really, really great distortions and manipulation by individuals within NGOs. So what do you need to look for within NGOs? Look at their governance model, look at their transparency, look at their financial reports, look at their annual reports, look at what their motivation really is, and look at their track record. Look for excellence like you do in anything else. Look for excellence in this organization, the integrity of the organization. There are NGOs that I greatly admire, but NGOs will not develop nations. I'm totally convinced of that. NGOs can make a contribution especially in times of crisis. It's a little bit like somebody drowning in your pool, you're going to throw them a lifeline. There's that role. And NGOs can do that very well. You see that currently maybe in Darfur and places like that where, hopefully, there's a short-term need and you're there to help. And I think that's an excellent role. Long-term development-most NGOs probably are not good at that and also not staffed with people who have that insight. Some NGOs really have built a record. You know, the board that I was on- that NGO has been around for 40-50 years and it indigenizes and it teaches people how to fish and, once people know how to do that, they teach them how to teach others, and they're out of there and going on to the next. So they don't make it a project. They indigenize their expertise and all the leaders, then, tend to be local leaders.

But even there, the danger still is that of becoming self-serving, as it is in business. You want to stay on—you don't want to work yourself out of a job, and that's dangerous, right? If you work yourself out of a job, then, "What am I going to do next?" So a lot of NGOs create this dependency, and dependency is fatal. It's like taking your child and when they're 20 years old you still have to hold them by the hand because you can't trust them how to cross the street. You haven't done a very good job as a parent and I think the same holds true for NGOs. So look for the NGOs that really have it together. And I'm afraid most NGOs do not–they tend to be somewhat self-serving. People with big hearts. I've seen so many people with big hearts doing all the wrong things and it's hard to say that to them. I have a good example of that. Some people at our local church found out I was going to Nairobi. Somebody knew of a school there and persuaded me—I really didn't want to do this-take along running shoes for the kids. And I'd been in Nairobi before and running shoes are readily available, more available than they are here and they have more choices there than I could find locally. Anyway, they got high school kids to give away their good running shoes and I took them all with me in a suitcase. And the funny part was when I drove up to the school, there's a guy standing out front of the school and he had as many running shoes hanging around his neck and arms than I had in my suitcase. And I ended up paying extra for luggage that the airline charged me. I could have bought shoes locally, cheaper than bringing them. I didn't have the heart to say no to the young lady who had worked there as a nurse, you know, but here was, to me, another classic example that I was doing totally the wrong thing.

FK: Is there a role for universities in longer term development in the area of capacity building and training of trainers?

HVL: Yes, absolutely there has to be a role, but the same role I think as holds true for the NGOs and even for private sector businesses and that is you really need to ask yourself what is the motivation first of all for doing this. So you need to ask yourself some pretty fundamental questions as to why you're doing this. And I think that will bring up some pretty interesting discussions just before you even go there.

I think absolutely there is a role. Secondly, what's the role of the universities and the other academic institutions? It is to bring to the table, I think, necessary solutions, the processes that help the local institutions to come to the point where they can become more self-sufficient.

And the danger is to go in, and leapfrog over ideas that they have locally without making the connection back to where they're at. It's a little bit like leapfrogging with ideas that don't have a context within the local scene. And I think that can be extremely disruptive and not helpful. So you have to, I think, have a very good understanding and appreciation for where the local academic institutions are at, first of all, and then in consultation with them try to bring to it ideas and processes and programs that can within a relatively short period of time take local ownership and grow it organically, locally.

FK: **Does the provision of technology from a western country undermine the technological ability of the country you're working with?**

HVL: It can but not necessarily so. I'll give you a little example, a little story. When I was in Nairobi-I was in Kenya not too long ago—Alex, a national, was my driver. He kind of drove me around because I found it quite chaotic trying to find my way around and Alex drove me around for a week, my wife and I. Alex had a cell phone. I said to him, "That's pretty interesting." My wife said, "I don't have a cell phone. Hank has one but I don't." And Alex said, "Well this one happens to be for the company that I drive for but my brothers and I bought one for our parents who live up country, about a day's travel by bus away from here. My dad has a little farm and so the three boys don't get up country very often so with our parents becoming older, we like to keep in touch. And the three of us bought them a cell phone and we have a cell phone here between the three of us and we taught them how to text message, and we send messages back and forth. And once in a while we ship them a SIM card so they can keep in touch. And between the three of us we can afford it." I said, "Alex, how much money do you earn—what's your income?" He says, "Well on a good day I might earn $5. And not so good days I might earn only $1." And I said, "You can afford a cell phone?" He said, "I couldn't by myself. I have a daughter who's in a special school. She has some certain learning disabilities and I'm paying to put her through a school for that purpose." So he said, "It's pretty tough" and "Some days I drink from the water that I shouldn't be drinking from, I become ill. And if I have diarrhea, I can't drive the taxi or my van and so I have no income for that day or for the next two days." And so that's the kind of typical circumstances that the average person lives in.

But he said, coming back to the cell phone for a moment, said, "You know, my dad always used to sell his crops from his little farm to a local entrepreneur who would come around and say "I'll pay you so many shillings for the sorghum and so much for your sweet potatoes" and my dad just sold it to him for that price. But now he text messages "My crop is ready. What do sorghum and sweet potatoes sell for in Nairobi?" And now the guy comes around to buy and says, "I'll buy the sorghum and the sweet potatoes for so many shillings a basket." And my dad says, "Oh, no you don't. I just got this message from my son. He says, 'It sells for that much.' I want this much." He more than doubled their income.

Now here's a great example of leapfrogging technology, as I call it. It's making a positive economic impact. The negative side is, also Alex would tell me that—which can be very detrimental— is that people are abusing women by giving them a cell phone and using them when they need them just by contacting them by cell phone. They give them a cell phone and give those girls a cell phone and when they need them for certain purposes, they will call those girls and have access to them at any time. And so, you know, it's like nuclear power. You can use it for creating energy or for creating destruction.

CHAPTER TWELVE

ENGINEERING AND INTERNATIONAL DEVELOPMENT

There are a good many different ways in which Canadian engineers** are involved in international development, including their roles...

- as volunteers

- as research partners

- as educators and trainers

- as consultants

- as contractors

- as entrepreneurs

- as Canadian government representatives

- as officials of multilateral organizations

- in emergency aid and mitigation of loss

- in non-engineering careers.

ENGINEERS AS VOLUNTEERS

Here are three examples concerning organizations where the engineering skills of volunteers are put to good use in international development. They are arranged according to increasing age of the volunteers: the first organization (EWB) has volunteers who, typically, are engineering students and recent

---

** Because one of the authors of this book (Keenan) is an engineer, engineering has been singled out in this chapter, from amongst other professions, for its contributions to international development. In future editions of this book, perhaps there will be similar chapters about other worthy professions.

graduates in their mid to late 20s, the second one attracts volunteers of all ages—a recent Habitat for Humanity project in Nicaragua had a team whose ages varied from 17 to 72, and the third one (CESO) utilizes volunteers most of whom are retired.

» Example: Engineers Without Borders

There are organizations in several countries that have the name Engineers Without Borders (e.g. Australia, Belgium, Canada, Denmark, Germany, India, Italy, Spain, Sweden, UK, USA). Each is a non-governmental organization involved in international development work. They are not formally affiliated with each other, although some of them have together created an international network to unite their actions.[229]

Engineers Without Borders Canada was formed in 2000: "Co-founders Parker Mitchell and George Roter were interested in tapping into the Canadian engineering profession-a group they believed to be passionate about improving the state of the world-to contribute to the Millennium Development Goals' pledge to halve world poverty by 2015…Engineering students, professionals and firms quickly became involved…In 2001 we sent the first EWB volunteer overseas and held the first National Conference…

"[There are now] 15 full time staff members, over 20,000 members, countless volunteers in Canada, more than 250 volunteers who have worked overseas, an Advisory Board of leading experts in their fields, a dedicated Board of Directors, and numerous partnerships with organisations overseas… In the coming years we will continue to strive to make Canada a model global citizen and to increase access to appropriate technologies in developing communities."[230]

Twenty-six Canadian engineering schools have local chapters of Engineers Without Borders Canada. EWB Canada volunteer Luke Brown wrote an article for The London Free Press of Saturday, March 25, 2006 that began:

"Eight months after graduating from the engineering faculty at the University of Western Ontario, I found myself leaving a country beset by rashes of criminal violence on its city streets, where charges of corruption were running to the highest levels of government, and worries about the outbreaks of killer diseases were weighing on the minds of many.

"That country was Canada. However, I was leaving for another continent—for Africa.

"I've been in Ghana, West Africa, for more than a month now, having been sent by the Canadian organization, Engineers Without Borders, to work on a water and sanitation project. Although I've barely

begun to scratch the surface in terms of understanding the challenges and opportunities this country faces, I have learned a great deal in my first month in Ghana.

"Perhaps the greatest lesson learned thus far is the destructive and misleading power of generalizations…"

» Example: Habitat for Humanity International

"Habitat for Humanity International is a nonprofit, ecumenical Christian housing ministry. HFHI seeks to eliminate poverty housing and homelessness from the world, and to make decent shelter a matter of conscience and action. Habitat invites people of all backgrounds, races and religions to build houses together in partnership with families in need.

"Habitat has built more than 225,000 houses around the world, providing more than 1 million people in more than 3,000 communities with safe, decent, affordable shelter. HFHI was founded in 1976.

"Through volunteer labor and donations of money and materials, Habitat builds and rehabilitates simple, decent houses with the help of the homeowner (partner) families. Habitat houses are sold to partner families at no profit and financed with affordable loans. The homeowners' monthly mortgage payments are used to build still more Habitat houses.

"Habitat is not a giveaway program. In addition to a down payment and the monthly mortgage payments, homeowners invest hundreds of hours of their own labor—sweat equity—into building their Habitat house and the houses of others…Habitat houses are affordable for low-income families because there is no profit included in the sale price. Mortgage length varies from seven to 30 years…"[231]

Other organizations through which engineers can provide voluntary services include the Canadian Executive Service Organization (CESO) (see the case *CESO & Gordon Cummings* in Chapter Nine) and several others listed in the section *Nongovernmental Organizations and Foundations* in Chapter Four.

ENGINEERS AS RESEARCH PARTNERS

Chapter Three, *Successful Development Projects: What Works and What Doesn't*, provides a comprehensive discussion of the results that are normally sought, and the approaches and methodologies that are usefully employed, in projects between research partners. Two examples in that chapter were of engineering projects—biomedical engineering and environmental engineering—*Cuba & biomedical engineering* and *Mongolia & mining*.

ENGINEERS AS EDUCATORS AND TRAINERS

Providing education and training to students from (and in) developing countries is a process by which engineers have contributed to international development over several decades. One method is by welcoming visa students, exchange students and graduate scholarship students to our classrooms and laboratories. Another method is by presenting lectures and workshops overseas as a visiting academic or as a collaboration project participant.

» Example: Philippines & Holy Angel University

Holy Angel University (HAU) is a 70-year-old well-respected private university that wants to make the transition from a teaching institution to one that also does research. HAU, which is located in Angeles City in the northern island of Luzon in the Philippines, approached the Canadian Executive Service Organization (CESO) in 2003 and asked for a Volunteer Advisor to teach research methodologies and to help develop a strategic plan that would lead to the creation of a research culture at HAU within the next five years.

CESO's VA accomplished these two objectives. With respect to the request to teach research methodologies, he responded in part by presenting workshops on Results-based Management to individuals who are planning to become researchers and research administrators at HAU. They wanted to learn RBM so that they could speak the same proposal language as prospective funding agencies for their research initiatives.

With respect to the request to help develop a strategic plan that would lead to the creation of a research culture at HAU within the next five years, the VA accomplished this by working with administrators and faculty members at HAU to first identify all the strengths and advantages that HAU has in attempting to become a research institution, and then identified all the issues and obstacles that will have to be dealt with. Finally, a package of proposals was assembled that should lead to the establishment of a research culture at HAU within the next five years, identifying the strategic decisions that will have to be taken by the Board of Trustees and President. These included:

- proactive support to faculty members to obtain doctorates (this is the main strategy)

- de-loading the teaching requirements for those committing to a research career
- providing seed money to get programs and projects started
- an announced commitment from the Administration to support research
- stronger assistance from the Administration in identifying sources of research funding and in preparing proposals to obtain financing
- enhanced library resources
- stronger graduate programs
- encouragement of academic publishing
- identification and utilization of mentors
- strengthened linkages with the private sector, with the Asian Development Bank, and with universities in other countries.

Things are changing, however. Even with the best will in the world, a teacher from a northern industrialized country will never *fully* understand the developing country environment within which she or he is teaching—the teacher from the north can not totally understand the opportunities, the motivations, the challenges and the impediments, for utilizing the information that is being transmitted.

As we all try to understand better what works in international development, Canadians are increasingly realizing that the most effective thing we can do is to make our information and experience available to our southern partners (rather than telling them what to do and what they need to know), and then let them get on with making the most appropriate use of it in their particular social-economic-educational-technical-cultural-religious-traditional environment.

In time, south-to-south sharing of relevant information may beneficially replace traditional north-to-south teaching.

ENGINEERS AS CONSULTANTS

(See the case *Peru & Wood Construction* in Chapter Thirteen.)

ENGINEERS AS CONTRACTORS

In Chapter Four, opportunities for Canadian consultants and contractors in CIDA-funded projects were described and funding sources were discussed both at CIDA and with the International Funding Institutions, such as the Asian Development Bank[232]. Remember to make your initial contact with the Canadian Executive Director[233] at the Bank you are approaching.

ENGINEERS AS ENTREPRENEURS

A good source of support for entrepreneurial ventures is the Industrial Cooperation Program (CIDA-INC) described in Chapter Four. This is probably a good place to remind the reader of the discussion of appropriate technology that appeared in Chapter Three because those concepts also apply to international entrepreneurial initiatives.

ENGINEERS AS CANADIAN GOVERNMENT REPRESENTATIVES

Engineers are well represented in the ranks of Canadian government officials who are working in international development, both overseas and at home. These professionals include staff members of embassies, high commissions, consulates and trade missions abroad. They also include staff of agencies such as the Canadian International Development Agency (CIDA). Descriptions of these organizations are in Chapters Four and Five of this book.

ENGINEERS AS OFFICIALS OF MULTILATERAL ORGANIZATIONS

Multilateral organizations were described in Chapter Five. Canada is a founding member of most of the multilateral institutions and continues to play an important role on their governing boards. About 40 percent of Canada's Official Development Assistance is channeled through multilateral institutions, which amounts to roughly 4 percent of their funding.

ENGINEERS IN EMERGENCY AID AND MITIGATION OF LOSS

Seven types of international assistance are:

- emergency aid
- post-disaster reconstruction
- development cooperation
- mitigation of human and financial loss

- finance
- trade liberalization
- debt relief

This book deals almost entirely with the third type, development cooperation, but engineers also make contributions in other areas of international assistance:

» Example: Mitigation of human and financial losses

The Boundary Layer Wind Tunnel Laboratory (BLWTL)[234] in the Faculty of Engineering at the University of Western Ontario is one of the leading organizations in the world in the area of wind engineering. By means of model studies and analytical techniques, engineers at the BLWTL determine the wind forces that should be considered in the design of very tall buildings (e.g. the CN Tower) and long span bridges. A large proportion of the world's tallest and longest structures have been studied at the BLWTL, which has always welcomed partners and students from developing countries. In helping structural designers to determine the correct wind forces to use in their designs, the BLWTL reduces the risk of failure of those structures and thus mitigates the consequent human and economic losses.

UWO's role in loss mitigation was expanded with the establishment of the Institute for Catastrophic Loss Reduction (ICLR)[235] in partnership with the Insurance Bureau of Canada. ICLR's objective is to reduce the likelihood of failures of civil engineering works caused by extreme natural events, e.g. by studying how to build houses with increased resistance to extreme wind events[236].

» Example: RedR Canada[237]

RedR (Registered Engineers for Disaster Relief) is an international federation of regional offices that cooperate to relieve suffering caused by natural and manmade disasters through selecting, training and providing competent and efficient personnel to humanitarian aid agencies world-wide.

The founding members of RedR Canada are the Association of Consulting Engineers of Canada (ACEC), the Canadian Council of Professional Engineers (now known as Engineers Canada), the Canadian Academy of Engineering, and the Engineering Institute of Canada (EIC).

RedR Canada's partners, sponsors and contributors include CIDA, Engineers Without Borders (EWB), several Canadian professional engineers, consulting engineering firms, and national and provincial engineering associations.

RedR Canada offers a range of training programs to its members, the public, and directly to agencies in North America for staff training. RedR Canada members have worked in Afghanistan, Bolivia, Congo and Guinea.

ENGINEERS IN NON-ENGINEERING CAREERS

It has often been said that an engineering education is good for more than just a career in engineering. What is meant is that the abilities to process information, to make decisions, to find solutions to challenges, to implement, and to evaluate, are useful attributes in a wide range of endeavors.

Interestingly, this list of engineering attributes is virtually identical to the case method process described in this book:

- to accumulate and organize available information,
- to establish various potential alternative courses of action,
- to set criteria for evaluating the various alternatives,
- to make the decision,
- to formulate plans for implementing the decision reached,
- to convincingly defend the decision and the implementation plans to peers, and
- to monitor and evaluate the implementation.

CHAPTER THIRTEEN

RESEARCH IN INTERNATIONAL DEVELOPMENT

Information on research actors and examples of research activities contributing to development have appeared previously in various locations throughout the book, including:

- Building capacity, including research capacity (Chapter Three)
- Example: Cuba & biomedical engineering (Chapter Three)
- Example: Mongolia & mining (Chapter Three)
- Example: Andean Pact countries & building products (Chapter Three)
- International Development Research Centre (Chapter Four)
- Example: Philippines & Holy Angel University (Chapter Twelve)

The following case derives directly from the ideas of the late former Canadian Prime Minister Lester Pearson. It supports the desire of partners in developing countries to build their own research and development capacity in order to take advantage of a development opportunity.

CASE: PERU & WOOD CONSTRUCTION

In July 1975 Steve Kingston, a civil/structural engineering graduate of the University of Toronto, was hired by an international development agency of the Government of Canada to assist a group of Peruvian engineers and architects who were starting up a project co-funded by Canada. The purpose of the project was to utilize the vast forest resources of Peru to create a plentiful

229

sustainable supply of forest products as safe, durable and economical building materials in the country. The Canadian contribution was C$ 5 million over six years.

Kingston would be acting as a resource person, not as a manager, but he had to decide which issues, information and experiences he should bring to the attention of his Peruvian partners. First of all, Kingston knew that there is often a temptation in an international forest utilization project to promote wood for all construction situations in the country (the "Wood is Good" syndrome), regardless of whether the use of wood products is really appropriate in all of those applications. In spite of the abundance of forest resources in Peru, Kingston suspected that manufactured wood products (consisting only of sawn lumber, sawn timbers, and plywood, at that time) might not be the right building materials for all construction uses in all parts of the country. He was aware that designers and builders should always look at competing materials and complementary materials.

AVAILABLE INFORMATION

Kingston and his Peruvian colleagues assembled the following information:

- Peru: geography and population (Exhibit 1)
- Peruvians and their structures (Exhibit 2)
- Peruvian attitudes towards wood as a building material (Exhibit 3)
- Peru's forest resources and harvesting (Exhibit 4)

Kingston shared what he had learned about the various types of wood products that were used in construction in Canada at that time (Exhibit 5), both engineered and non-engineered, and urged his colleagues to consider using what was appropriate for the Peruvian situations and to ignore what was not appropriate.

Above all, this was a collaborative development project and so Kingston and his colleagues reflected on the desirable results of such projects, and on the approaches and methodologies that have proven to be effective in achieving those results in international development activities (Chapter Three).

FIRST STEP

Kingston felt that, as a first step, he could encourage his Peruvian colleagues to make decisions as to what they should concentrate on in this wood utilization project. In particular:

a) Which parts of this highly variable country should be included (i.e., coast, highlands, jungle)?

b) Which socio-economic sectors of society (ranging from amazing wealth to extreme poverty) should be included?

c) What types of construction should be included (housing, industrial, commercial, tourism, prefabricated)?

d) What technical and non-technical issues should be addressed in their work plan?

» Exhibit 1: Peru: geography and population

The Republic of Peru, located on the western side of South America on the coast of the Pacific Ocean, had a population in 1975 of 15 million people on a land area of 1.3 million square km. Its neighbors were Ecuador and Colombia to the north, Brazil to the east, Bolivia to the southeast, and Chile to the south.

Peru is sometimes thought of as three countries in one:

- the dry desert strip along the shores of the Pacific Ocean (the western edge of the country)

- the highlands (the "sierra"): the multiple parallel ranges of the high Andes Mountains (the middle)

- the jungle, or more precisely the moist tropical forest, which is part of the enormous Amazon watershed (the eastern region of the country).

According to Teng:[238]

The whole of Peru's western seaboard along the Pacific coast is desert and this region constitutes one ninth of the country. One third of the population is concentrated in the desert, which is the economic heart of the country. From the coastal shelf the Andes rise steeply to a high sierra. This is composed of massive groups of high mountains and deep canyons. Only the land in the deeper valley basins is farmed and most of the highlands is covered with grass and shrubs. More than half of the population inhabit this sierra, which covers one fourth of the land area of the country. The eastern slopes of the sierra are composed of densely forested mountains and ravines. At the foot of the mountains lay the vast jungle lands of the Amazon basin. These constitute some 60 percent of the area of the country but are inhabited by only 10 percent of the population…

In the coastal region, temperatures are moderate and precipitation is very low, while in the sierra the climate is hot with very little rainfall on the lower slopes and changes with the altitude until in the very highest part of the region it is extremely cold. The jungle region is characterized by a hot, wet climate with high precipitation.

Lying on the "Pacific Ring of Fire", the Peruvian coast and highlands (but not the jungle) are seismically highly active.

The main language is Spanish, but Quechua and Aymara are also spoken in the highlands (both Spanish and Quechua are official languages), and Amerindian languages in the jungle.

In 1975, there had been ongoing steady migrations of poor people, generally small farmers (*campesinos*), from the highlands to the coast—especially to the capital Lima—in hope of employment and a better life. The result was widespread illegal construction of shanties and brick or adobe shelters without adequate sanitation, water or electricity in overcrowded conditions in the areas immediately surrounding the city. Many of these houses were not much more than hovels, especially considering the lack of facilities. This housing deficit numbered in the tens of thousands.

» Exhibit 2: Peruvians and their structures

There is often a temptation in a wood utilization program to develop wood construction for situations where it cannot really be justified. It is, therefore, useful to reflect on the appropriateness of wood construction in various situations in Peru. In doing this, one can review what building materials are presently being used, and ask whether or not manufactured wood products (specifically, sawn lumber and plywood) would be feasible and appropriate replacements for the building materials currently being used. Various geoclimatic zones can be examined, separate attention can be given to urban and rural locations, to housing and to industrial, commercial and tourism buildings, and to high-and low-income house builders.

In the jungle, the typical shelter built by the Indians is a pole frame structure having a living platform raised clear of the ground and with a steeply pitched roof made of palm leaves or thatch. The poles are fastened together using vines. This type of shelter seems to be perfectly in balance with the combined needs for ventilation, drainage, and protection from rain and from the ground. It is readily constructed from the materials at hand, costs little (if anything), and is adequately durable for a semi-nomadic lifestyle based on hunting, fishing and shifting agriculture. Houses made of manufactured wood products are clearly not applicable to this segment of society.

However, the picture is different for communities in the jungle that are organized or more permanent. One tends to see a great mixture of building materials in the large towns in the jungle: concrete, adobe, plaster, brick, steel, lumber, poles, palm and thatch. Manufactured wood products are seen here in all forms. In the shanty areas, poverty causes wood waste such as sawmill slabs and edgings and veneer mill clippings to be used as roof and wall coverings for the temporary shelters that come and go depending on the river levels at different seasons of the year. On the other hand, it is possible to see some well-designed houses that have the same overall architectural style as the "jungle clearing" house, i.e. a steeply pitched roof covered with palms or thatch, and a raised living platform, but with the walls and floors of sawn lumber, possibly treated with preservatives. This urban modification has provided more permanence and more privacy but has incorporated a large amount of verandah space for ventilation and for the opportunity to retain the "sheltered outdoor" lifestyle.

For this type of structure, the cooking area is often in a separate building some distance away and downwind from the main house for fire protection. Toilet and washing facilities are similarly often in a separate building. This appears to be a feasible, and appropriate, use for sawn lumber in housing. It is in an area where wood is abundant and where there are sawmills. It is, therefore, the natural material for the site and should be economically competitive. However, it is also clear that the successful use of wood here will benefit from wood technology: the species chosen must possess natural resistance to insect attack or be capable of being readily treated with preservatives; the design and detailing of the house must be such that moisture will not be trapped and lead to fungal attack; the species chosen should also be of low enough density that it can be nailed without splitting.

Some years ago, a very fine reinforced concrete tourist hotel was built in Pucallpa, a large forest products town in the Peruvian jungle. However, when the building was finished, it was unusable because it was too hot inside: the concrete roof didn't keep out the heat. Consequently, a second roof—this one made of lumber—was built on top of the concrete roof. Because of the good thermal insulating value of wood (and the shaded air circulation space provided under the second roof), the hotel is now very comfortable.

In the highlands, before the Spanish conquest the Incas had brought the art of stonemasonry to the highest levels. Wood poles and thatch were used for roofs. The Spaniards continued the tradition of using stone for their major structures in the highlands, largely by making use of the talents of the enslaved Incas. Currently in the cities and major towns, stonework and concrete are used for government buildings and for the houses of the more affluent in Peruvian society, with wood being used as plank floors, interior columns, staircases, window frames, doors and furniture.

For the low-income groups in the highlands the construction materials are adobe for the walls, and wood poles (round or partially hewn) for the roof framing, with a roof covering of tiles, thatch, or corrugated metal. Hewn wood pieces also appear as lintels over windows and doors; these are often extended around the full periphery of the house to provide a horizontal tying action for the adobe in case of earthquakes. The men of the highlands are skilled at building a house of adobe walls, and they can use the materials that are free on the land—mud, straw, water, and sun. It doesn't seem to be sensible, economically, to replace the adobe with lumber (even though wood construction can have a much better resistance to earthquakes). Unless the government pays to transport the lumber from the sawmills in the jungle up to the highlands, provides it, the tools, the nails, and the technical advice free to the occupants, it is difficult to see why wood would be used in place of adobe for the walls of these houses.

Moreover, there is a deep-seated conservatism in the rural Andes in cultural matters, including housing. Making a radical change in house construction in a rural community could make the house builder open to ridicule if any problems are encountered with housing innovations, in addition to possible unanticipated expenses.

The species of wood most commonly used for roof construction is Eucalyptus because of its availability in the highlands. However, Eucalyptus is hard to dry and to saw. Therefore, young trees are felled and these are used as poles, rather than being sawn into lumber. The resulting size is often larger than is necessary, and this increases the inertial mass of the roof, making it more susceptible to seismic damage. In this case, if wood technology were to lead to a reduction in the size of the roof timbers, this could simultaneously lower the cost of the roof as well as reducing the danger of earthquake damage to the walls.

One feasible and current use for wood in the highlands (and to some extent elsewhere) is for buildings for military camps and for mining, road building, irrigation, and forestry camps, i.e., structures that are suited to prefabrication, packaging, easy and quick transportation and erection, and possible reuse at another site later. Because of its relatively light weight and good workability, wood is ideally suited for such structures and has been used in this way for many years. Once again, continued success in this area will depend upon the results of research and development activity using the tropical hardwoods of the area.

Finally, in the desert regions (and in particular the river valleys that cut across the coastal plain), rural and urban areas can be considered separately. In the rural areas, the materials for low-income housing are mud, sticks, adobe, and also woven panels made of split cane supported on wood pole frameworks. The cane is free, or at least cheap, is locally available on the land (quite abundantly in some valley locations), and provides both ventilation and protection from sun, sand, and wind. This type of housing accompanies a rather primitive lifestyle; however, it is really the lack of amenities that renders the life-style primitive, not the house itself.

The urban areas have actually seen a decrease in the importance of wood as a building material over the years. In colonial times, many churches and cathedrals were constructed of stone but with heavy timber roofs. Several large public buildings used timber for the columns and the roofs. One outstanding example is the bullring in Lima that was built in 1768. Although founded on adobe, everything else is wood - the seats, columns, and roof. This gives an excellent testimonial to the possibility of using wood to build for permanence in an area of high earthquake activity.

A second important historical use of wood was in the form of "quincha" (or "bahareque" or "bajareque', names that hint at its Moorish origin). Quincha was used largely for walls and consisted of long vertical wood studs, spaced less than 2 feet apart, with diagonal braces at the lower end, and with split cane attached perpendicular to the studs. Mud and/or gypsum was then applied to the split cane. A common form of construction consisted of two-storey buildings, of which the lower storey had adobe walls and the upper storey walls were quincha. This system was often used in conjunction with timber columns, verandahs, and roofs.

Today, the modern commercial and government buildings are of reinforced concrete, specially designed to be earthquake-resistant and fireproof. Industrial buildings use steel and brick also. Private homes of the affluent use concrete, brick, and tiles, and sometimes wood but mainly for decorative reasons. For the lower-income groups, the housing materials are mainly brick, with some adobe, stone, concrete, and gypsum. Although bricks are quite inexpensive, a laborer will be able to buy only a few at a time and his house building progress will be slow. In fact, with the virtual absence of precipitation in Lima, he may never have a permanent roof on his house! However, from a sociological point of view, every brick that is worked for, purchased, and laid, represents a very tangible step in a man's building of a better life for himself and his family. At the present time, wood is more expensive than bricks, largely because of the great distances that it must travel from the jungle over the mountains to the coast, and also because of the unstable nature of the wood market caused by the transportation problems in the jungle due to the rain and the lack of roads. Another reason not to use wood in the crowded low-income urban areas is the risk of fire, particularly when one considers how poorly equipped many firefighting forces are.

Nevertheless, the pressures to provide large amounts of new housing in the vicinity of Lima are very great, and the need is urgent. Lima's population is growing rapidly because of the large-scale migration of workers and their families from the highlands. Brick construction is slow—in some cases, much too slow—and the more rapidly constructed wood houses are needed in spite of a cost disadvantage. Consequently, a number of companies and government organizations have been building prototype wooden houses in Lima, but these suffer from two disadvantages: they are not affordable by the lowest-income group in urban society, and their design and construction have not fully utilized the benefits obtainable from wood technology and construction technology.

Most of the foregoing pertains to housing, but wood can be a highly appropriate material for engineered structures such as buildings for industrial, commercial, or public assembly or tourism purposes; bridges; water towers; earth-retaining structures; cribs; wharves; electricity and communications towers; agricultural storage buildings; and concrete falsework and formwork. These uses of wood occur throughout the country but primarily on the coast and in the mountains. If the country's forest resources can be developed to produce wood products suitable for engineered construction, this will be to the economic benefit (and thus to the social benefit) of the people of Peru.

» Exhibit 3: Peruvian attitudes towards wood as a building material

Although there was an historical precedent for the use of wood in major public buildings and in the grander private residences in Peru, wood was currently regarded as "the poor man's building material" or, at best, as a temporary construction material. Consequently, where wood was currently used in construction, it appeared without benefit of professional design and thus was not resistant to the effects of earthquakes, fire and deterioration by insects and decay fungi.

Compounding the problem were shortages of engineers, architects and craftspersons trained in the proper use of tropical woods in construction. Also missing were courses and training programs that would help to create a wood construction human infrastructure. Nor, by and large, had there been any decisive action on the part of government, the financial institutions or the forest products industry to support the development of engineered wood products in construction.

Ironically, the problem of an underutilized and renewable resource of construction materials existed in a country plagued by chronic shortages of adequate housing.

» Exhibit 4: Peru's forest resources and harvesting

Peru had been blessed with rich and extensive forest resources that covered some 65 million hectares, i.e. over half of the country. The standing volume of forests is estimated to be 11 billion m^3. These forests, which are drained mainly by the Amazon River system, are almost entirely hardwoods and are highly diverse. In the natural forests, there were estimated to be approximately 2500 tree species.

This great resource, however, was being diminished. There were several causes. The most critical appeared to be uncontrolled destruction of the forest by migrants for conversion to agricultural land: in many cases this has led to rapid depletion of soil nutrients and to erosion, rendering the land unfit either for continued agricultural use or for reforestation.

Wood has been taken indiscriminately from the forest for fuelwood. Plans for hydroelectric power generation projects included the possibility of submerging extensive areas of forest. Many species had been selectively and extensively harvested for premium uses like decorative veneers and plywood, fine furniture and parquet. Of these, some (chanul, guayacan, balsamo, cedro and caoba are good examples) are not readily reforested. Moreover, forest utilization in many parts of the country was characterized by waste. This appeared in a number of forms: the less-preferred species are left unharvested to die and rot in the forest, about 40% of the harvested tree (tops, limbs, branches, stumps) is left in the forest, and much of the logs, another 30-40%, is unused mill residue in the form of slabs, edgings, trims, veneer clippings, sawdust and shavings. Another form of waste results from the fact that most wood products are in a relatively simple form—logs, sawn timber, veneer and plywood, but it is possible with further processing, to add more value to the products and to earn more from the same volume of wood.

Paul Richards, writing in Scientific American in 1973, summarized the global danger in these words: "One of the oldest ecosystems and a reservoir of genetic diversity, the wet evergreen tropical forest is threatened by the activities of man and may virtually disappear by the end of the 20th century." In Peru, the situation was possibly not as bleak as Richards suggested. The problem was early recognized by the Peruvian government and by international aid agencies such as the Canadian International Development Agency (CIDA) and by the International Development Research Centre (IDRC) of Canada. Several projects in silviculture, forest management, agroforestry and afforestation were currently under way and many more were planned for the future.

Of the 2500 tree species in the highly heterogeneous natural forests, only about 1,000 have been botanically identified and only about 50 species are regularly used by the wood industry. As another example, in Peru in 1979, some 170 species were used for industrial purposes but nine of these species represented more than 75% of the lumber and plywood in this region.

This variety brings with it another important characteristic - the very low representation of each species per unit of area. It is common to find, therefore, on the one hand, barely 1-8 specimens per ha and, on the other hand, as many as 50-80 different species per hectare. The maximum number of trees of the same species per hectare is in general less than 10.

Forest utilization in the Amazon basis is, therefore, extraordinarily selective. For several decades the interest has been solely in species of great world prestige, such as cedar (cedrela) and mahogany (swietenia) and, although the tendency is clearly toward a larger number of species, the process is still slow.

This practice, also known as "highgrading" or "cut and get out," entails the removal of desirable species leaving behind the inferior, unhealthy, or undesirable species to take over the area. It has been estimated that, during the selective harvesting of 10% of the trees in the rain forests of Malaysia, 55% of the remaining trees are severely damaged or destroyed and that only 35% are left undamaged. It can be assumed that similar damage occurs in the subregional tropical forests of South America under present logging practices.

The harvesting process begins with felling, which is mainly carried out with chainsaws. The use of axes, common a decade ago, is disappearing. Before a tree is felled it is cleared of vines and shrubs with machetes. Once felled, the crown is topped and the butt bucked if flare is extreme. The main stem is then bucked to appropriate dimensions, eliminating defective or damaged parts, so that it can be handled by the available hauling system. The crown, butt, and severed parts are left at the stump.

Primary transport is either manual or mechanized. Manual methods are labor intensive. In the lowlands, logs are either rolled along the ground or floated through flooded areas toward the nearest river. Hauling distances rarely exceed 2 km. On mountain slopes chutes are constructed in gullies to slide logs down to the roadside. Construction of the chute is simply a matter of clearing a gully and positioning small logs to act as ramps in the difficult parts of the tract. For mechanized primary transport, in lowland areas with good load-bearing soils, the common piece of equipment is the wheeled skidder. Skidding distances average 2.5 km but skids up to 10 km are frequent. On the eastern flank of the Andes range a combination of wheeled skidders and crawler tractors is preferred. Crawler tractors usually build the skid roads and often position themselves behind the skidder's load to assist the skidder up steep slopes. Old rebuilt trucks with A-frames and winches are also common. Mechanized skidding operations are limited to the dry season.

Secondary transport is mainly by river in the lowlands. The logs are either dumped into the river and assembled into rafts or loaded on to self-loading barges. In the highlands roads are the only means of transport. Logs are loaded onto trucks manually, or by using skidders and crawler tractors from elevated soil ramps or up planks onto the truck platform.

The amount of standing timber in these forests is enormous, with a possible value of US $ 36 billion. Nevertheless, production is low and the contribution of the forest sector to the gross national product has not exceeded 0.5%. One of the reasons for this is the high level of noncommercial use—in 1979 almost 90% of the wood harvested was used for firewood. Only 1-10 m^3/ha of timber is extracted for industrial purposes and the average is around 3 m^3/ha.

» Exhibit 5: wood products and components used in construction in Canada in 1975

Heavy timber construction:

- Sawn timbers, e.g. beams and columns
- Preservative treated sawn timbers
- Heavy timber trusses
- Glued-laminated timber ("glulam")
- Tongue & groove plank decking

Light wood construction:

- Sawn dimension ("2 by") lumber
- Prefabricated roof and floor trusses
- Moldings
- Hardwood flooring
- Plywood, e.g. for sheathing and siding
- Laminated particleboard, e.g. for furniture and cupboards
- Doors and windows
- Preservative treated sawn dimension lumber
- Preservative treated plywood

- Preservative treated shakes and shingles
- Fire retardant treated sawn dimension lumber
- Fire retardant treated plywood
- Fire retardant treated shakes and shingles

Engineered wood products: all of the above products are engineered, i.e. engineering skills are used to classify, grade and/or utilize them in structures, except for:

- Moldings
- Hardwood flooring
- Laminated particleboard
- Doors and windows
- Preservative treated shakes and shingles
- Fire retardant treated shakes and shingles

Sawn timbers, sawn dimension lumber, and plywood are used both in a non-engineered form and in an engineered form.

CHAPTER FOURTEEN

INTERNATIONAL EDUCATION AND STUDENT EXCHANGES

In Chapter Sixteen, we will talk about how to get started in international work. That information is directed both to those who wish to build life-long professional careers in international development, as well as to those who just feel an urge to do something, within their daily lives, to improve the quality of life of people in countries less well off than Canada.

In the present chapter we deal with one of the most enjoyable ways in which young people can get their initial taste of learning first-hand about life in other countries: by taking part in international education activities and, especially, by being a participant in an international student exchange program.

First, however, we want to explain how universities and colleges have evolved over the past two decades in order to provide a more international educational context for their students.

INTERNATIONALIZATION OF CANADIAN UNIVERSITIES AND COLLEGES

The last two decades have seen fundamental changes in the international attitudes and activities of Canada's universities. Twenty years ago, the typical situation consisted of an individual professor having a personal interest in cooperating with a friend or counterpart in a university in another country. Activities might have included faculty visits in both directions, guest lectures, joint scholarship and publication, and possibly a small student exchange program, usually without much involvement by the central administration. In most cases, the professors who were doing this already had tenure because not

241

much credit was given in the promotion and tenure process for international activities if they didn't result in the publication of refereed papers.

This situation was followed by the widespread emergence of requests by students for more international exchange and study abroad possibilities; by faculty, students and administrators who wanted to be of service to developing countries; by demands of faculty members for increased support from the central administration for their international initiatives; by an awareness on the part of the scholarly leaders of the university that they had to excel on the global stage if they were to be taken seriously as research institutions.

Most Canadian universities responded positively to these demands by creating administrative units to nurture student exchange and study abroad programs, to provide services to international students on campus, to support international development cooperation, and to enhance international scholarship and research[239]. Administrations typically also started allocating budgetary resources for these activities. Some universities formalized their international commitments by creating strategic plans for the internationalization of their institutions, which affirmed the value of their various forms of international engagement.

Universities in Canada differ widely as to how they administer their international activities. Usually, international education falls under the responsibility of the Vice President (Academic) or the Vice President (Research), although in a few rare cases the Office of the President or Rector takes direct responsibility. When these activities are under the VP (Research), projects of international development cooperation, international consulting and international research are central components in the range of activities. To provide oversight, there is often a senate-level committee to generate policies and to set standards, especially for international student exchange programs.

When universities became more serious about their international engagements, they often prepared a strategic plan for internationalization in which the universities' roles were seen in an international context, and much was done to enhance that role. At the point at which internationalism permeated the campus, responsibility for its management became shared between the central administrations and the individual faculties. Management of international activities, therefore, could take place under a consolidated model or under a dispersed model. The consolidated model of an international office could include many of the following functions[240]:

- providing a central forum and focus for all international matters at the institution

- disseminating comprehensive and timely information on international matters of potential interest to all parts of the institution
- encouraging faculty and students to consider involvement in international activities
- helping to obtain seed money for exploratory missions to meet with potential collaborators
- assembling multidisciplinary teams to respond to new scholarly challenges and funding opportunities
- assisting in preparing proposals for submission to funding agencies
- approving proposals on behalf of the President or Vice President
- negotiating with funding agencies
- approving interim and final reports on behalf of the President or Vice President
- providing follow-up to projects
- administering student exchange programs
- administering study abroad programs
- advising international students
- maintaining a database of current and potential international interests and capabilities
- publicizing and promoting the university's international activities and achievements
- maintaining contacts with the international community
- receiving international visitors on behalf of the institution and providing advice on protocol
- assisting in the development of the internationalization policy of the institution
- representing the institution at international meetings.

(Although the word "university" is used in the above, it is evident that it would apply equally to colleges.)

INTERNATIONAL EDUCATION

"International education" is a broad term encompassing a range of activities[241]:

- courses with international context and content
- study abroad credit courses
- short-term work experiences abroad
- individualized study or work abroad activities
- volunteer work programs
- internships
- advising foreign students in Canada
- international student exchanges.

In Canada, international student exchanges take place at the secondary school level and at the university and college level. We will concentrate here on student exchanges between Canadian universities and universities abroad.

UNIVERSITY-TO-UNIVERSITY INTERNATIONAL STUDENT EXCHANGE PROGRAMS

The starting point for such a program in a Canadian university often is the presence of a local "champion" for the program. This is usually a person who has a close association of some kind with the overseas institution—she or he may have done graduate or postdoctoral work there (in the case of an industrialized country), or was a visitor there or has a friendship with someone there (for both industrialized and developing country partner institutions). This is the individual with the enthusiasm for the exchange, who will work through the bureaucratic requirements to establish the program, who will probably be asked to administer the exchange, who will publicize it on campus, who will be the local source of information, who will interview and select the participating Canadian students, who will brief the participants and organize their travel, who will look after the arriving students from the partner institution, who will provide the main linkage between the visitors and the institution and the local community, and who will be constantly available by telephone and email to solve problems of the Canadian students who are studying at the host institution in the other country. Universities usually don't give much credit for this kind of activity in promotion and tenure evaluations, and so it is truly a "labor of love" to be an exchange program coordinator. In some Canadian universities, once the program is established, this administrative burden is eased by the presence of a student exchange officer, who will perform many of the activities listed.

This latter point hints at the second major requirement—the existence of a formal or informal culture in the university that welcomes student exchanges because of the richness they can bring to the campus, and the corresponding allocation of resources (such as a student exchange office) to support this activity. At the formal level, the university may have adopted a strategic plan for internationalization that explicitly includes and supports student exchange programs. The university may also have a committee, either at the central administration level reporting to a Vice President or at the faculty level reporting to a Dean, with authority to approve the establishment of individual exchanges and to prescribe regulations for the administration of the program. Of major concern to such committees are the academic quality of the partner institution (and the committee's willingness to accept courses taken abroad for equivalent credit at the home institution) and the security and wellbeing of visiting students in the light of social and health risks in the other country. It often falls to the local champion to provide assurances in these two areas of concern. These committees are often concerned about whether a particular proposed student exchange program fits with the university's strategy for internationalization, e.g. with respect to geographic region or for academic discipline.

Most exchange programs aim for numerical equity, i.e. the number of departing students is approximately equal to the number of arriving students. The students go from their "home" university to the "host" university. With such a system, students pay tuition fees at their home university, but the two universities often waive the requirement for the participating students to pay any tuition fees (whether these are international student fees or domestic student fees) at the host institution. This tuition waiver makes the exchange concept feasible for students from developing country universities, for whom the requirement to pay Canadian university tuition fees could represent an impossible hurdle. Nevertheless, visiting students may still have to pay some ancillary fees, such as athletic or student activity fees.

The exchange usually lasts a few weeks, one semester, two semesters, or even a whole year, although one semester in the third year is the most common arrangement.

Increasingly, risks to personal security and to health preoccupy exchange program managers and the parents of participating students. For this reason, it is essential that students who are considering participation in international exchange programs be thoroughly and competently briefed regarding the nature of the host country and the host university. The principles of "informed consent" are essential if the home university requires participating students to sign a waiver to relieve the university of responsibility and liability in the event of problems.

Similarly, visiting students have to be informed that provincial health plans will possibly not provide coverage for them in Canada, and they (or someone on their behalf) will have to purchase health insurance, e.g. from the University Health Insurance Plan.

Other items on the manager's checklist of issues or concerns are the following:

- Who is responsible for carrying out "due diligence" checks on the partner institution?

- If the language of instruction at the host institution is not the same as at the home institution, what provision for language training (or interpretation for short term exchanges) will be provided?

- What cultural briefing, or cross-cultural training, will be arranged?

- What health insurance, travel insurance and (if appropriate) what vehicle insurance is required?

- Who are the persons in each country responsible for the day-to-day running of the program?

- What communication network will be in place? Who are the contact persons on both sides, and can they contacted at all times when the students are at the host institutions?

- How many students should the program include (on each side), and how will they be chosen?

- What will be required of returning students, e.g. for reports or availability for the promotion of the following year's program?

- What programs—academic, cultural and promotional—will be organized for the visiting students?

- How will the visitors be treated in the crucially important first 48 hours at the host university, e.g. who will meet them at the airport or train station?

- Should there be a "peer" or "buddy" system in place to assist the visitors to settle in, and also to be available to help should some problems develop later?

- What about gifts?

- What should the formal agreement governing the exchange consist of? Should there be a public ceremony to mark the signing of the agreement?

- Will the students be responsible for all of their expenses, or will their home or host universities provide financial support? Should the institutions carry out fundraising campaigns as part of their public engagement?

- What are the liability implications for both the university and the individual faculty?

The current "bible" on pre-departure orientation and liability is *DepartSmart*[242] published by the University of Guelph. Another publication is: *Ready, Set, Go!*[243] CBIE has also published two papers on liability[244].

The following case, *Mexico & Robert Marino*, illustrates the many decisions that had to be made concerning the establishment of a student exchange program with a major Mexican university in the field of social work.

CASE ANALYSIS: MEXICO & ROBERT MARINO[245]

On July 27, 1993 Professor Robert Marino, Director of the School of Social Work at King's College[246] (KC), an affiliated college of the University of Western Ontario (UWO) in London, Ontario, had just returned from a conference of the International Association of Schools of Social Work held in Amsterdam. While there, he approached representatives of the School of Social Work at Universidad National Autónoma de México (UNAM), a major Mexican university, and discussed the concept of establishing an undergraduate student exchange program between King's and UNAM in the field of social work. Having reached agreement with UNAM to continue to explore this idea, Marino now started to formulate a list of all the issues, decisions and tasks that he would have to deal with in order to create and manage a valuable and sustainable student exchange program.

UNIVERSITY OF WESTERN ONTARIO

UWO had long been involved in international activities, including student and faculty exchanges, volunteer work, research collaborations, and international development assistance. Western's central administration supported these activities through its Office of International Research. The services of this Office were also available to the affiliated colleges.

KING'S COLLEGE

King's, one of the three affiliated colleges of UWO, was founded in 1954 as a Catholic, co-educational, liberal arts university college. King's students registered at UWO and received UWO credits. Programs offered were:

- Business, Mathematics, Administrative and Commercial Studies
- Arts
- Social Sciences
- Philosophy and Religious Studies
- History and Political Science
- Social Work (four year BSW degree)

King's took pride in its Catholic ethos of commitment to social justice, and (in the words of liberation theology) to "a preferential option for the poor". Not surprisingly, King's attracted faculty members who had an empathy with these underlying values. Prior to 1993 King's was focused largely on its national context, and there was no widespread interest and support for international activities. King's had no money specifically earmarked for student exchange programs or for any kind of international activity.

DR. ROBERT MARINO

Dr. Robert Marino was born into a culturally aware family of Italian heritage and, as a result, was raised within a caring, multilingual and cosmopolitan environment. Not surprisingly, early on he developed a fundamental sense of social responsibility, which manifested itself by his joining a religious order, the Redemptorist Fathers, and spending a year in a seminary in Italy. Subsequently, he became a social worker dealing with Italian and Portuguese immigrants in Toronto, and then was appointed to the position of Executive Director of the COSTI Educational Centre, a major Canadian social agency dealing with immigrants and refugees.[247] Following Ph.D. studies at the University of Toronto, and by virtue of his education, his experience and his temperament, he was well suited in 1976 to joining the School of Social Work at King's College. In 1982, Marino became Director of the School.

At KC, Marino was able to introduce into his courses the insights and sensitivities from his interactions with immigrants from a wide range of countries. Moreover, he had the vision that university graduates in general, and social work students in particular, should be enabled by their universities to have a broader view of the world. Consequently, a latent interest in the value of student exchanges, and the opportunities for KC students to interact with students of other countries, continued to grow. So, in 1993 when Marino attended the annual conference of the International Association of Schools of Social Work, he sought out the Director and her colleagues of UNAM's School of Social Work to discuss establishing an undergraduate student exchange program between KC and UNAM.

UNIVERSIDAD NATIONAL AUTÓNOMA DE MÉXICO (UNAM)

UNAM, located in Mexico City, is one of the largest and most prestigious public universities in Mexico. Marino's main contacts with UNAM were the Director of the School of Social Work, Lic. Nelia Tello Peon, and her colleagues, particularly Bertha Mary Rodriguez. These individuals were very enthusiastic and proactive in cooperating to set up an exchange program and, in this, they reflected an interest by their administration in having international links.

UNAM's School of Social Work had about 2000 students in a four-year program. Not all of the 2000 students intended to practice as social workers—many were interested in the school as the source of a good university education. Their program was based somewhat on the North American model, with an emphasis on community development and community organization. Their faculty members were particularly interested in the experience of King's in the areas of clinical social work, and skills in counseling and family therapy. UNAM had a focus on community organization, one aspect of which was that all students over the four-year period were working with a particular local neighborhood. In the first year, they did research on the community: Who is there? What were their concerns? The following year, they would start to get involved with organizing. In the third year, they would evaluate progress. This approach of having a longer-term connection with their neighborhoods, their institutions, the schools, the hospitals, the jails, was attractive to Marino. UNAM had connections with universities in other countries and thus had experience in working with international partners, and were keen on the idea of a collaboration with King's.

ISSUES, DECISIONS AND TASKS

Decision to proceed or not

Marino was driven by his conviction that students graduating from King's College—and social work students in particular—should have the opportunity to personally experience conditions in other parts of the world, especially the developing world. This was, quite simply, part of being an educated person. Moreover, cultivating a sense of social justice in young people was an important component of King's educational philosophy, as well as being close to Marino's heart. Another consideration was that future social work graduates would be dealing in large measure with clients who were recent immigrants to Canada, and thus an understanding of other cultures and some ability with languages would be professionally beneficial. A student exchange program was an attractive vehicle for accomplishing these ends, because it had the double benefit of Canadian students spending time in another culture in Mexico, and Mexican students coming north to influence the School of Social Work, the broader College and its various communities. More specifically, King's social work program included a required practicum experience, and Marino wondered if spending time at UNAM would be a valuable and feasible practicum opportunity.

So, Marino was convinced that King's should create an international student exchange program. He decided that his immediate tasks, in order, were:

a) as due diligence, to visit UNAM along with King's coordinator of field education, Susan O'Neil, to see the campus and to check out UNAM's approach to social work education and their experience and capacity for international cooperation,

b) to engage his academic colleagues in the School of Social Work and to get their cooperation (this was an important thing to do because it furthered the goals of the College and the School),

c) to convince the Principal and the Dean of the College and other senior colleagues to approve and support it,

d) to inform and enthuse the social work students about this opportunity,

e) to let the rest of King's College—students, administrators and academic colleagues—know about this effort, in the hope that these ideas would find fertile ground and widespread support throughout King's,

f) to seek formal approval of the College's governing bodies for the program, and

g) to enlist the help of the Director of UWO's Office of International Research in order to exploit his institutional expertise and experience in international engagements.

Participants from Canada

Which social work students at King's should be eligible to participate? Marino and his colleagues decided that the appropriate level was immediately following third year. They also decided that the number of participants should be limited (5 to 15 individuals) and they must be chosen carefully taking into account academic performance, cultural sensitivity, emotional maturity and motivation. What should they do in Mexico? What manner of educational, cultural and social work activities might they take part in? How to administer this? How to assure the safety of the students? What Spanish language proficiency is needed for this?

Participants from outside Canada

Mexico was a good choice for an international partner country because: (a) it was geographically close and easy to get to, (b) it was politically close through membership in NAFTA, (c) it had a different language but one that was not difficult for most English speakers to learn at a basic level, and (d) large parts of the country could be described as "developing". UNAM likewise was an excellent choice within Mexico because it was a most prestigious institution with wide experience in dealing with international students and partners, and it had a vibrant School of Social Work. But what were the expectations of UNAM? How should the Mexican students spend their time in Canada? How long a period of time should they come for? What level of English should they have, and what kinds of educational, cultural and social work activities should they observe or participate in? More generally who, on the Mexican side, would be the beneficiaries of a cooperation program with King's? Did "social work" in Mexico have a different meaning or a different context than in Canada?

Funding

This was difficult. It was evident that the program would have to be mainly self-funded by the participants, at least in the beginning. An important initial contribution was made by the local bishop, His Excellency Bishop John Sherlock, as a memorial to the recently deceased Director of Diocesan Social Services, Chuck Lyons. Marino then took it upon himself to do fundraising from a wide range of sources. These included the College itself, using the argument that, if internationalization was important to the College, then the College should provide some resources; service clubs; the Catholic Church communities, particularly the Sisters of St. Joseph; and others. (The cost per student was quite reasonable at that point benefiting from the recent drop in the Mexican peso: about $1400 for a one-month sojourn.) Marino also expected that the students themselves would be active in fundraising, such as organizing Mexico-related events on campus. He also surmised that their involvement in such activities would foster bonding among the members of the group, which would prove to be helpful as they encountered problems during their time in Mexico.

Preparation of the participants

a) King's participants: The period of preparation was to be virtually the entire academic year, from October right up to their departure in May. Marino decided to arrange for weekly elementary Spanish language training, and weekly seminars on Mexican history, culture, politics, anthropology and archaeology, and on health, safety, culture shock, difficulties on re-entry, etc. Should one or more faculty or staff members from King's accompany the students? Later, Marino arranged for a period of orientation and preparation at the Cuernavaca Centre for International Dialogue and Development for the King's students upon their arrival in Mexico.

b) UNAM participants: Likewise, what orientation and academic preparation should be arranged for the arriving UNAM students? How would housing and food be provided for them? What kind of practicum experience would be appropriate? How might the larger social work community play a role?

Re-entry and expectations of returning students and faculty

It was decided to have the students submit a written report on their experience, and this would become part of the "library" of the program. Also, participation in a debriefing session and oral presentations to audiences of potential participants the following year would be expected of the group, as well as ongoing mentoring, and assistance with fundraising. An indication of participation in the exchange would be included in the students' academic records. Should the students receive academic credit for participating in the exchange? What might be the "multiplier effect" of returning students talking to family and friends about their experiences and new insights?

Impact on King's College and relations with colleagues

As mentioned above, it was hoped that the Mexico exchange would inspire all of King's College to become more international in its outlook and activities, but would it? Would all faculty members share Marino's vision, or would they resent the potential draw on College resources that the program represented? Might it give rise to jealousy or to resentment? On the other hand, might it beneficially change the image of the College in the eyes of high school students trying to decide whether to apply to King's? What administrative support would the program require? What effect would the presence of the Mexican visitors have on the College? What impact would the increased internationalization of King's have on the content and context of its courses? On its research and scholarship? On its relationships with the London community? On the professional practice of social work in Canada? On the College's proposed new Social Justice and Peace Studies program?

Safety, risks, liability

What were the possible risks to the participants? How could their health and safety be assured, or the risks minimized? What liability might the College and UWO incur? Would waivers be appropriate? What must the College do to obtain defensible "informed consent" from the participants? What kind of insurance should the students and the College purchase?

Formal agreements and legal issues

What formal agreements among the parties needed to be drawn up? Should there be formal signing celebrations of these agreements? Would it be appropriate to present gifts? If so, what kinds of (distinctively Canadian) gifts should be offered?

Where to live in Mexico City?

Where should the students, staff and faculty stay while in Mexico? In student residences, or a hostel? In hotels? In private homes?

Timing

Marino and his colleagues decided to have the visit take place immediately after the end of the third academic year. How long should it last? One month? One semester? Two semesters? One calendar year? Did Marino have enough time to start the program immediately or should he wait until the following year? When and how should the program be advertised? When should the participants be selected? What should be the timing of their language and cultural preparation?

Sustainability

This was Marino's pet project as Director, but what steps should he take to ensure continuation, or even expansion, of the program when he was no longer in that role or no longer at King's? What would be the preferred administrative location (e.g. the field education office) for the exchange program most likely to ensure its continuation? Should there be a standing committee (comprising students and faculty) of the School Council responsible for exchange activities so that the program is embedded in the structure of the School and is no longer in the hands of just one person? Could he seek a separate line to be established in the budget of the School of Social Work to ensure ongoing funding?

CONCLUSION

Marino was enthusiastic and committed about establishing an undergraduate student exchange program between UNAM and King's College in the area of social work, and he now used his contemplation of the above issues to formulate a list of all the issues, decisions and tasks that he would have to deal with over the next few months in order to create a valuable and sustainable student exchange program.

Dr. Marino wishes to recognize and acknowledge the support of Dr. Ken Moffat, who accompanied and supported the first group of students going to Mexico; Dr. Joe Blom, who provided support and assistance to students both in Canada and in Mexico; Mary Lou Karley, the current field work coordinator, who eventually assumed responsibility for the project, which changed in a major way after the strike at UNAM.

CHAPTER FIFTEEN
MONITORING AND EVALUATION

Essential to the management of international activities are regular and systematic monitoring and evaluation of the completeness, the timeliness, the appropriateness and the effectiveness of your efforts. The process can be *informal*—in which it constantly pervades your mental processes during the ongoing work—or *formal*, which is usually a requirement of the funding agency or the executing agency. Normally, formal evaluations consist of mid-term evaluations and final evaluations, and utilize the disciplines and structures of Results-based Management.

Evaluations that are much less formal, usually more fun, and that are done early in a project can take the form of a Participatory Rural Appraisal (PRA).

MONITORING

» Example: Ethiopia & monitoring trips

When *Future Forests* board members made their annual monitoring trips to the four communities in the Bette Valley, they held public "update" meetings, at which the villagers talked about their activities, their concerns, their problems, their hopes for the future, in each of the project areas such as water, education, health, oxen loan programs. These meetings were lengthy and loquacious, necessitating interpretation from English to Amharic to Oromigna, and back again from Oromigna to Amharic to English. Of foremost importance was the showing of respect, as well as ensuring that there was enough time to hear all the things that the partners wanted to say.

PARTICIPATORY RURAL APPRAISAL

A highly useful technique in information gathering, transmission and sharing (and in participatory assessment, research, planning, and program design) at the village level is the use of Participatory Rural Appraisal (PRA) approaches. (Two major references in this field are by Robert Chambers: *Rural Appraisal: Rapid, Relaxed and Participatory* and *Whose Reality Counts? Putting the First Last.*)

PRA is a tool by which development workers can best learn the wishes and possibilities of their partner communities. It can take the form of the villagers jointly making a "ground map" of their community using stones, sticks and other materials at hand, arranged on the ground (and later transferred to paper). The process permits all the project participants to learn, in a very graphic way, about population, health, agriculture, water, etc. in the community and the associated problems.

Importantly, PRA enables the members of the community to take charge of the communication by making their physical portrayal of their villages and to reach consensus on the messages they wanted to give. PRA also gives the opportunity to "dig down" by asking increasingly detailed questions about the situation that each stick or stone represented, for example, to find out the locations of gardens and of cottage industries, such as weavers and potters. This "aerial view" of the villages is a very effective platform for developing cultural insights as to what men and women typically did each day in the villages.

A distinction should be made between the RRA (Rapid Rural Appraisal) methods developed in the late 1970s and 1980s, and PRA, from the late 1980s and 1990s: RRA is extractive, i.e. information flows from the villagers to the outsiders. PRA is participatory: the information is owned by, and used mainly by, the local people. Obviously, there is much common ground between RRA and PRA, but the objective of PRA is the empowerment of local people leading to sustainable local action and institutions.

In addition to being an effective means of communication, PRA can also be used as a participatory evaluation process, for such things as programs, seeds, crops, agricultural issues. One way of doing this is to set up a matrix of "good", "better", "best", and having the stakeholders place stones into the appropriate box(es) of the matrix. Then the stones in each box of the matrix are counted and the results tallied and shared and discussed with the participants. This way everyone (men and women) gets to vote using their experience with the program, or the certain seed, evaluation on basis of yield, drought resistance, and insect resistance. Also, it allows for the participants to actively be a part of the setup of the criteria for the evaluation.

When voting for or against a program, or an agricultural choice of seeds, etc. often a show of hands in a circle is not a true reading of feelings, because of the various pressures (between genders, within hierarchies, status) when people vote openly, but with the matrix they can come one at a time and make a vote by placing stones in the various squares in the matrix that represent their evaluation in somewhat of a "secret ballot" situation. "Voting systems don't make sense if late voters can see the earlier votes and so make more of a difference, and also be influenced by how people ahead of them have voted. There is, however, pocket voting, where people go behind a screen and put a seed or stone in a pocket – a form of secret ballot."****

MID-TERM EVALUATION

The mid-term evaluation (MTE) is usually conducted within the third year of a five or six year project. It provides an independent view (and therefore necessitates the hiring of a consultant who has had no prior involvement with the project) of how the project is proceeding and whether mid-course adjustments are needed.

Within an MTE, particular attention is paid to how the work has progressed in meeting its objectives, whether sustainability is being approached, what follow-up activities are being contemplated, how the various stakeholders are being engaged in the project, how gender equality is being achieved, whether the project management is working well, what are the lessons learned, and whether there are any unexpected results.

The report of the MTE will be used to guide decision-making concerning the future direction of the project. Usually, a round table meeting of the project team is held after the submission of the final report by the MTE consultant. At this conference, the final report is discussed and decisions are made: (a) whether to make adjustments to the project's remaining activities, for which a Project Completion Plan is prepared and submitted to the funding agency, and (b) on taking steps towards contemplated follow-up activities for the project. Modifications to the remaining budget are agreed upon at this point.

The methodology of an MTE consists of:

- examination of relevant documents
- small group and individual interviews in Canada and the partner country
- on-site observations in the partner country.

**** Chambers, Robert. Personal communication. August 16, 2007

Here are some typical questions and issues that an MTE consultant should be asked to address (Canadian institution is CI, the partner institution is PI, the partner country is PC):

- What is the nature of the partnership? Whose project is it?
- What is the relevance of the project? What are the links to the community? What is the strategic importance of this project to PC? Are the activities appropriate given the needs and priorities of the local partners?
- What results were achieved?
- Have there been any difficulties or obstacles?
- Have there been any unexpected results?
- Has PI been strengthened by the project? Does PI offer enhanced programming as a result of this project? Has CI been strengthened by this project?
- How has the project contributed to the internationalization of PI? How has the project contributed to the internationalization of CI, and to development education in Canada?
- To what extent has research been carried out in the project, and how important has research been to achieving expected results?
- How has the project addressed CIDA's development priorities?
- Has gender equality been achieved?
- How has this project targeted its intended beneficiaries?
- What is the environmental impact of the project?
- In what way does the project contribute to poverty reduction, and to the other Millennium Development Goals?
- Has CI or PI institutional policy, or PC government policy, been influenced by this project?
- To what extent are the results sustainable?
- How is the financial and operational management of the project?
- Has there been leveraging of other resources?
- What follow-up activities are contemplated?
- How have the partners regarded the Canadian Executing Agency's role?

- What are the lessons learned with respect to development results, capacity building (including capacity in monitoring and evaluation) and overall project management?

- Are any mid-course corrections needed?

Transparency of the MTE process when visiting the partner institutions should be paramount, and participation by the partners should be encouraged, in order (a) to remove the apprehension that an "inspector" has arrived to conduct an potentially punitive examination (a PowerPoint presentation on the first day can be helpful, as well as making a presentation before departing on the consultant's preliminary findings and recommendations), and (b) to build local capacity in evaluation as one aspect of local ownership.

CASE: THE GAMBIA & ALPHA JALLOW

Alpha Jallow, a Gambian citizen, was the associate evaluator for the mid-term evaluation of a project for which one intended impact was to establish a sustainable community-based policing (CBP) system in The Gambia. At the wrap-up meeting of the evaluation at the Gambia Police Force (GPF) headquarters on December 17, 2007, Jallow and the Canadian evaluator realized that the project was in serious trouble. The senior officials of the GPF had refused to continue with the planned activities that had been previously agreed upon for the project. The Canadian evaluator was obviously considering recommending that the project be terminated. Jallow, being acutely aware of the potentially great value of the project for the quality of democracy in his country, had to decide how to convince the Canadian evaluator and the funding authorities in Canada to find a satisfactory way not to shut down the project. Jallow also knew the Canadian evaluator was concerned about Jallow's professional reputation, and even Jallow's personal safety, in The Gambia if the project were terminated.

THE GAMBIA

The Gambia, a former British colony, is a small country occupying both banks of the Gambia River on the "bulge" of West Africa, and is surrounded on three sides by Senegal. It is about 338 km long (east to west) and less than 48 km wide (north to south), and contains fewer than two million people. Gambians comprise ten different ethnic groups and languages, in addition to the official language of English.

THE GAMBIA POLICE FORCE

Quoting from the original proposal for the project:

> *If placed within a framework of human rights and social justice, the maintenance and enhancement of stability within The Gambia is largely dependent upon the relationship between the civilian police force and the public. This proposed project is premised on the belief that good governance and enhanced economies are dependent upon internal security, which can only be achieved through effective and democratically based civilian policing that engages the public at large as a full partner in the process. Unfortunately, the relationship between the Gambia Police Force (GPF) and the Gambian public has deteriorated in recent years, and the GPF faces a crisis of confidence in its ability to act in a just and effective manner.*

In fact, many Gambian citizens with whom the evaluators came into contact alleged that the police regularly shake down drivers for money at police spot checks, are not sufficiently responsive to citizens' problems, and give preference to supporters of the ruling political party. Seldom did the evaluators hear anyone (other than members of the Gambia Police Force or officials of the government) say anything complimentary about the police.

COMMUNITY-BASED POLICING

The GPF was trying to improve its badly tarnished image in the country. They had turned to the principles and practices of community-based policing (CBP) in an attempt to build trust and confidence with the communities. Essentially, CBP: (a) engages the communities as partners in preventing crime, and (b) for less serious crimes, lets the existing and traditional structures in the community bring about a resolution of the offence without the permanently damaging effect of laying charges and going through the courts. (If the problem goes to court, much time and money may be consumed, there may be no effective remedy for the victim, and an ongoing state of hostility can subsequently prevail between the families of the offender and the victim.)

Quoting again from the project proposal:

> *The effort focuses on good governance at the front-line level of the criminal justice system, designed to promote police-community partnerships and enhance the effectiveness and accountability of the police. Importantly, the project will address a number of policing problems related to social*

justice concerns, especially those of women who currently live with certain cultural and traditional practices inconsistent with general principles of human rights in democratic societies.

RESTORATIVE JUSTICE

The principles and practices of restorative justice (RJ) are part of this process as the means by which attention is paid to finding adequate and appropriate remedies to the damage suffered by the victim, with corresponding accountability and responsibility for the damage and for the remedies on the part of the offender.

THE PROJECT: NOVA SCOTIA AGREES TO HELP

This project originated, the evaluators were told, in discussions between the man who later became the then-current Inspector General of Police and Burris Devanney, a founder of the Nova Scotia-Gambia Association. Devanney then approached Dr. Stephen Perrott, a former Halifax policeman and an Associate Professor in the Psychology Department of MSVU, about taking the lead to create a CBP and RJ collaborative capacity-building project in The Gambia. The project was designed, submitted, approved, funded by the Association of Universities and Colleges of Canada (AUCC) acting on behalf of CIDA, and became operational in 2004. The partners were:

- Mount Saint Vincent University (MSVU), Halifax (the lead Canadian institution)
- Halifax Regional Police (HRP)
- Nova Scotia Department of Justice, Restorative Justice Program (NSRJP)
- Gambia Police Force (GPF) (the lead Gambian institution)
- Gambia College (GC)

Other cooperants included:
- Nova Scotia-Gambia Association (NSGA)
- Island Community Justice Society (ICJS)
- Valley Restorative Justice Society (VRJS)
- Youth Crime Watch of The Gambia (YCW)

Using Results-based Management (RBM) language, the five intended outcomes of the project were:

- Improved capacity by 2009 of the Gambia Police Force to deliver training, particularly in the area of community-based policing and restorative justice, to new recruits (all recruits by 2009) as well as established police officers (100 by 2009) in three jurisdictions

- By 2010 improved relations between the GPF and three communities (urban Banjul, and rural Farafenni and Basse) and increased community awareness and support for CBP and RJ in those communities

- Improved capacity of the Gambia College by 2009 to train relevant human resources through the development and operation of a fully sustainable certificate program in Community-Policing and Restorative Justice (offered jointly by Gambia Police Force and Gambia College; courses taught at both Gambia College and Gambia Police Force training school) and through the improvement of faculty and student research skills

- Improved ability by 2007 of the Gambia Police Force and Gambia College to educate new recruits and existing police officers in three jurisdictions in areas related to gender equality, particularly in relation to community-based policing and RJ

- Enabling environment by 2008 within Gambia Police Force for women to join the police profession and to be promoted to positions of influence within the GPF.

The first phase of the project was achieving institutional commitment to community-based policing on the part of the senior officials of the Gambia Police Force and a sensitization to CBP on the part of all ranks of the GPF in three major jurisdictions: Banjul, Farafenni and Basse. Activities in this phase included travel by Gambia Police Force (and GC) personnel to Canada for training in CBP and RJ, and travel by Halifax Regional Police (and MSVU and NSRJP) personnel to The Gambia to transfer knowledge, skills and attitudes regarding CBP and RJ (including gender issues, communication and leadership) to their counterparts. In particular, the face-to-face communication between Gambian and Halifax police officers was a highly effective means of sharing skills and attitudes, and the sensitization of those members of the GPF to CBP. It was also valuable for the Halifax police as they serve an increasingly diverse community in Canada.

In addition to the increase in awareness and skills in CBP on the part of the lower ranks of the GPF, there had been several declarations by the "High Command" of the GPF that they totally support the concept of CBP.

This two-pronged achievement meant that the first phase of the project had come successfully to an end. This accomplishment was expected to lead to a heightened receptivity by the GPF to the potential advantages of the certificate program in CBP to be created by Gambia College in the second phase of the project. Therefore, the time had come for emphasis in the project to evolve from sensitization to CBP to capacity-building and training in CBP.

Within its first three years of operating, the project had encountered a number of problems, e.g. delays, promises allegedly not being kept, disagreements, personality conflicts, and so the Canadian Project Director and AUCC therefore agreed to hold the mid-term evaluation at the earliest possible moment. Accordingly, a Canadian evaluator was hired and the Canadian asked Alpha Jallow to be the associate evaluator. The Canadian evaluator knew about Jallow from the case the Canadian had written entitled *The Gambia & Don Sawyer*. Jallow's excellent role in the formation of the West Africa Rural Development Centre in The Gambia was well known, and the Canadian evaluator sought and received invaluable and insightful information from him about the local context and the cultural appropriateness of the recommendations.

ALPHA JALLOW

Jallow, a Gambian citizen and former police officer, received an MBA in Human Resources Management from the Centre for Management Studies and Development in Switzerland. He had also achieved Certificates as a Rural Adult Instructor, in Participatory Rural Appraisal and in Building and Managing an Effective Training Administration.

In his 20 years of practical field experience in education and community development training, he worked with the American Peace Corps/The Gambia and Save The Children USA as a trainer and spent six years as Development Area Coordinator of Action Aid's Basic Education and Literacy Programme, in the Gambia;

Jallow was the founding Programme Director of the West Africa Rural Development (WARD) Centre, a CIDA-funded project, and also served as the in-country Supervisor for the International Youth Internship Program (CIDA) in the Gambia and was instrumental in building closer links between

Okanagan University College (OUC), Saint Mary's University (SMU) in Canada, The Gambia Technical Training Institute (GTTI), The West Africa Rural Development (WARD) project, and other indigenous organizations operating in The Gambia.

In addition to his administrative role, Jallow was engaged in curriculum research and writing, training (especially training of trainers) and facilitating the Rural Community Development Practitioners Diploma program in The Gambia and Ghana. He has co-authored and contributed in the development of culturally appropriate, interactive and experiential learning materials for the training of West African Rural Development workers and project managers.

Jallow was currently the Head of Training of the Gambia Revenue Authority and served as a trainer consultant for the National Women's Bureau of The Gambia. He had been a member of a team of experts assigned to develop modules on community development and leadership for the project being evaluated.

THE WRAP-UP MEETING WITH THE GAMBIA POLICE FORCE

The Canadian evaluator's usual practice when conducting mid-term evaluations was, on the second last day in the partner country, to present the findings and the draft recommendations of the evaluation team to the local stakeholders and to seek their further input and their reactions to the draft recommendations.

During that meeting, the senior officials of the Gambia Police Force (the Command) refused to cooperate with Gambia College as the project attempted to move from its initial phase to the capacity-building phase. The Command refused to accept that GC was a partner in the project, and held the position that the community policing project had been imposed on them. The Command stated that they would continue to be involved only if the project would support the Police Academy instead of Gambia College. The establishment of a Police Academy had been mentioned as part of the immediate plans of the GPF, but the reality was that the institution did not exist.

JALLOW HAS TO DECIDE WHAT TO DO

The Canadian evaluator felt that the GPF had effectively prevented the project from continuing, and that it was not a good use of Canadian taxpayers' money being spent in attempting to keep the project going. Unless some means of resolving the current impasse could be found, he was in favour of recommending that the project be terminated and all uncommitted funds and recoverable expenditures be returned to AUCC. Jallow, however, knew how potentially important this project could be in improving the struggling democracy in his country, and tried to find some means of keeping the project going. Jallow also appreciated that there was some concern about his own career and personal safety in The Gambia if the project were shut down.

CASE ANALYSIS: MEXICO & ERIC DILLMANN[248]

A project entitled "Connecting Campus and Community" was a collaboration involving the University of Calgary, la Universidad Autónoma del Estado de Morelos in Mexico, and the University College of Belize. Approximately halfway through the project, Dr. Eric Dillmann became the Canadian Project Director, replacing the original person in that position. On May 21, 2003, shortly after assuming his new responsibilities, Dillmann had just finished reading the report of the mid-term evaluation of the project. He was surprised and disheartened at what he regarded as the harshness of the criticisms leveled at the project, and he had to decide what to do.

AVAILABLE INFORMATION

- The original goal of the project was to enhance the abilities of the Mexican and Belizean universities to respond to the development needs of local communities, especially rural and indigenous communities, and particularly women. The key activities to accomplish this included the design and implementation of community-based development activities, preparation and design of various training modalities, curriculum design, development of teaching materials for diploma education and short courses, continuing education, and participatory development research.

- The project effectively began in 2000. In the first two years, AUCC became concerned that the narrative reporting did not make sense. Accordingly, they recommended that a mid-term evaluation be carried out in 2002, which was somewhat earlier than usual in the project cycle. By the time the evaluator was hired and was able to travel to Mexico, however, it was the spring of 2003. Unfortunately, the visit coincided with *la semana santa*, the major Easter holiday, and many participants were not sufficiently available.

- Eric Dillmann, before he became Canadian Project Director, had been in Mexico in November of 2002 for other work but happened to visit the project team at UAEM. He was highly impressed with the abilities and the dedication of the participants.

- In early 2003, there was widespread corporate change (and consequent partial loss of institutional memory) in all three partner institutions: at the University of Calgary, at UAEM and at the University College of Belize.

- The MTE found that many activities of the project were spread so thin that they had very little impact, and recommended a major reorganization with increased focus on a smaller number of outputs. The MTE also found that, in Mexico, the project essentially had no identity because the project activities had been largely subsumed into the work of the partner institution. One of the main conclusions of the MTE was:

> The combination of: inheriting a project design that was highly ambitious; inexperience among core team members in the implementation of participatory community development and program / curricular development; lack of an identifiable group of tutors working long-term in and with communities supporting ongoing development work; frequent coordinator and personnel changes; lack of clear criteria, as well as a sense of dis-empowerment for decision making on implementation; are reflected in the lack of coordinated and cumulative learning strategies and continuity of actions in communities; lack of coherence between actual project activities and workplans; and no, low, or inappropriate activity in certain project areas (e.g., micro-projects). Overall, these issues have affected program performance and have strained the bilateral relations between the U of C and UB, and the U of C and UAEM. With additional project management changes looming in both Calgary and Belize, the project is at a critical decision-making point. The UB and UNICEDES-UAEM, in consultation with the U of C – IC, need to decide if the time, resources, and personal / institutional commitment are present to re-create a coherent project out of CCC supported activities, and to map a reasonable performance level achievable through a programmed effort, in order to continue the project to its current slated completion

date – OR – to explore other options for continuing the linkages.

- When Dillmann tried repeatedly to engage the University College of Belize in discussions about their role, they were essentially non-responsive. In contrast, UAEM was open to such discussions, but were likely to lose morale and momentum unless Dillmann moved quickly.

ALTERNATIVE COURSES OF ACTION

After reviewing all the information in the section above, Dillmann conceived of three possible things he could do:

- Terminate the project.
- Continue the project, but carry out a major restructuring with the existing partners.
- Continue the project, but carry out a major restructuring and drop the Belizean partner.

CRITERIA FOR EVALUATING THE ALTERNATIVE COURSES OF ACTION

1. Based on his contacts with the Mexican partners, he had developed a great deal of respect for their commitment and their capacity to bring about successes in the field of community development, and he wanted to give them a chance to do so. He did not have the same feelings about the partners in Belize, however, who seemed to have lost interest in the project.
2. The University of Calgary's International Centre had a good track record of operating projects of international development cooperation, and Dillmann wanted to contribute to that track record, rather than avoiding problems by terminating the project.
3. At the same time, he knew that the best choice might be to shut down the project if he couldn't see a way to resurrect it. He knew he had to make a sincere and honest decision in the circumstances.
4. He knew he had to maintain strict accountability to the Government of Canada (via AUCC and the UPCD program) because taxpayers' dollars were being spent on this project.

THE DECISION

Criteria 3 and 4 urged Dillmann towards Alternative A: terminate the project. Criterion 2 argued for Alternatives B and C: continue the project. He gave greatest weight, however, to Criterion 1, which led him to decide on Alternative C: continue the project, but carry out a major restructuring and drop the Belizean partner.

PLANS FOR IMPLEMENTING THE DECISION

After a mid-term evaluation has been carried out on a project, the project managers are required to prepare and submit a Project Completion Plan to AUCC a few months after the MTE final report has been released. The PCP was, in effect, the implementation plan for Dillmann's decision. The PCP contained the following highlights:

- The University College of Belize, because of its non-responsiveness, was dropped from the project.

- The project was redefined within a conceptual framework that was more tightly focused on results that were clearly defined, measurable and achievable.

- Because the previous work had been excessively dispersed over a large number of communities, the project now concentrated on just three carefully selected communities.

- The level of contact between the University of Calgary and the project implementation unit at UAEM was intensified, via telephone, Internet and face-to-face contacts. Communication among team members in Mexico was also increased.

- The project reporting structure was tightened up, with increased emphasis on performance indicators.

- A phase-out plan was designed to begin after another 15 months of field activities. Responsibility for ongoing activities would be transferred to the Mexican partner institution and to community-based groups.

- Creation of a Master's program was postponed to a future project.

FINAL EVALUATIONS

Final evaluations take place shortly after the end of the duration of the period of funding of the project, i.e. typically after five or six years. These are less useful from an operational point of view than MTEs because there is no longer any budget money with which to act on the findings of this evaluation. Nevertheless, final evaluations are highly desirable because they provide a record and a recognition of the results of the work of the project team and of the investment of the donor agency. Typically, a final report is required of the project team, but this does not benefit from the independent view that characterizes a mid-term evaluation.

With respect to the RBM framework, it is usually premature (after only five or six years of effort) to see any definite results at the level of Impact, i.e. the long-term contribution to the fundamental development issue to which this project was intended to make a contribution), but undoubtedly there will (or should) be measurable results at the Outcome level. Some commentators, such as Dr. Jim Shute of the University of Guelph, are of the opinion that results at the Impact level will not really be observable in periods of less than ten years[249].

CHAPTER SIXTEEN

HOW TO GET STARTED IN INTERNATIONAL WORK

EARLY INFLUENCES

What kinds of people choose to go into international work? Are there any common characteristics that they possess, or are there similarities in their backgrounds—family, community, educational, ethical, religious—that have attracted them to international development?

In an attempt to shed some light on this, we looked at the backgrounds of three of the focal points of the cases in this book. Not surprisingly, they were all unique, but we identified some early influences that possibly prepared them for subsequently making international contributions.

> » **Robert Marino** (Case Analysis *Mexico & Robert Marino* in
> Chapter Fourteen

Dr. Robert Marino was born into a culturally aware family of Italian heritage and, as a result, was raised within a caring, multilingual and cosmopolitan environment. Not surprisingly, early on he developed a fundamental sense of social responsibility, which manifested itself by his joining a religious order, the Redemptorist Fathers, and spending a year in a seminary in Italy. Subsequently, he became a social worker dealing with Italian and Portuguese immigrants in Toronto, and then was appointed to the position of Executive Director of the COSTI Educational Centre, a major Canadian social agency dealing with immigrants and refugees.

» **Christine Gilmore** (Case Analysis *Ethiopia & Christine Gilmore* in Chapter Nine)

Born in Oshawa, Christine Gilmore grew up in the 1950s in a unilingual white Anglo-Saxon Canadian environment that had a strong community and social consciousness as a core part of their family values. Resulting in part from the grandparents' farming background, one of the things they naturally did was to watch out for others in the community–keeping an eye on the neighborhood children, noticing if anyone was away and their grass needed cutting, bringing in meals or groceries for someone who was ill, swapping clothing that children outgrew, and making things for the bazaar to raise money for church programs or for families in hard times. Gilmore, early on, had a well-developed sense of outrage against unfairness and injustice, and frequently found herself "sticking up for the underdog". She was often vociferous and proactive on matters of principle–she organized a sit-in when she was in Grade 8 to protest a name change for her school that had been arrived at without consultation with the students.

» **Andrew Nelson** (Case Analysis *Peru & Andrew Nelson* in Chapter Ten)

Dr. Andrew Nelson (together with his wife, Christine Nelson) has been working in Peru for many years, principally in archaeological and osteological investigations of the Moche (approximately 100 AD to 750 AD) and later cultures of the northern coast. Nelson, whose father was born in Peru, led teams that contained many indigenous workers, some of whom were probably descendants of the Moche. As they excavated skeletal remains and artifacts from ancient graves in this area, Nelson realized that the indigenous workers were highly curious about these discoveries and quite proud of their pre-European cultural heritage. The Nelsons understood that awareness of the cultural patrimony of indigenous peoples was a valuable aspect of development through increasing self-confidence, and resolved to help create a museum that would celebrate their heritage.

Are there common characteristics that were nurtured by these early influences? Reading the backgrounds of these three, as well as thinking of the many other fine people in international development we have come to know over the years, we note that a strong sense of social justice comes high on the list. Another characteristic is the desire to make oneself useful in doing something that is genuinely needed by the partners—good intentions alone don't help very much in a village—what works is either having a useful skill or the initiative to find out what needs to be done and then rolling up one's sleeves. Languages, curiosity, a desire to help bring about beneficial change, are all helpful. We know of no one who has done it for the money or the prestige.

GETTING YOUR FEET WET

Countless opportunities are available for obtaining a first taste—almost always unpaid—of international work. In this section, we will list a sampling of these opportunities. (The mention of any organization should not necessarily be construed as an endorsement of the organization.) This list is far from being complete, and so we refer the reader to a most comprehensive handbook called *The BIG Guide to Living and Working Overseas* by Jean-Marc Hachey, Intercultural Systems, Toronto, for additional information.

- Trips to other countries organized by high schools, colleges and universities

- International student exchange programs organized by high schools, colleges and universities (see Chapter Fourteen)

- Study abroad programs

- Participation in local international development events such as CIDA's International Development Week

- Attending "Go Abroad" fairs

- Volunteering with a non-governmental organization, either a Canadian NGO with an overseas project or an NGO of a developing country. Chapters Four and Twelve have a lot to say about volunteers and NGOs–here are some programs of interest to young people:

- Canada World Youth[250]

- Canadian Crossroads International[251]

- CUSO[252]

- Engineers Without Borders[253]

- Habitat for Humanity[254]

- CIDA Internships[255]

- International work vacations

- Service overseas:

CASE: NICARAGUA & MIRA NOORDERMEER

Mira Noordermeer knew something was wrong. Her aunt Judy Noordermeer and the Dignidad para el Pueblo Team Leader Cora Walker had just arrived back at Dignidad's site in the village of Ojo de Agua in Nicaragua on July 13, 2006 from a trip into the capital Managua, and Judy was obviously upset. Judy took Mira behind the camp to get some privacy, and explained that the pains in her jaw that had started before the trip had been getting worse every day. Two separate dentists in Managua had both recommended root canal surgery. Judy greatly preferred to have the root canal work performed by her own dentist back in Canada. Because Mira was seventeen years old, Judy was her legal guardian in Nicaragua. While in Managua, Judy had already arranged flights back to Canada for the two of them. Mira and Judy had to pack and leave the village within 30 minutes in order to get transportation back to Managua. Mira then also became distraught because, until that point, she had been having a wonderful time with the villagers and with the other volunteers who were building houses in partnership with the Nicaraguan families who would live in them. Judy initially assumed that she couldn't leave Mira in Nicaragua. Cora thought that there just might be a way legally to arrange it. If there *were* such a possibility, Mira had to decide what she should urge her aunt to do.

JUDY NOORDERMEER

Judy had worked in international development prior to this trip. Inspired by an older brother, she spent three months as a volunteer with Canada World Youth in rural Ecuador almost twenty years ago and, subsequently, worked in villages in northern Ethiopia as a member of the Future Forests NGO. She had also spent time as a visitor in Indonesia. These experiences had created in Judy an awareness of the richness and formative value of living and working as a volunteer overseas, and she wanted to share this with her niece Mira. After first seeking the blessing of Mira's parents, Judy invited Mira to take such a trip with her. They studied the various organizations that provide this type of experience, and the countries in which they work. Mira and Judy finally decided on Dignidad para el Pueblo's house building project in the village of Ojo de Agua in Nicaragua, which is about two hours travel from Managua. They decided to spend two weeks, from July 8 to 23, 2006 in Nicaragua.

MIRA NOORDERMEER

Mira was delighted with her Aunt Judy's idea, and accepted immediately. The Noordermeer family was accustomed to international travel, and to the principle of service to others, and thus Mira's parents were highly supportive of the trip. Because Mira was seventeen years old at the time, Judy would be her legal guardian in Nicaragua. In addition to her family's positive attitude, Mira was sustained by her religious views, which included the importance of assistance to developing countries.

Mira and Judy then embarked on a campaign to raise the money for Mira's travel, and Mira had the opportunity to speak in public about the purposes and anticipated benefits of the trip.

NICARAGUA

Nicaragua's Human Development Index ranks it as 121st out of 175 countries[256]. It is one of the poorest and least developed countries in the Western Hemisphere—only Haiti is lower in the rankings. Nicaragua is now a democracy, but with an economy in dire straits after decades of political strife, especially the *Contra* war with the Sandinista-led government.

Both urban and rural dwellers suffer from a dire lack of adequate housing. As a result of the 1972 earthquake, approximately 53,000 residential units were destroyed or seriously damaged in the Managua area. The Sandinistas launched housing construction and tree-planting programs, but were hampered by a shortage of hard currency to pay for the construction equipment required. Hurricane Mitch in 1998 also destroyed thousands of dwellings[257].

"With more than 5 million inhabitants, Nicaragua presents a housing deficit of over 500,000 houses. Of the total number of existing houses, 250,000 are in need of repairs. Natural disasters, social and economic instability, migrations from the countryside to the city and the formation of new families give rise to the need for 30,000 new houses every year. Approximately 3,750,000 people in urban and rural areas currently live in sub-human conditions. Overcrowding, a lack of sanitary conditions, squatting and an increase in crime are among some of the other side effects of poverty housing." [258]

DIGNIDAD PARA EL PUEBLO

Dignidad para el Pueblo is a nonprofit, ecumenical Christian housing ministry. Dignidad seeks to eliminate poverty housing and homelessness in Central America, and to make decent shelter a matter of conscience and action. Dignidad invites people of all backgrounds, races and religions to build houses together in partnership with families in need.

Through volunteer labor and donations of money and materials, Dignidad builds and rehabilitates simple, decent houses with the help of the homeowner (partner) families. Dignidad houses are sold to partner families at no profit, financed with affordable loans. The homeowners' monthly mortgage payments are used to build still more Dignidad houses. Dignidad is not a giveaway program. In addition to a down payment and the monthly mortgage payments, homeowners invest hundreds of hours of their own labor--sweat equity--into building their Dignidad house and the houses of others.

Dignidad houses are affordable for low-income families because there is no profit included in the sale price. Mortgage length varies from seven to 30 years. The monthly payments, during a 10-year term, are of approximately US$18 per family, a minuscule amount compared to rent payments, which hover around US$100 or more. Large-scale purchases of materials permit lower house costs and guarantee their control and distribution.

Dignidad para el Pueblo's work is accomplished at the community level by affiliates—independent, locally run, nonprofit organizations. Each affiliate coordinates all aspects of Dignidad home building in its local area—fund raising, building site selection, partner family selection and support, house construction and mortgage servicing.

Families in need of decent shelter apply to local Dignidad affiliates. The affiliate's family selection committee chooses homeowners based on their level of need, their willingness to become partners in the program and their ability to repay the loan. Every affiliate follows a nondiscriminatory policy of family selection. Neither race nor religion is a factor in choosing the families who receive Dignidad houses.

Dignidad's houses are made of confined masonry with concrete blocks, zinc sheet roofs over a metallic panel structure and floors of domestic tile. They (typically, but not always) consist of a living-dining room, two dormitories, a bathroom and a kitchen. They are designed to resist frequent severe storms.

Once the construction is finished, Dignidad, together with volunteer community leaders, request the installation of basic services for electricity, water and public lighting in order to create convenient and secure conditions for partner families.

JUDY HAS TO LEAVE

Judy had visited her dentist ten days before her departure from Canada, and no problems were detected. Therefore, when she had some minor dental discomfort a few days before the trip, she paid little attention to it.

In Nicaragua, pains in her jaw grew steadily worse and she decided to travel into Managua with Cora, the Dignidad Team Leader, to visit a dentist. The dentist said Judy needed root canal work. This was most worrisome and so Judy sought a second opinion from another dentist, who came to the same conclusion. Judy much preferred to have the work done by her dentist in Toronto and, because of the pain, wanted to leave Nicaragua at the earliest possible moment. Judy, as Mira's guardian, assumed that she couldn't leave Mira in Nicaragua. Assisted by Cora, Judy booked flights that departed the following morning to Canada for Mira and herself.

During the drive with Cora back to Ojo de Agua from Managua, Judy felt full of guilt-guilt to Mira for cutting short Mira's Nicaraguan experience, guilt to the people who had donated money for their trip, guilt to Dignidad and the Nicaraguan villagers for not living up to her commitment. Then, Cora mentioned that there was a possibility that Judy could transfer her guardianship of Mira to Cora (and thus Mira could stay in Nicaragua for the remainder of the assignment) provided that Mira, Judy, Mira's parents, and Dignidad's head office all approved.

MIRA HAS TO DECIDE

Judy arrived back in Ojo de Agua and told all this to Mira. Now Mira was also in tears (and was comforted by a four year old Nicaraguan girl who sensed Mira's dismay and held her hand). Mira had to quickly sort through all the considerations facing her, and had to decide what she should urge her aunt to do. She started by mentally listing all the reasons for returning to Canada with Judy, and all the reasons for remaining in Nicaragua while Judy returned to Toronto.

BUILDING A CAREER IN INTERNATIONAL DEVELOPMENT

"Foreign Service Examination and Career Counselling Inc.[259] (FSECC) provides comprehensive international careers training, as follows:

- Personal coaching to experienced professionals seeking advancement within or outside their present field of work;

- Application assistance, test preparation materials and interview training to individuals seeking diplomatic, development, or other government or multilateral institution positions and internships;

- Workshops on international opportunities at educational institutions and conferences.

"Established in 1984, FSECC works with individual and institutional clients across North America, in Europe and worldwide. It is the only organization that offers such an extensive array of international career development expertise and training.

"*Career Development Coaching*: gives a valuable edge to professionals in the government, non-governmental, multilateral, academic, media, legal and corporate sectors who are competing for highly sought-after international positions. We develop tailored *Resumes* and *Cover Letters* that demonstrate candidate strengths related to job requirements. We also deliver *In-basket, Executive Simulation, Presentation Skills* and *Personal Interview* coaching for behaviorally-based hiring and promotion processes.

"*Foreign Service Entry Training:* prepares candidates for complex recruitment competitions carried out by the countries listed below:

Canada: Foreign Service, Management/Consular, and CIDA officer *Application Statements, Examinations and Interviews*

United Kingdom: Diplomatic Service *E-tray and Fast Stream Assessment* processes

United States: Foreign Service Officer *Oral Assessment* and *Statement of Interest* preparation, and Foreign Service Specialist *Application* and *Oral Assessment* exercises.

"*International Careers Workshops:* enable students, teachers and counsellors to learn about the spectrum of international opportunities and how to pursue them in an informed manner. Our *International Careers Workshop* is a presentation sponsored by professional development associations, universities, and international baccalaureate and independent secondary schools. We also facilitate a *Strategic Planning Workshop* for educational administrators responsible for developing, managing and expanding international co-op, student exchange and internship programs.

CHAPTER SEVENTEEN

PREPARING YOURSELF FOR INTERNATIONAL ASSIGNMENTS

INTERCULTURAL EFFECTIVENESS

A very useful unit of the Canadian government is the Centre for Intercultural Learning[260] (CIL) of the Canadian Foreign Service Institute of the Department of Foreign Affairs and International Trade (DFAIT). One of CIL's programs is the provision of a three-day workshop to persons who are about to go overseas on CIDA-funded projects, e.g. many of CIDA's International Interns participate in this program, as well as CESO Volunteer Advisors and people involved in UPCD projects. (If spouses are also traveling, they are encouraged to attend.) The workshop is entitled the *Pre-departure Course in Intercultural Effectiveness*.

A book used in the workshops is CIL's *Profile of the Interculturally Effective Person*[261], which describes actual behaviors linked to nine intercultural competencies:

- **Adaptation skills:**
  Interculturally Effective Persons (IEPs) have the ability to cope personally, professionally, and in their family context with the conditions and challenges of living and working in another culture.

- **An attitude of modesty and respect:**
  IEPs demonstrate modesty about their own culture's answers to problems and a respect for the ways of the local culture, are humble about their knowledge of the local context, and

are therefore willing to learn much and consult with locals before coming to conclusions on issues.

- **Understanding the concept of culture:**
  IEPs have an understanding of the concept of culture and the pervasive influence it will have on their life and work abroad.

- **Knowledge of the host country and culture:**
  IEPs possess knowledge of the host country and culture and try constantly to expand that knowledge.

- **Relationship-building:**
  IEPs possess good relationship-building skills, both social/personal and professional.

- **Self-knowledge:**
  Knowledge of one's [own] background, motivations, strengths and weaknesses

- **Intercultural communication:**
  IEPs are effective intercultural communicators.

- **Organizational skills:**
  IEPs strive to improve the quality of organizational structures, processes, and staff morale, and promote a positive atmosphere in the workplace.

- **Personal and professional commitment:**
  IEPs have a high level of personal and professional commitment to the assignment and the life experience in another culture.

In summary, an Interculturally Effective Person "is someone who is able to live contentedly and work successfully in another culture". Attending a CIL workshop is an excellent way to nurture the skills and attitudes for becoming an IEP.

In Chapter Three, we mentioned that CIL has studied the effectiveness of training in international projects and has published *Re-examining the role of training in contributing to international project success: A literature review and an outline of a new model training program*[262], which is recommended reading for Canadians who will be trying to create or deliver training activities in other countries.

CIL has also published *International Projects: Some Lessons on Avoiding Failure and Maximizing Success*[263]. CIL notes that performance improvement is needed both for individuals and for organizations (such as companies and government agencies). With respect to individuals, the training in intercultural effectiveness described above is a means of improving performance. With respect to organizations, CIL proposes "Ten Keys to Becoming an Internationally Effective Organization":

- Examine and prioritize your motives and strategic objectives. Are they consistent with those of a partner organization so that a cooperative, win-win relationship is likely?

- Select partner organizations that have compatible or complementary competencies, management practices, and organizational cultures.

- Be clear on and ensure agreement with partners on operational goals and performance targets.

- Be realistic in setting objectives and performance targets.

- Have clear and unambiguous governance mechanisms and definitions of the roles and responsibilities of the partner organizations and the middle and senior project managers.

- Consult and build consensus. Seek out the views of local partners and stakeholders in the community and try to integrate the best of the management traditions of the host country as much as is possible, consistent with corporate or project goals.

- Ensure the commitment of senior management at headquarters by having a project champion and providing services to ease the life of expatriates.

- Constantly assess the sociopolitical and economic environment of the project, weighing its feasibility in the first place, making ongoing adjustments during implementation, and having programs to consult with and influence local and international stakeholders and build community support.

- Recognize the importance culture will have on project management, and select and train personnel to be culturally sensitive and effective collaborators with people of another culture.

- Trust your partners until proven wrong.

It is reassuring that these recommendations from CIL resonate well with suggestions made throughout the rest of this book.

An important cross-cultural issue is sexual orientation and how a visiting development worker should deal with various situations that may arise. Very useful and pragmatic advice is provided by Carrie McLaren in the following conversation.

A CONVERSATION WITH CARRIE MCLAREN, LESBIAN

Carrie McLaren teaches French and Spanish at Sir Oliver Mowat Collegiate Institute in Toronto, and has recently become the Head of Modern Languages at this high school. Carrie is also a co-author of a high school textbook on Spanish language and culture called *El Idioma y La Cultura Española* currently being written. Frederick Keenan interviewed Carrie on December 3, 2009.

FK: Carrie, are you a lesbian?

CM: Yes, I do identify as a lesbian. I came out at age 18. At the time, my best friend identified as a lesbian and in the process of her exploring her own sexual orientation, I realized I, too, was gay and she became my first partner for two years.

I'm now working as a high school teacher and head of a department in a local school here in Toronto, and I'm out not only to students but also to staff. And I've recently started the first-ever gay-straight alliance at my school, which is a group of students that come together with staff to talk about issues around homophobia and how to make our school a better and a safer place for everybody.

FK: I'm interested in your experiences when you travel. Have you travelled in developing countries, either as a tourist or working there, and have you been recognized as a lesbian and if so, what's happened? What has the impact been on you?

CM: Sure. At age 21, which is a few years after I came out, I went on an exchange to Mexico through York University. I spent a year there and, at that time, I had short hair and I dressed mainly in men's clothing, and I was very much out of the closet. When I first arrived I couldn't believe how difficult it was to find a community or a place where I actually felt I fit in and where I wasn't mistaken for a man.

Initially, when I would get on a local public bus and I'd go to sit down, people would get up and move away from me. So there was a lot of unspoken homophobia but I think I was less of a threat because I was a tourist or because I was studying there and I wasn't one of them. A month into the exchange, I was able to see the other side of the coin when I started dating a local Mexican girl and I could see her struggle as a Mexican woman, living in her own country where she was oppressed and of course people would say hurtful things. A friend of ours was beaten up because he was a gay man. In my experiences, I found that the gay men tend to have a harder time with homophobia because they tend to be more out. The men that I met in Mexico tended to be a little more flamboyant and so they became more of a threat and more of a target for homophobia. But in my own experience as a traveler, it's been difficult for people to know what to do with me. It was challenging to assert myself and to feel secure in my own identity before I left and certainly when I came back.

FK: In Mexico, how were you treated by other people? Tell us more about how they reacted to you.

CM: Sure. There are some examples I can give. First of all, oftentimes when people would come into contact with me the first thing that they would say was "amigo" or "señor." Just based on the length of my hair, I'd be called "friend" or "sir" but they would use the masculine form of "friend" [amigo, rather than amiga]. Some more offensive things that happened: I was teaching English at the time and one of the teachers spread rumors around about me being a lesbian and my students started dropping out of my course and asking for their money back, and it became a real issue at the school. Thank goodness that the owner took a really good stance on the situation and said, "Fine, you may go but we're not giving you your money back". He didn't fire me but, it's certainly something that I think a lot of people face.

Mexico isn't unlike other countries. I've also travelled in other Latin American countries and I get a similar response. Not that it's necessarily in-your-face homophobia but, when I've been out with a partner, I've been called a "torta", or a "tortuga".

Sorry, these are slang words for lesbians. "Torta" could be a cake or a pie, but it's also the word that they use. I'm not really sure of the origin of "tortuga" but I mean, certainly I could guess. You know, it's some sort of relation to turtle but, again, it's unclear to me how that relates to a lesbian. "Puto" is a very offensive word for a gay man. I haven't been called that because I'm not a man but certainly in the mistaken identity there have been a lot of words that have been exchanged.

I've certainly heard the argument that there are no Mexicans who are gay, and that's certainly completely untrue. There are a number of gay bars in Mexico City and in all of the main cities. Even in the small town where I was studying, Cholula, one of my roommates said to me, "Oh, do not go to this bar that's behind the school because it's a gay bar" and I said, "Oh, thank you. Thank you so much." And then of course the next night a bunch of my new foreign friends and I all went, who were also gay or gay-friendly and it was a very positive experience.

But a lot of things are incognito. Oftentimes it's hard to find the communities. They're so hidden because they're afraid of people finding out and then targeting them for graffiti or for homophobic words or fights. So oftentimes it's word of mouth and for people who are not out, it becomes hard for them as well to find the community. The positive side of this isolation is that it really brought us together and we really looked out for one another.

But certainly looking the part made it that much easier for me to find communities. I know a friend of mine who went to Mexico and she has long hair and, while she identifies as a lesbian, it was much harder for her to find where the community was because they didn't associate her with being gay. So stereotypes become really important and you must be sensitive to the language you use and your own internalized homophobia. It is something that we all must unlearn, because our society raises us as straight by default. So being inclusive and aware that you might be talking to somebody who isn't straight and using, gender-neutral words such as "partner" and not going right for "sir" or "madam" as titles because sometimes you're going to be wrong. So I think that that's something really important to keep in mind.

FK: **Many of the developing countries I've worked in have in fact denied that there's any homosexuality in their countries. You've just talked about your experience in Mexico. What do you think the situation might be in other developing countries? I've noticed this particularly in Muslim countries.**

CM: I think it's safe to say that there are going to be gay and lesbian people in all countries, in all walks of life. There does exist a Kinsey scale, and I don't know how much research has been done to validate the findings but I think it's an accepted statistic that one in ten people are gay or lesbian. So it's safe to say, if you're in a large group of people, there will be at least one person in the room who is gay or lesbian.

In terms of my own travels, I've also lived and studied in Spain and Costa Rica, as well as Cuba, France, England and St. Martins. I have plans to go to Peru. But I certainly know that within those countries there will be certain areas that will be "unsafe" or homophobic. Bigger cities tend to be a little bit more open than the smaller towns where everyone knows everybody. And then, there are certain countries such as Spain and Argentina that recognize gay rights and are moving ahead with gay marriages and promoting gay-friendly spaces and truly trying to make it a gay-accepting, if not gay-positive, country.

And while my experience has been when I've travelled to these countries and you're looking in the guidebook under the section where it says "This neighborhood is gay-friendly", you go to those neighborhoods and it becomes really difficult to see where the community starts because you're looking for signs of gayness. Usually it's a rainbow sticker, somewhere, that will indicate that oh, okay, this is a gay shop or this is a gay friendly space. And you're also looking for other people who are going to identify as gay or lesbian and it becomes very challenging because oftentimes they don't want to be stigmatized either.

I think it's safe to say that there are gay people in all countries and I think a lot of them, if they're not out or if it's not commonly known where the gay area is, it's because they're oppressed and so it's word of mouth. So people find each other and then they stay in close contact with each other in order to feel safe and protected that a group will provide for you.

I know that when my partner was living and working in Japan, because of the isolation she and many others felt, they would organize these lesbian retreats for foreigners and Japanese. There was a need for a space where, women could come together and not feel so alone and isolated. These spaces become so critical for the gay and lesbian community because it is a place where they can go and be themselves. For women, it is even more difficult because most of the gay bars are predominately men focused. But that's yet another form of, inequality where, within the gay community, lesbians really have to fight to have their own spaces. So it's something else to be aware of.

FK: Talking again about developing countries, for people who are nationals of that country and who are homosexual, what has been your experience about stigma applied to those people or to discrimination being shown to them?

CM: In the countries that I've visited and the women that I've dated or the friends that I've made, I find it can be very oppressive and it leads to a lot of insecurities and self-loathing because they're always trying to not only fit into society but they're also trying to be true to themselves. It's an internal conflict and it's something that must be resolved.

But, always finding that sense of community has allowed people to connect with other people and to not feel so isolated. Isolation, as everybody knows, can be very painful and very difficult.

With one particular woman that I dated, we were thrown out of a "straight bar" that we had gone to several times before but on this particular occasion we were thrown out because we had been seen kissing in a corner. This was a real eye opener for me because on so many other occasions, we had been admitted into the bar even before other people. We would bypass the line because we were white and I looked like a foreigner – someone with money. We tried going back there the following weekend but they refused to let us in. And, upon my partner's questioning it, they said, "You're not welcome here, you lesbians." Well they said a derogatory word for dyke but that's what the sense is. They want tourism and they want to promote their bar, yet they want a certain image of the kind of establishment that they are. This is the kind of bar we are and anything that doesn't fit into this stereotype is not wanted or not welcome.

FK: **Finally, Carrie, what would your advice be to young Canadian engineers who are going to work in developing countries as to how they should factor homosexuals as a group that's discriminated against in their work in international development in that country?**

CM: Well number one, I would say use appropriate language and be sensitive. What I mean by that is, when you're meeting somebody for the first time, try to be inclusive in your language so say "partner", say, "Yes, so and so." Try to get away from the titles because I find even in Canada people are still calling me "Sir", not because I look like a man but because I have short hair and so at first glance, that's what they see and so they follow their stereotype. So that always irritates me and it puts me in a bad mood being called "Sir." And while now I can sort of laugh it off, after a while it grates on your nerves.

So, use appropriate language, be sensitive, be aware. Be aware that if one in ten people are gay, you're going to meet gay people so you don't want to come across as a close-minded heterosexual if that's in fact how you identify.

When you're thinking about working in certain countries, people like to talk to each other a little bit closer, people are a little bit more touchy in certain countries, so don't equate that with homosexuality. Be comfortable with that, welcome that. I mean, these are normal forms of greetings and salutations and ways that people talk to one another. It doesn't have to mean that they're gay or that you are.

I find that people who are secure in themselves and in their own sexual orientation are not threatened by any person who is gay or lesbian. I wouldn't suggest that you get into a debate about whether it's right or wrong, or whether it's moral or immoral, whether it's Christian or Catholic. That religion argument, you're never going to win that one so try to avoid it. It seems to be a popular discussion these days: Is it legal? Is it not? Is it right? Is it wrong?

Apparently in the news recently there was an African country, which one was it?

FK: Uganda.

CM: Uganda, that said it was illegal to be gay? That's a move backwards. Obviously, there are gays and lesbians in Uganda. There are gays and lesbians everywhere. They've been around for—as long as the Greeks have been around, there have been known cases or known people who were gay and it was acceptable back then and, I don't know, at one point we started to say that this is wrong who people choose to love. How people choose to identify shouldn't be a question for other people to debate about.

BUSINESS ETIQUETTE IN OTHER CULTURES

The business press in Canada regularly contains alarming articles about the hazards of making cultural gaffes when doing business overseas. "For international business travelers, a misused chopstick can kill a big deal" appeared in the Globe and Mail a few years ago.[264] More reassuringly, the Globe subsequently contained a quote concerning international etiquette, "It's like a sport, you have to train hard. But once you train and know the rules, it all comes naturally." A comprehensive treatment of these topics is contained in the following four very useful books:

- *Kiss, Bow or Shake Hands: How to Do Business in Sixty Countries* by Terri Morrison, Wayne A. Conaway and George Bowden, Adams Media Corporation, Holbrook, Massachusetts. 1994.
- *Do's and Taboos of Preparing for Your Trip Abroad* by Roger E. Axtell and John P. Healy, John Wiley & Sons, Inc. 1994.
- *Do's and Taboos of Hosting International Visitors* by Roger E. Axtell, John Wiley & Sons, Inc. 1990.
- *Do's and Taboos of International Trade* by Roger E. Axtell, John Wiley & Sons, Inc. 1989.

For business and other information concerning the country you are heading for, you could make contact with the Canadian Embassy or High Commission and the Canadian Consulates in the country where you will be working, the corresponding offices of that nation in Canada, and bilateral trade associations (both in Canada and in the host country) such as the Canada-Peru Chamber of Commerce or the Canadian Colombian Professional Association.

DFAIT has a number of useful sources of information, including:

- Booklets:
    o "Bon Voyage, But…"
    o "Working Abroad: Unravelling the Maze"
    o "Her Own Way: Advice for the Woman Traveller"
    o "Canadian Consular Services: Providing Assistance to Canadians Abroad"

- Links to:
    o Country Insights[265]
    o Travel Warnings[266]
    o Country Travel Reports[267]

On a lighter note, a wonderful guide to exotic food in other countries is *Fierce Food: The intrepid diner's guide to the unusual, exotic, and downright bizarre,* by Christa Weil, Penguin, 2006. Have you ever eaten marmot, grasshoppers, jellyfish, ants, durian, smoked blubber, waterbugs, snakes or guinea pigs?

CORRUPTION AND ETHICS

In Chapter Eleven, there is a section entitled *Coping with Corruption*. A few of the highlights from that section are:

There is no end of anecdotal evidence—real or apocryphal—about corruption in international development, and Canadian companies working overseas will need to take a proactive informed position on this issue before getting started.

Transparency International[268] publishes two interesting indices:

   o *Corruption Perceptions Index: "CPI Score relates to perceptions of the degree of corruption as seen by business people and country analysts, and ranges between 10 (highly clean) and 0 (highly corrupt)." In 2006, the top five in a list of 163 countries were Finland, Iceland, New Zealand, Denmark, Singapore. (Canada ranked 14th.) At the other end of the list (reading from the bottom upwards) were Haiti, Myanmar, Iraq, Guinea, Sudan.*

o   *Bribe Payers Index: "The BPI is a ranking of 30 of the leading exporting countries according to the propensity of firms with headquarters within their borders to bribe when operating abroad." In 2006, the top five (least likely to bribe) were Switzerland, Sweden, Australia, Austria, Canada. At the other end of the list (reading from the bottom upwards) were India, China, Russia, Turkey, Taiwan.*

In recent years, the World Bank has committed to combat corruption in its operations and internally: "To reduce the corrosive impact of corruption in a sustainable way, it is important to go beyond the symptoms to tackle the causes of corruption. Since 1996, the World Bank has supported more than 600 anticorruption programs and governance initiatives developed by its member countries."[269]

There is an International Code of Ethics for Canadian Business[270]. It is reported that the following companies have adopted the code: Alcan Aluminum; Beak International, Inc.; Cambior Inc.; Chauvco Resources Ltd.; John Neville Inc.; Komex International Ltd.; Liquid Gold Resources Inc.; Profco Resources and Pulsonic Corporation.

HEALTH

Fortunately, the level of expertise in Canada in travel medicine is quite high, both for knowledge of necessary inoculations and advice before going abroad, and for the diagnosis of diseases picked up in other countries. Give yourself sufficient time before departure and seek out an experienced specialist or clinic in travel medicine.

Another source of expertise in Canada is the International Association for Medical Assistance to Travellers (IAMAT):

IAMAT is a non-profit membership organization. Since its founding in 1960, IAMAT has been a leader in the field of travel medicine, advising travelers about health risks, the geographical distribution of diseases, immunization requirements, sanitary conditions of water, milk and food, and environmental and climatic conditions around the world. IAMAT maintains a network of physicians-general practitioners and specialists, hospitals and clinics around the world-who have agreed to treat IAMAT members in need of medical care during their journey.

Our aim is to make competent care available to travelers anywhere in the world, even in very remote locations, by doctors who speak English and have had medical training in North America or Europe. IAMAT continuously inspects clinics in an attempt to ensure that travelers receive competent medical care. Any individual traveler can belong to IAMAT. There is no charge for membership, although a donation is appreciated to help support and expand IAMAT's work."[271]

CUSO[272] prepares publications such as "Health Advice for Living Overseas" and "Get Ready! Hints for a Healthy Short-Term Assignment Overseas".

Other useful sources of travel health information are:

*   World Health Organization (WHO)[273]
*   Health Canada[274]
*   Centres for Disease Control & Prevention[275]
*   Canadian Public Health Association[276]

SECURITY AND LIABILITY

One of the current "bibles" on these issues is Mitchell, L., Myles, W. and Jagdeosingh, G., 2006. *DepartSmart*. Ver. 2.0 edn. Guelph: University of Guelph.

> Another publication is *Ready, Set, Go!* http://www.uoguelph.ca/cip/page.cfm?id=33

> Two papers on liability published by CBIE are at http://www.cbie.ca/publication/index_e.cfm?page=research_e

An excellent practical and comprehensive guide is *Personal Safety Abroad* published by the Centre for Intercultural Learning (CIL), which was mentioned earlier in this chapter. It contains information on:

*   Minimizing the risks
*   Terrorism
*   Crime
*   Fire safety
*   Natural disasters

Another guide, *Living Overseas: Security Orientation,* is published by DFAIT. Its recommendations are:

- Assess your security needs.

  The more you know about the country where you will be residing, the better equipped you will be to adopt habits for that particular environment.

- Know and respect the customs and laws of the host country.

  Frustrating or alarming confrontations can sometimes occur simply because the visitor was not aware of local customs and laws.

- Keep a low profile.

  A relatively wealthy foreigner, unfamiliar with the ways of the host country, can appear to be an attractive or easy target for crime.

- Choose a secure place to live in.

  The area you choose to live in and the security features of your home can dissuade criminals and give you greater confidence in your safety.

- Keep your home secure.

  Potential burglars will usually assess the risks and will be deterred by well-maintained security. A home with all the necessary physical deterrents may still be entered easily if household members are not cautious about allowing people access. Information about the family, vacation plans, school hours, valuable belongings or work is highly useful to criminals or terrorists seeking an opportunity.

- Avoid potentially dangerous situations.

  The enjoyment of discovering a new country and a different culture does not need to be curtailed if you consciously avoid placing yourself in vulnerable situations.

- Stay alert.

  Being aware of what is going on around you will help you detect unusual events or occurrences. Thieves are less likely to assault you if they see that you are alert and confident.

- Stay informed, and inform others.

  Keeping up to date about local conditions and political

events that may affect your security will enable you to plan appropriate security precautions.

- Plan, rehearse, continually reassess your security procedures and be prepared to respond.

    Effective personal safety depends on you – on how well you plan, how automatic your family's daily security plans are and how you are prepared to respond quickly. The ability to respond quickly and effectively to threats to your safety depends on knowing in advance what you would do, and on having the necessary aids available quickly.

- Be aware of drugs and the law.

    Being involved with drugs, whether knowingly or otherwise, can lead to serious legal consequences in both a host country and in Canada – not to mention having a possible adverse impact on your career.

» Example: Shelly Steffler & safety in French Africa

Student Shelly Steffler wrote:

I'm really keen on working in Africa in a French-speaking area so that I can hone my skills, but most of the countries that speak French are ones that I associate with political instability, and I definitely want to feel safe. Your thoughts?

Our reply:

It is true, generally speaking, that there is political instability in some parts of Francophone Africa, but there is also some level of instability in many Anglophone, Lusophone and Arab African countries as well. There are some places (such as eastern Congo, Darfur in Sudan, Liberia and Cote d'Ivoire) that you will absolutely want to stay well clear of. Do your own research on the country situation using the Internet, rather than relying on someone else's opinion.

However, other than areas that are experiencing armed conflict, it seems that much personal risk stems from random individual acts of robbery and violence. It is grossly unfair that young white women on their own are most at risk, but that is the sad reality. Therefore, you may wish to choose your destination according to whether:

a) *you will always be part of a group, rather than being frequently alone,*

b) *you are in the country under the auspices of a well organized and highly experienced organization, and*

c) *whether you will be working in a rural area, rather than an urban area. Ironically, there is often more personal danger in certain parts of large cities than in small farming communities.*

Above all, trust your instincts. If a situation looks a little fishy to you, get out. And don't feel obliged, for reasons of political correctness, to do things in another country that your instincts and values would tell you not to do in Canada.

This is gloomy talk. We are talking here about worst case scenarios. Please don't let this conversation deter you from the wonderful life-altering experiences that you can have building friendships and experiencing different cultures that can come from spending a few weeks in a village in Africa. Speaking for ourselves, we can hardly wait to get back to Africa.

CHECKLISTS[277]

BEFORE YOU GO

Doing these essential things before you leave will help ensure a safer trip:

1. Get a Canadian passport. Be sure to check if your destination country requires your passport to be valid for six months beyond your date of entry (review the Foreign Affairs Canada Travel Report for such information).

2. Get a visa. Some countries require a visa for entry. Check with the Foreign Government Office in Canada or the country's Travel Report.

3. Get medical insurance and take the necessary medical precautions (i.e. immunizations). Check out the Health Canada Travel Medicine Program or the Centers for Disease Control and Prevention: Traveler's Health for more information.

4. Obtain the contact information of the nearest Canadian Government Office in your destination country. Register

with the office upon arrival and maintain contact throughout your stay.

5. Provide a friend or family member with a copy of your itinerary [and a photocopy of your passport], and inform them of changes while you are away. Also, reconfirm your hotel and flight arrangements before traveling.

6. Make arrangements for how you can obtain additional funds if needed. Foreign travel is often more expensive than people plan for.

7. Learn about the country you are going to visit. Consult the Foreign Affairs Canada Travel Report for your destination country for the latest information about security and safety issues.

PRECAUTIONS TO TAKE WHILE ABROAD:

1. Check your travel documents carefully to ensure all dates are correct, and that flights connect and are confirmed.

2. Leave your overseas postal address with family and friends.

3. You will not be able to avoid culture shock! Try to take it in slowly and do not be worried.

4. If you are unwell, go to a reputable Western educated doctor. DO NOT TRY LOCAL DRUGS OR ANTIDOTES. DO NOT TRY TO TREAT YOURSELF.

5. Take a small first aid pack with some basic medication in case you are not in contact with a good doctor.

6. Be careful as to what you eat and drink. Check on the safety of local water; boil all drinking water; avoid uncooked foods, including salads; in many areas it may be necessary to do without ice, as impure water is often used to make it.

7. Do not take unnecessary "luxury" items such as jewellery, etc. Do not take too much clothing, but do check carefully that you take everything you need.

8. Remember that cameras, transistor radios, and watches are at risk of being stolen in many countries.

9. Do not keep large sums of cash with you.

10. Do not give excessively to beggars. Ask the advice or your colleagues or a local friend.
11. Remember local customs are part of your host country's heritage. Respect them so far as you can-you will not change them.

RE-ENTRY TO CANADA

For some travelers, coming back to Canada can be as stressful—but unexpectedly so—as going abroad. One immediate problem is difficulty sleeping. For others, especially those who worked in emergency assistance or in relief camps, the adjustment is more difficult.

» Example: Ethiopia and re-entry

As so often happens, when the emergency eased, and the volunteers returned to Canada, they could not simply pick up their domestic lives where they had left off many months before. For many members of the medical and nursing teams, in particular, the re-entry back to Canadian life was difficult (in fact, every bit as demanding as preparing to go overseas in the first place). Many had trouble adjusting from living in a community in which everything was in desperate scarcity back to Canadian environments of bewildering abundance.

On a lighter note, after spending time in the camps, in the communities and in the markets of their host countries, many Canadians fear that they have lost their sense of smell when they are back in Canada!

ACKNOWLEDGEMENTS

Before it was published, this textbook was used in manuscript form in courses in the Civil Engineering and International Development program at the University of Western Ontario. The students who took these courses in the years 2008 to 2010 were enormously helpful in finding ambiguities, unsubstantiated facts and opinions, errors in logic, topics that should have been covered but were not yet in the book, and whether the various cases were engaging and pertinent. Thanks go to all the students: Taryn Meyers, Tyler Rosen, Jordan Atherton, Lindsay Christink, Justin Philippi, Adam Crookes, Jessica Barker, Anne Lombardi, Katayoon Pejman, Romain Martel, David Marmor, Leanna King, Gabriela Avila, and Megan Moore.

Sincere appreciation is due to Penny Keenan for her painstaking, insightful and thorough editing of several drafts of the material in the book.

A debt of gratitude is owed to all those individuals who have contributed to the book in so many ways, including the provision of information, enthusiastic support, sound advice, willingness to be interviewed, and permission to quote. With apologies in advance for having unintentionally neglected anyone, the following should be mentioned: Jim Shute, Art Headlam, Saruul Ayurzana, David Dacks, Rob Carson, Tim Newson, Michael Bartlett, Clare Robinson, Ernest Yanful, Paul Beamish, James Erskine, Michiel Leenders, Hank Vander Laan, Nigel Fisher, Carrie McLaren, Mira and Judy Noordermeer, Peter Ross, Greg Weiler, Don Sawyer, Alpha Jallow, Andrew and Christine Nelson, David Cechetto, Shelly Steffler, Ian Smillie, Alison Casey, Robert Chambers, Tadesse Mesfin, Laura Guzman, Katherine McKenna, Aldo Chircop, Pat Rodee, Shafique Pirani, Gordon Cummings, Kathy Engle, Kate Archer Ramadori, Krista Pettit, Eric Dillmann, Robert Marino, Jana Janakiram, Juan Lorenzo-Ginori, Edward Rubaduka, Jen Avaz, Bernie Gilmore, Charles Ruud, Ed

Biden, Stephen Perrott, Jessica Whitbread, Lumen Abad, Martin Connell, Mamsamba Joof, Tina Motley, Alicia Cueva, James Fox, Judy Barbeau, Jennifer Humphries, Jarda Dostal, Ochir Gerel, Yondon Majigsuren, Nguyen Bich Luu, Lan Gien, Michael Campbell, Marcel Hamelin, Joanne MacDonald, Kimberly Gibbons, Doug MacDonald, Maureen Woodhouse, Jean Loubert, Larry Gemmel, Mario Ramirez, Gina Delph, Anna Weston, Maria Pascual, Stan Kutcher, Scott Umstattd, Kevin Perkins, Brenna Donohue, Nadia Sallese, Jenna Hoyt, Micol Zarb, and Barry Yeates.

Several of the cases and case analyses in this book were written by Frederick Keenan specifically for this publication. Some of the case analyses were written by Keenan for the Association of Universities and Colleges of Canada (AUCC)[278], and are reprinted with the permission of AUCC.

All photographs were taken by Frederick Keenan unless otherwise acknowledged in the caption under the photograph.

All material taken from the website of the Canadian International Development Agency (CIDA) is reproduced with the permission of the Minister of Public Works and Government Services, 2007.

All web site references to Foreign Affairs and International Trade Canada are reproduced with the permission of Her Majesty the Queen in Right of Canada, represented by the Minister of Foreign Affairs, 2007.

The authors and publisher gratefully acknowledge the permission granted to reproduce the copyright material in this book. Every effort has been made to trace copyright holders and to obtain their permission for the use of copyright material. We apologize for any errors or omissions and would be grateful to be notified of any corrections that should be incorporated in future reprints or editions of this book.

ABOUT THE AUTHORS

FREDERICK KEENAN, PHD, PENG

Until 2004, Frederick was the Director of International Research at The University of Western Ontario (UWO), London, Canada and is now the President & CEO of International Project and Protocol Services Inc. in Toronto. He has been doing international development work for more than 30 years in South and Central America, Asia, East and West Africa, Europe and the Former Soviet Union. From 1985 to 1988, he was with the United Nations as the Director of the Forest Industries Division of the Food and Agriculture Organization (FAO), based in Rome, working towards sustainable forest utilization.

In the private sector, in 1988-90, Frederick was CEO of an information technology company in Ottawa and Toronto that provided information and technical services to the Canadian construction industry and, previously, he was a division manager of a consulting engineering firm in Toronto. He has received lifetime achievement awards from the Canadian and Peruvian forest products industries.

In the voluntary sector, he served on the Boards of the London Cross-Cultural Learner Centre and of Future Forests, has taught for Frontier College in northern Ontario, and has carried out assignments in Malaysia and the Philippines as a Volunteer Advisor for the Canadian Executive Service Organization. He is currently a Professor of Civil and Environmental Engineering at the University of Western Ontario, and teaches graduate and undergraduate courses in international development.

CHRISTINE GILMORE, MSM

Christine devoted more than 15 years to working in rural community development in Ethiopia as the Administrator of the London-based nongovernmental organization called *Future Forests, Partners in African Community Development*. As Administrator, she was responsible for securing funding through proposal writing to CIDA as well as travelling to Ethiopia for the express purposes of monitoring, evaluating, and reporting on the project's progress and problems. Her responsibilities also extended to reporting the project's financial status to the Board of Directors as well as monitoring all of the donors' funds. Keeping donors interested and informed about the project and the Ethiopian staff led Christine to designing and writing the Future Forests annual newsletter.

She oversaw the complex task of fundraising and coordinating work to help recovery in the drought and famine-stricken Bette Valley of Ethiopia, and in making the transition from emergency relief to rural community development. Since its inception, Future Forests' work included establishing tree nurseries and distributing seedlings, encouraging community wood lots, improving the quality of drinking water, enhancing agricultural and sanitation practices, economics, skills training, developing community leaders and improving literacy.

Christine has been involved with an international project running out of the University of Western Ontario's Schulich School of Medicine Nursing Faculty. Her work took her to Rwanda twice to research and report on what non-governmental organizations were doing with programs to train health care workers, specifically nursing students. The second trip involved an in-depth look at gender issues and policies within the Rwandan government and nongovernmental organizations.

She represented *Future Forests* at the 50th Anniversary of the Food and Agriculture Organization of the United Nations (FAO) and presented her overseas work to a workshop on Food Security and Partnership Participation.

In 2000, the Governor General of Canada awarded Christine the Meritorious Service Medal in recognition of her African work.

ACRONYMS AND ABBREVIATIONS

ABC	Abstinence/ Be faithful/ use a Condom
ACCC	Association of Canadian Community Colleges
ACEC	Association of Consulting Engineers of Canada
ADWAC	Agency for the Development of Women and Children
AFRRI	African Farm Radio Research Initiative
AIDS	Acquired Immune Deficiency Syndrome
AUCC	Association of Universities and Colleges of Canada
AVU	African Virtual University
BLWTL	Boundary Layer Wind Tunnel Laboratory
BME	Biomedical Engineering
CBIE	Canadian Bureau for International Education
CBP	Community-based Policing
CCI	Canadian Crossroads International
CCIC	Canadian Council for International Cooperation
CCPP	Canadian College Partnership Program
CECI	Canadian Centre for International Studies and Cooperation
CENCEC	Centro Nacional Coordinador de Ensayos Clínicos
CEO	Chief Executive Officer
CESO	Canadian Executive Service Organization

CIDA	Canadian International Development Agency
CIDA-INC	CIDA's Industrial Cooperation Program
CIL	Centre for Intercultural Learning
CIS	Commonwealth of Independent States
CITEmadera	Centro de Innovación Tecnológica de la Madera
COO	Chief Operating Officer
COSTI	Centro Organizzativo Scuole Tecniche Italiano
CPB	Canadian Partnership Branch
CUSAC	Commonwealth Universities Study Abroad Consortium
CWY	Canada World Youth
DCFRN	Developing Countries Farm Radio Network
DFAIT	Department of Foreign Affairs and International Trade
ED	Executive Director
EDC	Export Development Canada
EHM	Economic Hit Man
EIC	Engineering Institute of Canada
ÉUMC	Entraide universitaire mondiale du Canada
EWB	Engineers Without Borders
FAO	Food and Agriculture Organization of the United Nations
FCM	Federation of Canadian Municipalities
FF	Future Forests
FSECC	Foreign Service Examination and Career Counselling Inc.
FSU	Former Soviet Union
GDP	Gross Domestic Product
GRAIT	Gambia Rural Adult Instructor Training
GTTI	Gambia Technical Training Institute
HAU	Holy Angel University
HDI	Human Development Index
HDR	Human Development Report
HFHI	Habitat for Humanity International
HIV	Human Immunodeficiency Virus

HRD	Human Resource Development
HSC	Hospital for Sick Children
HSP	Human Security Program
HYV	High Yielding Variety
IAE	International Assistance Envelope
IAMAT	International Association for Medical Assistance to Travellers
ICLR	Institute for Catastrophic Loss Reduction
ICMD	International Centre for Municipal Development
ICZM	Integrated Coastal Zone Management
IDRC	International Development Research Centre
IEP	Interculturally Effective Person
IFI	International Financial Institution
IMF	International Monetary Fund
INC	Instituto Nacional de Cultura
IOHE	Inter-American Organization for Higher Education
IPPS	International Project and Protocol Services Inc.
ISPJAE	Instituto Superior Politécnico "José Antonio Echeverría"
IYIP	International Youth Internship Program
JICA	Japan International Cooperation Agency
KAR	Key Agency Result
KC	King's College
KHI	Kigali Health Institute
LDC	Less Developed Country
LEADER	Leading Education and Development in Emerging Regions
LFA	Logical Framework Analysis
LOI	Letter of Intent
MBA	Master of Business Administration
MDG	Millennium Development Goal
MEOP	Medical Electives Overseas Program
MNE	Multinational Enterprise
MSF	Médecins sans frontières/Doctors Without Borders

MSM	Meritorious Service Medal
MTE	Mid-term Evaluation
MUST	Mongolian University of Science and Technology
NAFTA	North American Free Trade Agreement
NEPAD	New Partnership for African Development
NGO	Nongovernmental Organization
NTC	Northern Tourism Circuit
NUR	National University of Rwanda
OCIC	Ontario Council for International Cooperation
ODA	Official Development Assistance
OECD	Organization for Economic Cooperation and Development
OUC	Okanagan University College
PAC	Partnership Africa Canada
PAC	Project Advisory Council
PCP	Project Completion Plan
PEMD	Program for Export Market Development
PEng	Registered Professional Engineer
PEPFAR	President's Emergency Plan for AIDS Relief
PMC	Project Management Committee
PPP	Purchasing Power Parity
PRA	Participatory Rural Appraisal
PRSP	Poverty Reduction Strategy Paper
PSD	Private Sector Directorate
PTP	Partnerships for Tomorrow Program
RBM	Results-based Management
RedR	Registered Engineers for Disaster Relief
RJ	Restorative Justice
RRA	Rapid Rural Appraisal
SDP	Social Development Priority
SME	Small and Medium Sized Enterprise
SUCO	Solidarité Union Coopération

SWAP	Sector-Wide Approach
TB	Tuberculosis
TFAP	Tropical Forestry Action Plan
TOR	Terms of Reference
UAEM	Universidad Autónoma del Estado de Morelos
UCLV	Universidad Central "Marta Abreu" de Las Villas
UK	United Kingdom
ULSA	University of Labor and Social Affairs
UN	United Nations
UNAIDS	Joint United Nations Programme on HIV/AIDS
UNAM	Universidad National Autónoma de México
UNB	University of New Brunswick
UNCTAD	United Nations Conference on Trade and Development
UNDP	United Nations Development Programme
UNFPA	United Nations Population Fund
UNICEF	United Nations Children's Fund
UNIDO	United Nations Industrial Development Organization
UO	Universidad de Oriente
UPCD	University Partnerships in Cooperation and Development
USAID	United States Agency for International Development
UWO	University of Western Ontario
VA	Volunteer Advisor
VCA	Volunteer Cooperation Agency
VERCON	Virtual Extension & Research Communication Network
VP	Vice President
VSO	Volunteer Sending Organization
WARD	West African Rural Development Centre
WB	World Bank
WBI	World Bank Institute
WHO	World Health Organization
WTO	World Trade Organization

WUSC   World University Service of Canada

$ Canadian Dollar

NOTES

1. As explained in *Learning with Cases, Writing Cases,* and *Teaching with Cases*, all written by James A. Erskine, Michiel R. Leenders and Louise A. Mauffette-Leenders, and published by the Richard Ivey School of Business at the University of Western Ontario in London, Ontario.

2. For three cases in this book, *disguises* have had to be used. For a variety of reasons, the actual names of individuals, the actual names of organizations, locations, or numerical data can not be used and disguises have had to be employed.

3. http://hdr.undp.org/aboutus/ accessed August 20, 2007

4. http://hdr.undp.org/hd/ accessed August 20, 2007

5. http://hdr.undp.org/reports/global/2004/ accessed August 20, 2007

6. *A Developing World,* Canadian International Development Agency

7. http://www.canadiangeographic.ca/worldmap/cida/CIDAWorldMap.aspx?Language=EN&Resolution=1024x768 accessed September 12, 2007

8. http://www.un.org/millenniumgoals/ accessed August 20, 2007

9. http://www.unmillenniumproject.org/index.htm accessed August 20, 2007

10. "Millennium Development Goals", The World Bank Group, updated October 2004

11. "Poverty Net", The World Bank Group, 2005

12. http://www.imf.org/external/np/prsp/prsp.asp accessed September 5 2008

13. *CIDA in brief.* Canadian International Development Agency.

14. "The 0.7-per-cent solution", The Globe and Mail, January 18, 2005

15. Westoby, Jack. The purpose of forests. Blackwell, Oxford. 1987

16. Westoby, Jack. The purpose of forests. Blackwell, Oxford. 1987

17. Keenan, F.J. 1988. Forest products research and forest industries for socio-economic development. Proceedings, International Union of Forestry Research Organizations Division 5 Conference, Sao Paulo, Brazil.

18. http://www.un.org/millenniumgoals/ accessed August 20, 2007

19. http://unstats.un.org/unsd/mdg/Resources/Static/Products/Progress2006/MDGReport2006.pdf accessed August 20, 2007

20. The bottom 1.4 billion. The Economist August 30 2008

21. *The Bottom Billion: Why the Poorest Countries Are Failing and What Can Be done About It* by Paul Collier, Oxford University Press 2007

22. http://oraweb.aucc.ca/pls/cupid/show_project_e?project_no_in=45/S61268-258/E accessed August 20, 2007

23. http://www.ceso-saco.com/ accessed August 20, 2007

24. http://www.indexmundi.com/canada/distribution_of_family_income_gini_index.html accessed May 1 2010

25. https://www.cia.gov/library/publications/the-world-factbook/fields/2172.html accessed May 1 2010

26. Smillie, Ian. Mastering the Machine. Broadview Press, 1991

27. Cook, O.F. 1925. Peru as a center of domestication. Journal of Heredity 16: 33–46; 95–110. Blackwell, Oxford

28. Lost Crops of the Incas: Little-Known Plants of the Andes with Promise for Worldwide Cultivation (1989) http://books.nap.edu/openbook.php?record_id=1398&page=1 accessed August 20, 2007

29. http://en.wikipedia.org/wiki/Green_Revolution accessed August 20, 2007

30. http://mdgs.un.org/unsd/mdg/Resources/Static/Products/Progress2006/MDGReport2006.pdf accessed August 20, 2007

31. Fisher, Nigel. Personal communication, September 12 and 24, 2007

32. http://oraweb.aucc.ca/pls/cupid/show_project_e?project_no_in=165/S61268-322/F accessed August 20, 2007

33. Known in other countries as the Vietnam War

34. http://www.dfait-maeci.gc.ca/cfsi-icse/cil-cai/home-en.asp accessed August 20, 2007

35. Daniel J. Kealey, David R. Protheroe, Doug MacDonald, Thomas Vulpe. 2005. *Re-examining the role of training in contributing to international project success: A literature review and an outline of a new model training program.* International Journal of Intercultural Relations 29 (2005) 289-316. Elsevier.

36. http://mdgs.un.org/unsd/mdg/Resources/Static/Products/Progress2006/MDGReport2006.pdf accessed August 20, 2007

37. Canadian International Development Agency: CIDA's Framework for Assessing Gender Equality Results, April 2005, CIDA-CPB Framework for Integration of Gender Equality, 2003, CIDA's Policy on Gender Equality, 1999, Gender Equality: How To Perform Evaluations, No. 4, May 2001, Questions about culture, gender equality and development cooperation, 2001.

38. http://www.aucc.ca/upcd-pucd/_pdf/resources/2006_gender_resources_e.pdf accessed August 20, 2007

39. http://oraweb.aucc.ca/pls/cupid/show_project_e?project_no_in=102/S61268-443/H accessed August 20, 2007

40. http://oraweb.aucc.ca/pls/cupid/show_project_e?project_no_in=128/S61268-549/I accessed August 20, 2007

41. http://oraweb.aucc.ca/pls/cupid/show_project_e?project_no_in=158/S61268-486/H accessed August 20, 2007

42. "Nuclear fallout", *The Economist,* April 22, 2006 p. 77

43. http://mdgs.un.org/unsd/mdg/Resources/Static/Products/Progress2006/MDGReport2006.pdf accessed August 20, 2007

44. http://www.stephenlewisfoundation.org/grassroots/archive/0507/youasked.htm accessed May 1 2007

45. For more information about the legislation, see the website of the Canadian HIV/AIDS Legal Network at www.aidslaw.ca.

46. Kiddell-Monroe, Rachel. *Canada's generic drug law is all talk, no action.* Globe and Mail. August 14, 2006.

47. Nolen, Stephanie. *U.S. gets this war right,* The Globe and Mail, August 19, 2006

48. Fox, Maggie. *Polio could follow smallpox as next scourge to be eradicated,* Globe and Mail April 13, 2005

49. http://mdgs.un.org/unsd/mdg/Resources/Static/Products/Progress2006/MDGReport2006.pdf accessed August 20, 2007

50. http://en.wikipedia.org/wiki/Child_soldiers accessed August 20, 2007

51. Jones, Lynne. *The boys of war.* Book review of *A Long Way Gone: Memoirs of a Boy Soldier* by Ishmael Beah, Douglas & McIntyre, *Globe & Mail* March 3, 2007

52. http://oraweb.aucc.ca/pls/cupid/show_project_e?project_no_in=37/S61268-275B/E accessed August 20, 2007

53. Scott, Norvall. *Global warming will hit poor countries harder, report says,* Globe and Mail, April 2, 2007

54. The Tropical Forestry Action Plan. Food and Agriculture Organization of the United Nations, Rome.

55. http://www.fadr.msu.ru/rodale/agsieve/txt/vol4/issue1/4.html accessed August 20, 2007

56. http://oraweb.aucc.ca/pls/cupid/show_project_e?project_no_in=102/S61268-443/H accessed August 20, 2007

57. Carson, Rachel. *Silent Spring*, Boston, Houghton Mifflin Company (2002); The new 40th Anniversary Edition of *Silent Spring* with a new introduction by Linda Lear and afterword by E.O. Wilson. Boston: Houghton Mifflin Company, 2002.

58. Our Common Future, the report of the World Commission on Environment and development, Oxford University Press 1987

59. Atwood, Roger. 2004. *Stealing History*. New York: St. Martin's Griffin.

60. Jean Vanier, Roméo Dallaire and Stephen Lewis were ranked 12th, 16th and 17th, respectively, in the CBC's List of Top 100 Greatest Canadians. Lester Pearson was number six and Pierre Elliott Trudeau was third.

61. http://www.stephenlewisfoundation.org/grassroots/archive/0507/youasked.htm accessed August 20, 2007

62. http://www.grameen-info.org/ accessed August 20, 2007

63. http://www.leaderproject.com/article.php?pn=advisoryboard accessed August 20, 2007

64. http://mdgs.un.org/unsd/mdg/Resources/Static/Products/Progress2006/MDGReport2006.pdf accessed August 20, 2007

65. Keenan, Frederick and Eva. *Peru's Northern Tourism Circuit and the Pacasmayo Museum*. Report for Dr. Andrew Nelson, University of Western Ontario. September 25, 2006. International Project and Protocol Services Inc., Toronto

66. Alison Casey, a native of Canmore, Alberta, is currently a Uniterra volunteer in Tamale, Northern Region, Ghana, where she is working with the Girls' Education Unit in the Ghana Education Service as a Gender Advocacy Advisor. This is her second time in Ghana and her fourth on the continent: when she was 16, she spent a year in South

Africa as a Rotary Youth Exchange Student, and in 2002, returned to Southern Africa as a tourist. In 2003-04, she was a CIDA-funded Intern through the Okanagan University College's International Development Center. In June of 2006, she completed an MA in gender and peacebuilding at the UN-mandated University for Peace in San José, Costa Rica.

67.   Schumacher, E.F. Small is Beautiful. Harper & Row 1973

68.   Smillie, Ian. Mastering the Machine. Broadview Press 1991

69.   Keenan, F.J. et al. 1986. Forest industries in socio-economic development. Unasylva 38(153):2-9.

70.   Yen, Hope. *81 journalists killed in 2006*, Society of Professional Journalists PressNotes

71.   Publication IDRC-TS49e, "Tropical Timber for Building Materials in the Andean Group Countries of South America" by F.J. Keenan and Marcelo Tejada (1984), and as Publication IDRC-TS49s, "Maderas Tropicales como Material de Construccion en los paises del Grupo Andino del America del Sur" (1987).

72.   http://oraweb.aucc.ca/pls/cupid/show_project_e?project_no_in=38/S61268-391/G accessed August 20, 2007

73.   See Sawyer, Don. *For a few dollars more*. The Ottawa Citizen. August 8 2006.

74.   www.iog.ca accessed August 20, 2007

75.   http://www.iog.ca/publications/swap.PDF accessed August 20, 2007

76.   http://www.sfcg.org/programmes/indonesia/programmes_indonesia.html accessed August 20, 2007

77.   Le Carré, John. *The Constant Gardener*, Penguin Books 2001

78.   http://www.communityradionetwork.org/leftlinks/crs_howto accessed August 20, 2007

79.   http://www.farmradio.org/ accessed August 20, 2007

80.   *Civic voice: Empowering the Poor through Community Radio*. The World Bank Group.

81. David Dacks, personal communication April 2, 2007 rev. May 10, 2010

82. Commonwealth of Learning

83. Chambers, Robert. 1992. *Rural Appraisal: Rapid, Relaxed and Participatory.* Sustainable Agriculture Program, International Institute for Environment and Development, University of Sussex.

84. Chambers, Robert. 1997. Whose Reality Counts? Putting the First Last, Intermediate Technology Publications (now Practical Action Publications), Rugby, UK

85. http://ideas.repec.org/f/pch385.html accessed August 20, 2007

86. Chambers, Robert. 1992. *Rural Appraisal: Rapid, Relaxed and Participatory.* Sustainable Agriculture Program, International Institute for Environment and Development, University of Sussex.

87. Chambers, Robert. Personal communication. August 16, 2007.

88. Gilmore, Bernard. 1993. *A Practical Plan for Village-based Education in Ethiopia.* Report prepared for the Ethiopian Orthodox Church/DICAD and the Village of Wake Tiyo.

89. Keenan, F.J. and L. Vallée. 1994. Management of international affairs in universities. Inter-American Organization for Higher Education, Quebec. Also published in Spanish as: Keenan, F.J. y L. Vallée, 1994. La gestión de los asuntos internacionales en la universidad, and in Portuguese as Keenan, F.J. e L. Vallée. 1995. A Gestáo dos Assuntos Internacionais na Universidade.

90. http://www.un.org/millenniumgoals/ accessed August 20, 2007

91. Jean Vanier, Roméo Dallaire and Stephen Lewis were ranked 12th, 16th and 17th, respectively, in the CBC's List of Top 100 Greatest Canadians. Lester Pearson was number six and Pierre Elliott Trudeau was third.

92. http://www.dfait-maeci.gc.ca/canada_un/cdn_un-en.asp#02 accessed August 20, 2007

93.   http://www.cbc.ca/greatest/top_ten/nominee/pearson-lester.html accessed August 20, 2007

94.   Christopher Ondaatje and Robert Catherwood. 1967. The Prime Ministers of Canada 1867-1967. Miller Publishing, Toronto.

95.   The Canadian Encyclopedia

96.   For example, the Latin American Cultural Centre of Canada regularly organizes public events to celebrate multiculturalism in Canada and the role of Trudeau; see http://www.centrolatinocanadiense.com/home_eng.htm accessed August 20, 2007

97.   Leman, Marc. *Canadian Multiculturalism*, Publication 93-E, Political and Social Affairs Division, Library of Parliament

98.   http://www.acdi-cida.gc.ca accessed August 20, 2007

99.   *International Policy Statement: A Role of Pride and Influence in the World*

100. "Martin won't commit to foreign-aid target", The Globe and Mail, April 19, 2005

101. Jeffrey Sachs and John MacArthur, "Promises aren't enough", The Globe and Mail, April 22, 2005

102. Bailey, Sue. "Bono is 'annoyed' with Paul Martin's delay on foreign aid hike", Canada Press Online April 22, 2005

103. Welsh, Jennifer. *At Home in the World: Canada's Vision for the 21ˢᵗ Century*, Toronto: Harper Collins, Toronto 2004.

104. "PM seeks answers from Oxford scholar", The Globe and Mail, February 5, 2005

105. http://www.acdi-cida.gc.ca/acdi-cida/acdi-cida.nsf/eng/JUD-51895926-JEP accessed May 14, 2010

106. http://www.dfait-maeci.gc.ca/ accessed August 20, 2007

107. *CIDA in brief.* Canadian International Development Agency

108. http://www.acdi-cida.gc.ca/index-e.htm accessed August 20, 2007

109. http://www.acdi-cida.gc.ca/organi-e.htm accessed August 20, 2007

110. *CIDA in brief.* Canadian International Development Agency

111. www.acdi-cida.gc.ca accessed August 20, 2007

112. Pratt, Cranford. *Alleviating Global Poverty or Enhancing Security: Competing Rationales for Canadian Development Assistance.* In Freedman, Jim. 2000. Transforming Development: Foreign Aid for a Changing World. University of Toronto Press.

113. Lorinc, John. November 2004. *The Best Aid Plans.* In: Saturday Night pages 44 – 50.

114. *Aid and Ebb Tide: A History of CIDA and Canadian Development Assistance* by David R. Morrison, Wilfrid Laurier University Press (October 1, 1998).

115. http://www.idrc.ca accessed August 20, 2007

116. http://www.idrc.ca/en/ev-68017-201-1-DO_TOPIC.html accessed August 20, 2007

117. http://www.voyage.gc.ca/main/foreign/can_offices_desc-en.asp accessed August 20, 2007

118. http://www.dfait-maeci.gc.ca/world/embassies/mission-en.asp?MID=119 accessed August 20, 2007

119. Keenan, F.J. 1996. Chapter: "Managing an Office of International Affairs, and the Internationalization of Higher Education" in International Educator's Handbook, Canadian Bureau for International Education, Ottawa.

120. http://www.aucc.ca/ accessed August 20, 2007

121. http://www.aucc.ca/upcd-pucd/projects/index_e.html accessed August 20, 2007

122. http://www.aucc.ca/publications/auccpubs/series/upcd_fact_sheets_e.html accessed August 20, 2007

123. http://www.accc.ca/ accessed August 20, 2007

124. http://www.accc.ca/english/about/ accessed August 20, 2007

125. http://www.accc.ca/english/publications/accc_international.htm accessed August 20, 2007

126. http://www.cbie.ca/ accessed August 20, 2007

127. http://www.oui-iohe.qc.ca/

128. Keenan, F.J. and L. Vallée. 1994. Management of international affairs in universities. Inter-American Organization for Higher Education, Quebec. Also published in Spanish as: Keenan, F.J. y L. Vallée, 1994. La gestión de los asuntos internacionales en la universidad, and in Portuguese as Keenan, F.J. e L. Vallée. 1995. A Gestão dos Assuntos Internacionais na Universidade.

129. http://www.charityvillage.com/cv/guides/guide4.asp accessed August 20, 2007

130. http://www.ccic.ca/e/home/index.shtml accessed August 20, 2007

131. www.web.net/acgc accessed August 20, 2007

132. www.aqoci.qc.ca accessed August 20, 2007

133. www.acic-caci.org accessed August 20, 2007

134. place2b.org/bccicweb accessed August 20, 2007

135. www.escape.ca/~mcic accessed August 20, 2007

136. http://www.ocic.on.ca/ accessed August 20, 2007

137. www.earthbeat.sk.ca accessed August 20, 2007

138. Gibbons, Kimberly. Email message to Frederick Keenan September 4, 2007

139. http://www.cwy-jcm.org/en accessed August 20, 2007

140. http://www.cciorg.ca/welcome.html accessed August 20, 2007

141. http://www.foodgrainsbank.ca/ accessed August 20, 2007

142. http://www.cpar.ca/ accessed August 20, 2007

143. http://care.ca/ accessed August 20, 2007

144. http://www.cuso.org/index.php accessed August 20, 2007

145. http://www.ewb.ca/en/index.html accessed August 20, 2007

146. http://www.akfc.ca/ accessed August 20, 2007

147. http://www.crcid.org/index.html accessed August 20, 2007
148. http://www.doctorswithoutborders.org/ accessed August 20, 2007
149. http://www.habitat.ca/ accessed August 20, 2007
150. http://www.oxfam.ca/ accessed August 20, 2007
151. http://www.unicef.ca/portal/SmartDefault.aspx accessed August 20, 2007
152. http://www.acdi-cida.gc.ca/CIDAWEB/acdicida.nsf/En/JUD-122012222-MZ3 accessed August 20, 2007
153. http://www.globalcitizensforchange.ca/en/ivca accessed August 20, 2007
154. http://www.afscanada.org/can_en/home accessed August 20, 2007
155. http://www.akfc.ca/ accessed August 20, 2007
156. http://www.cwy-jcm.org/en accessed August 20, 2007
157. http://www.ceci.ca/ceci/en/index.html accessed August 20, 2007
158. http://www.cciorg.ca/welcome.html accessed August 20, 2007
159. http://www.ceso-saco.com/ accessed August 20, 2007
160. http://www.cuso.org/index.php accessed August 20, 2007
161. http://www.ewb.ca/en/index.html accessed August 20, 2007
162. http://www.wusc.ca/ accessed August 20, 2007
163. http://www.oxfam.qc.ca/ accessed August 20, 2007
164. http://www.suco.org/ accessed August 20, 2007
165. http://www.vsocanada.org/ accessed August 20, 2007
166. http://www.wusc.ca/ accessed August 20, 2007
167. http://www.yci.org/ accessed August 20, 2007
168. http://www.acdi-cida.gc.ca/CIDAWEB/acdicida.nsf/En/JUD-3311056-KPR?OpenDocument accessed August 20, 2007

169. http://www.stephenlewisfoundation.org/ accessed August 20, 2007

170. http://www.akdn.org/agency/akf.html accessed August 20, 2007

171. http://www.calmeadow.com/ accessed August 20, 2007

172. http://www.littlevoice.ca/ accessed August 20, 2007

173. http://www.ipps.net/ accessed August 20, 2007

174. http://www.hicklinginternational.ca/ accessed August 20, 2007

175. http://www.snc-lavalin.com/ accessed August 20, 2007

176. http://www.aucc.ca/upcd-pucd/index_e.html accessed August 20, 2007

177. 174

178. http://www.aucc.ca/upcd-pucd/projects/index_e.html accessed August 20, 2007

179. www.acdi-cida.gc.ca accessed August 20, 2007

180. http://www.aucc.ca/ptp-ppa/index_e.html accessed August 20, 2007

181. http://www.acdi-cida.gc.ca/cidaweb/acdicida.nsf/En/JUD-62183519-GS5 accessed August 20, 2007

182. http://www.acdi-cida.gc.ca/CIDAWEB/acdicida.nsf/En/JUD-112912183-NAU accessed August 20, 2007

183. http://www.acdi-cida.gc.ca/cidaweb/acdicida.nsf/En/NIC-54102116-JUN accessed August 20, 2007

184. http://www.acdi-cida.gc.ca/CIDAWEB/acdicida.nsf/En/NIC-54153252-QX4 accessed August 20, 2007

185. http://www.merx.com/ accessed August 20, 2007

186. http://www.acdi-cida.gc.ca/CIDAWEB/acdicida.nsf/En/JUD-131122129-ND5 accessed August 20, 2007

187. http://www.fcm.ca/english/international/international.html accessed August 20, 2007

188. http://geo.international.gc.ca/cip-pic/library/humansecurityprogram-en.asp accessed August 20, 2007

189. http://www.acdi-cida.gc.ca/CIDAWEB/acdicida.nsf/En/ JUD-3692051-JU4 accessed August 20, 2007

190. http://www.acu.ac.uk/scholarships/cusac.html accessed August 20, 2007

191. Picard, Andre. *Thanks, Rotary, for fighting polio: Next, please take on HIV*, Globe and Mail May 26, 2005

192. http://www.soros.org/ accessed August 20, 2007

193. "Muhammad Yumus has won the Nobel peace prize for his role in promoting financial services for the poor", *The Economist,* October 21, 2006

194. *Microloan pioneer and bank win Nobel Prize* by Estanislao Oziewicz Globe and Mail October 14, 200

195. Calmeadow's chairman is Martin Connell, co-founder of Ace Bakery in Toronto.

196. http://www.calmeadow.com/ accessed August 20, 2007

197. RBM Handbook on Developing Results Chains, RBM Division, CIDA December 2000

198. One of the authors of this book (Frederick Keenan) used an adaptation of the case method in teaching design of engineering structures at the University of Western Ontario. It proved to be effective in the fostering of skills in assembling, assessing and utilizing data and engineering theory in designing an actual building. This important and relevant skill was learned and was then carried into professional practice by the graduating students. Admittedly not all the students who were subjected to the case method of teaching engineering design liked it—the better students, once they had become accustomed to the approach, appreciated its potentially very positive impact on their professional development—but there, unfortunately, remained some students who would have happily preferred a more readily regurgitated approach to education.

199. In preparation for writing this book, Keenan participated in the 2004 Case Writing Workshop presented by Professors James A. Erskine and Michiel R. Leenders of Ivey, who provided invaluable advice to us in utilizing

the case method for the management of international development activities. Three central references to the case method are *Learning with Cases, Writing Cases, and Teaching with Cases*, all written by James A. Erskine, Michiel R. Leenders and Louise A. Mauffette-Leenders, and published by Ivey.

200. Erskine, J.A. and Leenders, M.R., *Learning with Cases*, © 1997, Richard Ivey School of Business.

201. This case analysis was written by Frederick Keenan solely to provide material for class discussion. The Author does not intend to illustrate either effective or ineffective handling of a managerial situation.

202. This case analysis was written by Frederick Keenan for the Association of Universities and Colleges of Canada (AUCC). It was prepared solely to provide material for class discussion. The Author does not intend to illustrate either effective or ineffective handling of a managerial situation. Copyright © AUCC 2006. Reprinted by permission.

203. For more information about this project, see the project's profile on AUCC's web site at http://oraweb.aucc.ca/pls/cupid/show_project_e?project_no_in=128/S61268-549/I.

204. This case analysis was written by Frederick Keenan for the Association of Universities and Colleges of Canada (AUCC). It was prepared solely to provide material for class discussion. The Author does not intend to illustrate either effective or ineffective handling of a managerial situation. Copyright © AUCC 2006. Reprinted by permission.

205. This case was written by Frederick Keenan for the Association of Universities and Colleges of Canada (AUCC). It was prepared solely to provide material for class discussion. The Author does not intend to illustrate either effective or ineffective handling of a managerial situation. Copyright © AUCC 2006. Reprinted by permission.

206. This case was written by Frederick Keenan solely to provide material for class discussion. The Author does not intend

to illustrate either effective or ineffective handling of a managerial situation.

207. This case was written by Frederick Keenan solely to provide material for class discussion. The Author does not intend to illustrate either effective or ineffective handling of a managerial situation.

208. http://ideas.repec.org/f/pch385.html accessed August 20, 2007

209. This information was kindly provided by Don Sawyer and Mamsamba Joof, ADWAC's Executive Director.

210. This information was kindly provided by Don Sawyer.

211. Mambo Press, Senga Road, PO Box 779, Gweru, Zimbabwe

212. http://styluspub.com/books/SeriesDetail.aspx?id=78 accessed August 28, 2007

213. According to the US Small Business Administration

214. This case analysis was written by Frederick Keenan solely to provide material for class discussion. The Author does not intend to illustrate either effective or ineffective handling of a managerial situation.

215. http://www.ipps.net/ accessed August 20, 2007

216. http://www.hicklinginternational.ca/ accessed August 20, 2007

217. http://www.snc-lavalin.com/ accessed August 20, 2007

218. http://www.snc-lavalin.com/ accessed August 20, 2007

219. Yakabushi, Konrad. *Building the world, Canadian Style*, Globe and Mail Report on Business, August 26, 2006.

220. http://www.acdi-cida.gc.ca/inc accessed August 20, 2007

221. http://www.acdi-cida.gc.ca/CIDAWEB/acdicida.nsf/En/NIC-54153252-QX4 accessed August 20, 2007

222. http://www.acdi-cida.gc.ca/CIDAWEB/acdicida.nsf/En/JUD-112912750-N4F accessed August 20, 2007

223. http://ww1.transparency.org/index.html accessed August 20, 2007

224. http://www.worldbank.org/ accessed August 20, 2007

225. Perkins, John, *Confessions of an Economic Hit Man*, Penguin Books, 2004

226. http://www.dfait-maeci.gc.ca/cfsi-icse/cil-cai/home-en.asp accessed August 20, 2007

227. Daniel J. Kealey, PhD, David R. Protheroe, Doug MacDonald, and Thomas Vulpe. *International Projects: Some Lessons on Avoiding Failure and Maximizing Success.* 2006. www.ispi.org March 2006, p.46.

228. This section is based on information kindly provided by Peter M. Ross, who provides legal counsel on intellectual property matters to The University of Western Ontario, and is a principal of Ross & Associates of London, Canada.

229. http://en.wikipedia.org/wiki/Engineers_Without_Borders accessed August 20, 2007

230. www.ewb.ca accessed August 20, 2007

231. http://www.habitat.org/ accessed August 20, 2007

232. http://www.adb.org/ accessed August 20, 2007

233. http://www.adb.org/Documents/Fact_Sheets/donors/CAN.pdf accessed August 20, 2007

234. http://www.blwtl.uwo.ca/Public/Home.aspx accessed August 20, 2007

235. http://www.uwo.ca/univsec/board/minutes/1999/9909iclr.html accessed August 20, 2007

236. http://www.uwo.ca/research/docs/faces/3littlepigs.pdf accessed August 20, 2007

237. http://www.redr.ca/ accessed August 20, 2007

238. Teng, I. 1971. Review of the use of wood in housing in Peru. Vancouver, Canada. World Consultation on the Use of Wood in Construction.

239. Keenan, F.J. 1996. Chapter: "Managing an Office of International Affairs, and the Internationalization of Higher Education" in International Educator's Handbook, Canadian Bureau for International Education, Ottawa.

240. Keenan, F.J. and L. Vallée. 1994. Management of international affairs in universities. Inter-American Organization for Higher Education, Quebec.

241. CBIE's International Educator's Handbook. Canadian Bureau for International Education, Ottawa, 1996

242. Mitchell, L., Myles, W. and Jagdeosingh, G., 2006. *DepartSmart*. Ver. 2.0 edn. Guelph: University of Guelph.

243. http://www.uoguelph.ca/cip/page.cfm?id=33 accessed August 20, 2007

244. http://www.cbie.ca/publication/index_e.cfm?page=research_e accessed August 20, 2007

245. This case was written by Frederick Keenan solely to provide material for class discussion. The Author does not intend to illustrate either effective or ineffective handling of a managerial situation.

246. Now "King's University College at the University of Western Ontario"

247. According to their web site: "Formally incorporated as COSTI-IIAS Immigrant Services in 1981, COSTI is Canada's largest education and social service agency with a specific mandate to provide services to newcomers and their families. The agency is the result of the amalgamation of the Italian Immigrant Aid Society (founded in 1952) and COSTI (founded in 1962).

248. This case analysis was written by Frederick Keenan for the Association of Universities and Colleges of Canada (AUCC). It was prepared solely to provide material for class discussion. The Author does not intend to illustrate either effective or ineffective handling of a managerial situation. Copyright © AUCC 2006. Reprinted by permission.

249. Shute, J.C.M. "Assessing the Medium-Term Impact of an Institutional Strengthening Project". *Canadian and International Education*, 24,2 (Dec 1995),85-94.

250. http://www.cwy-jcm.org/en accessed August 20, 2007

251. http://www.cciorg.ca/welcome.html accessed August 20, 2007

252. http://www.cuso.org/index.php accessed August 20, 2007

253. http://www.ewb.ca/en/index.html accessed August 20, 2007

International Development

254. http://www.habitat.ca/ accessed August 20, 2007

255. http://www.acdi-cida.gc.ca/internships accessed August 20, 2007

256. http://hdr.undp.org/statistics/data/cty/cty_f_NIC.html accessed August 20, 2007

257. http://www.nationsencyclopedia.com/Americas/Nicaragua-HOUSING.html accessed August 20, 2007

258. http://www.habitat.org/intl/lac/145.aspx accessed August 20, 2007

259. http://www.foreignserviceexamprep.com/index.html accessed August 20, 2007

260. http://www.dfait-maeci.gc.ca/cfsi-icse/cil-cai/home-en.asp accessed August 20, 2007

261. Thomas Vulpe, Daniel Kealey, David Protheroe and Doug Macdonald. 2000. *A Profile of the Interculturally Effective Person.* Centre for Intercultural Learning, Canadian Foreign Service Institute, Department of Foreign Affairs and International Trade.

262. Daniel J. Kealey, David R. Protheroe, Doug MacDonald, Thomas Vulpe. 2005. *Re-examining the role of training in contributing to international project success: A literature review and an outline of a new model training program.* International Journal of Intercultural Relations 29 (2005) 289-316. Elsevier.

263. Daniel J. Kealey, PhD, David R. Protheroe, Doug MacDonald, and Thomas Vulpe. *International Projects: Some Lessons on Avoiding Failure and Maximizing Success.* 2006. www.ispi.org March 2006, p.46.

264. Eligh, Blake. *Cross-cultural etiquette 101 – For international business travelers, a misused chopstick can kill a big deal,* Globe and Mail October 4, 2003.

265. http://www.dfait-maeci.gc.ca/cfsi-icse/cil-cai/home-en.asp accessed August 20, 2007

266. http://www.voyage.gc.ca/dest/sos/warnings-en.asp accessed August 20, 2007

267. http://www.voyage.gc.ca/dest/ctry/reportpage-en.asp accessed August 20, 2007

268. http://www.transparency.org/ accessed August 20, 2007

269. http://www.worldbank.org/ accessed August 20, 2007

270. http://www.lib.uwo.ca/business/intlethi.htmlhttp://www.lib.uwo.ca/business/intlethi.html accessed August 20, 2007

271. http://www.iamat.org/ accessed August 20, 2007

272. http://www.cuso.org/index.php accessed August 20, 2007

273. http://www.who.int/en/ accessed August 20, 2007

274. http://www.hc-sc.gc.ca/ accessed August 20, 2007

275. http://www.cdc.gov/ accessed August 20, 2007

276. http://www.cpha.ca/ accessed August 20, 2007

277. Courtesy of the Medical Electives Overseas Program (MEOP) at the University of Western Ontario http://www.med.uwo.ca/students/meop/ accessed August 20, 2007

278. http://www.aucc.ca/upcd-pucd/resources/documents/use_of_case_study_in_upcd_e.pdf accessed August 20, 2007

INDEX

Pages with notation 'n' or 'nn' refer to Notes in back of book
Pages with notation 'fn' refer to footnotes
Pages with notation 'ph' refer to photographs

Ondaatje, Christopher, 93, 313*n*94
Ontario Council for International
 Cooperation, 109
Open Society Institute, 124
Our Common Future (Report of the
 World Commission), 49, 310*n*58
outcomes, RBM definition of, 133–135
outputs, RBM definition of, 133, 135
Overcoming 40 Years Of Failure, report
 (International Trade of the Senate of
 Canada), 102–103
Oxfam-USA, 172

P

Pakistan, measles in, 44
Pan-American Health Organization,
 122
Participatory Rural Appraisal (PRA),
 71, 84–85, 170
partners
 choosing, 75
 listening to, 70–71
 long-term partnerships, 88–89
Partnerships for Tomorrow Program II,
 116–117
Patent Cooperation Treaty (PCT), 208
patents, 208
PCT (Patent Cooperation Treaty), 208
Pearson, Lester Bowles, 71, 92, 93, 104,
 229
PEMD (Program for Export Market
 Development), 204
Penny, Dr. Norgrove, 160
PEPFAR(US President's Emergency
 Plan for AIDS Relief), 43, 309*n*47
performance indicators (indicators),
 RBM definition of, 133, 136–137
Perkins, John, 205–206, 321*n*225
Perrott, Stephen, 261
Persepolis (Satrapi), 79
Personal Safety Abroad (CIL), 290
Peru, Republic of
 about, 231–232
 CITEmadera in, 72

creating Northern Tourism Circuit
 in, 21, 60–61
north coast of Peru, map of, 200
Peru and Andrew Nelson case
 business plan, 191, 201–202
 establishing museum of cultural
  history, 4–5, 55–56, 56*ph*, 188,
  189–191, 320*n*214
 financial plan, 198–199
 management of museum, 196–197
 market analysis, 191–193
 marketing plan, 198
 Museum of Cultural History,
  concept of, 189–191
 Northern Tourism Circuit of Peru,
  190–191
 map of, 201
 other attractions and museums in
  area, 193–195
Peru and wood construction case,
 229–240
 about, 229–231
 attitudes towards wood as building
  material, 236–237
 geography and population, 231–232
 harvesting forests, 237–239
 structures in Peru, 232–236
 wood products and components used
  in Canada, 239–240
pesticides, Green Revolution and, 25
Philippines, Holy Angel University and,
 224–225
*Phool-e-Rangeena Government School
 (Afghanistan),* 28*ph*
Pirani, Shafique, 38–39, 159–160
plays, using as communication tool,
 79–80
PMC (Project Management
 Committee), decision making body
 for ICZM Cuban project, 156–158
policing, community-based, 66–68
polio
 eliminating, 43, 124
 example of Norbile, 173–174

women
  empowering, as MDG, 11, 31–32
  maternal mortality ratios, 44
  prevention of violence against
    women, 45–46
  professional geologists (Mongolia),
    34–36
  rapes in Rwanda, 37
wood construction case, Peru and,
  229–240
  about, 229–231
  attitudes towards wood as building
    material, 236–237
  geography and population, 231–232
  harvesting forests, 237–239
  structures in Peru, 232–236
  wood products and components used
    in Canada, 239–240
"Wood is Good" syndrome, 229
World Bank (WB)
  economic hit men and, 206
  on empowerment of poor through
    community radio, 81–82, 311n80
  evaluating MDGs, 12–13, 307n10
  funding development activities, 112,
    203
  Global Strategy and Booster
    Programme, spurring malaria
    control interventions, 41
  initiating African Virtual University
    network, 59
  lead agency for, 122
  partnership for conserving tropical
    forests, 47
  poverty line criterion, 19, 307n20
  PRSPs and, 13, 76
  struggles against corruption, 205–
    209
World Health Organization (WHO)
  funding for, 122
  recommendations on generic drugs,
    42, 309n45
World Intellectual Property
  Organization (WIPO), 208
World Rain Forest Movement, 48

World Resources Institute, 47, 48
World Trade Organization (WTO),
  member countries producing generic
  drugs for export, 42, 309n45
World University Service of Canada
  (WUSC), 22
WUSC (World University Service of
  Canada), 22

Y

Yakabuski, Konrad, 03, 320n219
Yunus, Muhammad, 125, 318nn193–
  194

Z

Zimbabwe, HIV/AIDS in, 41